DEMOSTHENES, SPEECHES 18 AND 19

THE ORATORY OF CLASSICAL GREECE
Translated with Notes • *Michael Gagarin, Series Editor*

VOLUME 9

DEMOSTHENES, SPEECHES 18 AND 19

Translated with introduction and notes by

Harvey Yunis

 UNIVERSITY OF TEXAS PRESS, AUSTIN

This book has been supported by an endowment dedicated to classics and the ancient world and funded by the Areté Foundation; the Gladys Krieble Delmas Foundation; the Dougherty Foundation; the James R. Dougherty, Jr. Foundation; the Rachael and Ben Vaughan Foundation; and the National Endowment for the Humanities. The endowment has also benefited from gifts by Mark and Jo Ann Finley, Lucy Shoe Meritt, the late Anne Byrd Nalle, and other individual donors.

Material from the introduction to *Demosthenes: On the Crown,* edited by Harvey Yunis, reprinted with the permission of Cambridge University Press.

First edition, 2005

Requests for permission to reproduce material from this work should be sent to Permissions, University of Texas Press, P.O. Box 7819, Austin, TX 78713-7819.

⊗ The paper used in this book meets the minimum requirements of ANSI/NISO Z39.48-1992 (R1997) (Permanence of Paper).

Library of Congress Cataloging-in-Publication Data

Demosthenes.
    [On the crown. English]
    Demosthenes, speeches 18 and 19 / translated with introduction and notes by Harvey Yunis.— 1st ed.
        p.   cm.— (The oratory of classical Greece ; v. 9)
    Includes bibliographical references and index.
    ISBN 978-0-292-70578-4

    1. Demosthenes—Translations into English.   2. Speeches, addresses, etc., Greek—Translations into English.   3. Athens (Greece)—Politics and government—Early works to 1800.   I. Yunis, Harvey.   II. Demosthenes. On the dishonest embassy.   III. Title.   IV. Series.
    PA3951.E5   2005
    885'.01—dc22

                                                                    2004008741

CONTENTS

SERIES EDITOR'S PREFACE

This is the ninth volume in a series of translations of *The Oratory of Classical Greece*. The aim of the series is to make available primarily for those who do not read Greek up-to-date, accurate, and readable translations with introductions and explanatory notes of all the surviving works and major fragments of the Attic orators of the classical period (ca. 420–320 BC): Aeschines, Andocides, Antiphon, Demosthenes, Dinarchus, Hyperides, Isaeus, Isocrates, Lycurgus, and Lysias. This is the third volume of Demosthenes to appear, and it includes his most famous speech, *On the Crown*—often considered the greatest example of Greek oratory—together with *On the Dishonest Embassy,* the other great speech we have from his battles with Aeschines over Athenian foreign policy. These two speeches, together with Aeschines 2 and 3, are the only instances where both speeches from the same trial survive.

Once again I would like to thank all those at the University of Texas Press who have worked with this volume and the others in the series, Director Joanna Hitchcock, Humanities Editor Jim Burr, Managing Editor Carolyn Wylie, Copyeditor Nancy Moore, and the production staff.

—M. G.

TRANSLATOR'S ACKNOWLEDGMENTS

The introduction to the volume and the introductions to the individual speeches include, with alterations, material from the introduction to my book *Demosthenes: On the Crown,* published by Cambridge University Press. The material is reprinted here with the permission of the press, for which I am most grateful. I am also grateful to Michael Gagarin, who improved the translations immensely. And thanks again to Tom Elliott for his help with the map.

—H. Y.

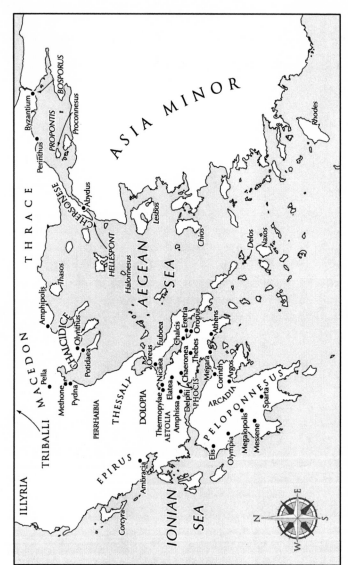

Greece, Macedon, and the Aegean

SERIES INTRODUCTION
Greek Oratory

❧❧

By Michael Gagarin

ORATORY IN CLASSICAL ATHENS

From as early as Homer (and undoubtedly much earlier) the Greeks placed a high value on effective speaking. Even Achilles, whose greatness was primarily established on the battlefield, was brought up to be "a speaker of words and a doer of deeds" (*Iliad* 9.443); and Athenian leaders of the sixth and fifth centuries,[1] such as Solon, Themistocles, and Pericles, were all accomplished orators. Most Greek literary genres —notably epic, tragedy, and history—underscore the importance of oratory by their inclusion of set speeches. The formal pleadings of the envoys to Achilles in the *Iliad,* the messenger speeches in tragedy reporting events like the battle of Salamis in Aeschylus' *Persians* or the gruesome death of Pentheus in Euripides' *Bacchae,* and the powerful political oratory of Pericles' funeral oration in Thucydides are but a few of the most notable examples of the Greeks' never-ending fascination with formal public speaking, which was to reach its height in the public oratory of the fourth century.

In early times, oratory was not a specialized subject of study but was learned by practice and example. The formal study of rhetoric as an "art" (*technē*) began, we are told, in the middle of the fifth century in Sicily with the work of Corax and his pupil Tisias.[2] These two are

---

[1] All dates in this volume are BC unless the contrary is either indicated or obvious.

[2] See Kennedy 1963: 26–51. Cole 1991 has challenged this traditional picture, arguing that the term "rhetoric" was coined by Plato to designate and denigrate an activity he strongly opposed. Cole's own reconstruction is not without prob-

scarcely more than names to us, but another famous Sicilian, Gorgias of Leontini (ca. 490–390), developed a new style of argument and is reported to have dazzled the Athenians with a speech delivered when he visited Athens in 427. Gorgias initiated the practice, which continued into the early fourth century, of composing speeches for mythical or imaginary occasions. The surviving examples reveal a lively intellectual climate in the late fifth and early fourth centuries, in which oratory served to display new ideas, new forms of expression, and new methods of argument.[3] This tradition of "intellectual" oratory was continued by the fourth-century educator Isocrates and played a large role in later Greek and Roman education.

In addition to this intellectual oratory, at about the same time the practice also began of writing speeches for real occasions in public life, which we may designate "practical" oratory. For centuries Athenians had been delivering speeches in public settings (primarily the courts and the Assembly), but these had always been composed and delivered impromptu, without being written down and thus without being preserved. The practice of writing speeches began in the courts and then expanded to include the Assembly and other settings. Athens was one of the leading cities of Greece in the fifth and fourth centuries, and its political and legal systems depended on direct participation by a large number of citizens; all important decisions were made by these large bodies, and the primary means of influencing these decisions was oratory.[4] Thus, it is not surprising that oratory flourished in Athens,[5] but it may not be immediately obvious why it should be written down.

The pivotal figure in this development was Antiphon, one of the fifth-century intellectuals who are often grouped together under the

---

lems, but he does well to remind us how thoroughly the traditional view of rhetoric depends on one of its most ardent opponents.

[3] Of these only Antiphon's *Tetralogies* are included in this series. Gorgias' *Helen* and *Palamedes,* Alcidamas' *Odysseus,* and Antisthenes' *Ajax* and *Odysseus* are translated in Gagarin and Woodruff 1995.

[4] Yunis 1996 has a good treatment of political oratory from Pericles to Demosthenes.

[5] All our evidence for practical oratory comes from Athens, with the exception of Isocrates 19, written for a trial in Aegina. Many speeches were undoubtedly delivered in courts and political forums in other Greek cities, but it may be that such speeches were written down only in Athens.

name "Sophists."[6] Like some of the other sophists he contributed to
the intellectual oratory of the period, but he also had a strong practical
interest in law. At the same time, Antiphon had an aversion to public
speaking and did not directly involve himself in legal or political affairs (Thucydides 8.68). However, he began giving general advice to
other citizens who were engaged in litigation and were thus expected
to address the court themselves. As this practice grew, Antiphon went
further, and around 430 he began writing out whole speeches for others to memorize and deliver. Thus began the practice of "logography,"
which continued through the next century and beyond.[7] Logography
particularly appealed to men like Lysias, who were metics, or noncitizen residents of Athens. Since they were not Athenian citizens, they
were barred from direct participation in public life, but they could
contribute by writing speeches for others.

Antiphon was also the first (to our knowledge) to write down a
speech he would himself deliver, writing the speech for his own defense at his trial for treason in 411. His motive was probably to publicize and preserve his views, and others continued this practice of
writing down speeches they would themselves deliver in the courts
and (more rarely) the Assembly.[8] Finally, one other type of practical
oratory was the special tribute delivered on certain important public
occasions, the best known of which is the funeral oration. It is conve-
nient to designate these three types of oratory by the terms Aristotle
later uses: forensic (for the courts), deliberative (for the Assembly), and
epideictic (for display).[9]

---

[6] The term "sophist" was loosely used through the fifth and fourth centuries
to designate various intellectuals and orators, but under the influence of Plato,
who attacked certain figures under this name, the term is now used of a specific
group of thinkers; see Kerferd 1981.

[7] For Antiphon as the first to write speeches, see Photius, *Bibliotheca* 486a7–11
and [Plut.], *Moralia* 832c–d. The latest extant speech can be dated to 320, but we
know that at least one orator, Dinarchus, continued the practice after that date.

[8] Unlike forensic speeches, speeches for delivery in the Assembly were usually
not composed beforehand in writing, since the speaker could not know exactly
when or in what context he would be speaking; see further Trevett 1996.

[9] *Rhetoric* 1.3. Intellectual orations, like Gorgias' *Helen,* do not easily fit into
Aristotle's classification. For a fuller (but still brief) introduction to Attic oratory
and the orators, see Edwards 1994.

THE ORATORS

In the century from about 420 to 320, dozens—perhaps even hundreds—of now unknown orators and logographers must have composed speeches that are now lost, but only ten of these men were selected for preservation and study by ancient scholars, and only works collected under the names of these ten have been preserved. Some of these works are undoubtedly spurious, though in most cases they are fourth-century works by a different author rather than later "forgeries." Indeed, modern scholars suspect that as many as seven of the speeches attributed to Demosthenes may have been written by Apollodorus, son of Pasion, who is sometimes called "the eleventh orator." [10] Including these speeches among the works of Demosthenes may have been an honest mistake, or perhaps a bookseller felt he could sell more copies of these speeches if they were attributed to a more famous orator.

In alphabetical order the Ten Orators are as follows: [11]

- AESCHINES (ca. 395–ca. 322) rose from obscure origins to become an important Athenian political figure, first an ally, then a bitter enemy of Demosthenes. His three speeches all concern major public issues. The best known of these (Aes. 3) was delivered at the trial in 330, when Demosthenes responded with *On the Crown* (Dem. 18). Aeschines lost the case and was forced to leave Athens and live the rest of his life in exile.

- ANDOCIDES (ca. 440–ca. 390) is best known for his role in the scandal of 415, when just before the departure of the fateful Athenian expedition to Sicily during the Peloponnesian War (431–404), a band of young men mutilated statues of Hermes, and at the same time information was revealed about the secret rites of Demeter. Andocides was exiled but later returned. Two of the four speeches

[10] See Trevett 1992.

[11] The Loeb volumes of *Minor Attic Orators* also include the prominent Athenian political figure Demades (ca. 385–319), who was not one of the Ten; but the only speech that has come down to us under his name is a later forgery. It is possible that Demades and other fourth-century politicians who had a high reputation for public speaking did not put any speeches in writing, especially if they rarely spoke in the courts (see above n. 8).

in his name give us a contemporary view of the scandal: one pleads for his return, the other argues against a second period of exile.

- ANTIPHON (ca. 480–411), as already noted, wrote forensic speeches for others and only once spoke himself. In 411 he participated in an oligarchic coup by a group of 400, and when the democrats regained power he was tried for treason and executed. His six surviving speeches include three for delivery in court and the three Tetralogies—imaginary intellectual exercises for display or teaching that consist of four speeches each, two on each side. All six of Antiphon's speeches concern homicide, probably because these stood at the beginning of the collection of his works. Fragments of some thirty other speeches cover many different topics.

- DEMOSTHENES (384–322) is generally considered the best of the Attic orators. Although his nationalistic message is less highly regarded today, his powerful mastery of and ability to combine many different rhetorical styles continues to impress readers. Demosthenes was still a child when his wealthy father died. The trustees of the estate apparently misappropriated much of it, and when he came of age, he sued them in a series of cases (27–31), regaining some of his fortune and making a name as a powerful speaker. He then wrote speeches for others in a variety of cases, public and private, and for his own use in court (where many cases involved major public issues), and in the Assembly, where he opposed the growing power of Philip of Macedon. The triumph of Philip and his son Alexander the Great eventually put an end to Demosthenes' career. Some sixty speeches have come down under his name, about a third of them of questionable authenticity.

- DINARCHUS (ca. 360–ca. 290) was born in Corinth but spent much of his life in Athens as a metic (a noncitizen resident). His public fame came primarily from writing speeches for the prosecutions surrounding the Harpalus affair in 324, when several prominent figures (including Demosthenes) were accused of bribery. After 322 he had a profitable career as a logographer.

- HYPERIDES (389/8–322) was a political leader and logographer of so many different talents that he was called the pentathlete of orators. He was a leader of the Athenian resistance to Philip and

Alexander and (like Demosthenes) was condemned to death after Athens' final surrender. One speech and substantial fragments of five others have been recovered from papyrus remains; otherwise, only fragments survive.

- ISAEUS (ca. 415–ca. 340) wrote speeches on a wide range of topics, but the eleven complete speeches that survive, dating from ca. 390 to ca. 344, all concern inheritance. As with Antiphon, the survival of these particular speeches may have been the result of the later ordering of his speeches by subject; we have part of a twelfth speech and fragments and titles of some forty other works. Isaeus is said to have been a pupil of Isocrates and the teacher of Demosthenes.

- ISOCRATES (436–338) considered himself a philosopher and educator, not an orator or rhetorician. He came from a wealthy Athenian family but lost most of his property in the Peloponnesian War, and in 403 he took up logography. About 390 he abandoned this practice and turned to writing and teaching, setting forth his educational, philosophical, and political views in essays that took the form of speeches but were not meant for oral delivery. He favored accommodation with the growing power of Philip of Macedon and panhellenic unity. His school was based on a broad concept of rhetoric and applied philosophy; it attracted pupils from the entire Greek world (including Isaeus, Lycurgus, and Hyperides) and became the main rival of Plato's Academy. Isocrates greatly influenced education and rhetoric in the Hellenistic, Roman, and modern periods until the eighteenth century.

- LYCURGUS (ca. 390–ca. 324) was a leading public official who restored the financial condition of Athens after 338 and played a large role in the city for the next dozen years. He brought charges of corruption or treason against many other officials, usually with success. Only one speech survives.

- LYSIAS (ca. 445–ca. 380) was a metic—an official resident of Athens but not a citizen. Much of his property was seized by the Thirty during their short-lived oligarchic coup in 404–403. Perhaps as a result he turned to logography. More than thirty speeches survive in whole or in part, though the authenticity of some is doubted. We also have fragments or know the titles of more than a hundred others. The speeches cover a wide range of cases, and he may have delivered one himself (Lys. 12), on the death of his brother at the hands of the Thirty. Lysias is particularly known for his vivid narratives, his *ēthopoiïa*, or "creation of character," and his prose style, which became a model of clarity and vividness.

THE WORKS OF THE ORATORS

As soon as speeches began to be written down, they could be preserved. We know little about the conditions of book "publication" (i.e., making copies for distribution) in the fourth century, but there was an active market for books in Athens, and some of the speeches may have achieved wide circulation.[12] An orator (or his family) may have preserved his own speeches, perhaps to advertise his ability or demonstrate his success, or booksellers may have collected and copied them in order to make money.

We do not know how closely the preserved text of these speeches corresponded to the version actually delivered in court or in the Assembly. Speakers undoubtedly extemporized or varied from their text on occasion, but there is no good evidence that deliberative speeches were substantially revised for publication.[13] In forensic oratory a logographer's reputation would derive first and foremost from his success with jurors. If a forensic speech was victorious, there would be no reason to alter it for publication, and if it lost, alteration would probably not deceive potential clients. Thus, the published texts of forensic speeches were probably quite faithful to the texts that were provided to clients, and we have little reason to suspect substantial alteration in the century or so before they were collected by scholars in Alexandria (see below).

In addition to the speaker's text, most forensic speeches have breaks for the inclusion of documents. The logographer inserted a notation in his text—such as *nomos* ("law") or *martyria* ("testimony")—and the

---

[12] Dover's discussion (1968) of the preservation and transmission of the works of Lysias (and perhaps others under his name) is useful not just for Lysias but for the other orators too. His theory of shared authorship between logographer and litigant, however, is unconvincing (see Usher 1976).

[13] See further Trevett 1996: 437–439.

speaker would pause while the clerk read out the text of a law or the testimony of witnesses. Many speeches survive with only a notation that a *nomos* or *martyria* was read at that point, but in some cases the text of the document is included. It used to be thought that these documents were all creations of later scholars, but many (though not all) are now accepted as genuine.[14]

With the foundation of the famous library in Alexandria early in the third century, scholars began to collect and catalogue texts of the orators, along with many other classical authors. Only the best orators were preserved in the library, many of them represented by over 100 speeches each (some undoubtedly spurious). Only some of these works survived in manuscript form to the modern era; more recently a few others have been discovered on ancient sheets of papyrus, so that today the corpus of Attic Oratory consists of about 150 speeches, together with a few letters and other works. The subject matter ranges from important public issues and serious crimes to business affairs, lovers' quarrels, inheritance disputes, and other personal or family matters.

In the centuries after these works were collected, ancient scholars gathered biographical facts about their authors, produced grammatical and lexicographic notes, and used some of the speeches as evidence for Athenian political history. But the ancient scholars who were most interested in the orators were those who studied prose style, the most notable of these being Dionysius of Halicarnassus (first century BC), who wrote treatises on several of the orators,[15] and Hermogenes of Tarsus (second century AD), who wrote several literary studies, including *On Types of Style*.[16] But relative to epic or tragedy, oratory was little studied; and even scholars of rhetoric whose interests were broader than style, like Cicero and Quintilian, paid little attention to the orators, except for the acknowledged master, Demosthenes.

Most modern scholars until the second half of the twentieth century continued to treat the orators primarily as prose stylists.[17] The

---

[14] See MacDowell 1990: 43–47; Todd 1993: 44–45.

[15] Dionysius' literary studies are collected and translated in Usher 1974–1985.

[16] Wooten 1987. Stylistic considerations probably also influenced the selection of the "canon" of ten orators; see Worthington 1994.

[17] For example, the most popular and influential book ever written on the orators, Jebb's *The Attic Orators* (1875) was presented as an "attempt to aid in giving Attic Oratory its due place in the history of Attic Prose" (I.xiii). This modern focus

reevaluation of Athenian democracy by George Grote and others in the nineteenth century stimulated renewed interest in Greek oratory among historians; and increasing interest in Athenian law during that century led a few legal scholars to read the orators. But in comparison with the interest shown in the other literary genres—epic, lyric, tragedy, comedy, and even history—Attic oratory has been relatively neglected until the last third of the twentieth century. More recently, however, scholars have discovered the value of the orators for the broader study of Athenian culture and society. Since Dover's groundbreaking works on popular morality and homosexuality,[18] interest in the orators has been increasing rapidly, and they are now seen as primary representatives of Athenian moral and social values, and as evidence for social and economic conditions, political and social ideology, and in general those aspects of Athenian culture that in the past were commonly ignored by historians of ancient Greece but are of increasing interest and importance today, including women and the family, slavery, and the economy.

GOVERNMENT AND LAW IN CLASSICAL ATHENS

The hallmark of the Athenian political and legal systems was its amateurism. Most public officials, including those who supervised the courts, were selected by lot and held office for a limited period, typically a year. Thus a great many citizens held public office at some point in their lives, but almost none served for an extended period of time or developed the experience or expertise that would make them professionals. All significant policy decisions were debated and voted on in the Assembly, where the quorum was 6,000 citizens, and all significant legal cases were judged by bodies of 200 to 500 jurors or more. Public prominence was not achieved by election (or selection) to public office but depended rather on a man's ability to sway the majority of citizens in the Assembly or jurors in court to vote in favor of a pro-

---

on prose style can plausibly be connected to the large role played by prose composition (the translation of English prose into Greek, usually in imitation of specific authors or styles) in the Classics curriculum, especially in Britain.

[18] Dover (1974, 1978). Dover recently commented (1994: 157), "When I began to mine the riches of Attic forensic oratory I was astonished to discover that the mine had never been exploited."

posed course of action or for one of the litigants in a trial. Success was never permanent, and a victory on one policy issue or a verdict in one case could be quickly reversed in another.[19] In such a system the value of public oratory is obvious, and in the fourth century, oratory became the most important cultural institution in Athens, replacing drama as the forum where major ideological concerns were displayed and debated.

Several recent books give good detailed accounts of Athenian government and law,[20] and so a brief sketch can suffice here. The main policy-making body was the Assembly, open to all adult male citizens; a small payment for attendance enabled at least some of the poor to attend along with the leisured rich. In addition, a Council of 500 citizens, selected each year by lot with no one allowed to serve more than two years, prepared material for and made recommendations to the Assembly; a rotating subgroup of this Council served as an executive committee, the Prytaneis. Finally, numerous officials, most of them selected by lot for one-year terms, supervised different areas of administration and finance. The most important of these were the nine Archons (lit. "rulers"): the eponymous Archon after whom the year was named, the Basileus ("king"),[21] the Polemarch, and the six Thesmothetae. Councilors and almost all these officials underwent a preliminary examination (*dokimasia*) before taking office, and officials submitted to a final accounting (*euthynai*) upon leaving; at these times any citizen who wished could challenge a person's fitness for his new position or his performance in his recent position.

---

[19] In the Assembly this could be accomplished by a reconsideration of the question, as in the famous Mytilenean debate (Thuc. 3.36–50); in court a verdict was final, but its practical effects could be thwarted or reversed by later litigation on a related issue.

[20] For government, see Sinclair 1988, Hansen 1991; for law, MacDowell 1978, Todd 1993, and Boegehold 1995 (Bonner 1927 is still helpful). Much of our information about the legal and political systems comes from a work attributed to Aristotle but perhaps written by a pupil of his, *The Athenian Constitution* (*Ath. Pol.*—conveniently translated with notes by Rhodes 1984). The discovery of this work on a papyrus in Egypt in 1890 caused a major resurgence of interest in Athenian government.

[21] Modern scholars often use the term *archōn basileus* or "king archon," but Athenian sources (e.g., *Ath. Pol.* 57) simply call him the *basileus*.

There was no general taxation of Athenian citizens. Sources of public funding included the annual tax levied on metics, various fees and import duties, and (in the fifth century) tribute from allied cities; but the source that figures most prominently in the orators is the Athenian system of liturgies (*leitourgiai*), by which in a regular rotation the rich provided funding for certain special public needs. The main liturgies were the *chorēgia,* in which a sponsor (*chorēgos*) supervised and paid for the training and performance of a chorus which sang and danced at a public festival,[22] and the trierarchy, in which a sponsor (trierarch) paid to equip and usually commanded a trireme, or warship, for a year. Some of these liturgies required substantial expenditures, but even so, some men spent far more than required in order to promote themselves and their public careers, and litigants often tried to impress the jurors by referring to liturgies they had undertaken (see, e.g., Lys. 21.1–n5). A further twist on this system was that if a man thought he had been assigned a liturgy that should have gone to someone else who was richer than he, he could propose an exchange of property (*antidosis*), giving the other man a choice of either taking over the liturgy or exchanging property with him. Finally, the rich were also subject to special taxes (*eisphorai*) levied as a percentage of their property in times of need.

The Athenian legal system remained similarly resistant to professionalization. Trials and the procedures leading up to them were supervised by officials, primarily the nine Archons, but their role was purely administrative, and they were in no way equivalent to modern judges. All significant questions about what we would call points of law were presented to the jurors, who considered them together with all other issues when they delivered their verdict at the end of the trial.[23] Trials were "contests" (*agōnes*) between two litigants, each of whom presented his own case to the jurors in a speech, plaintiff first, then de-

---

[22] These included the productions of tragedy and comedy, for which the main expense was for the chorus.

[23] Certain religious "interpreters" (*exēgētai*) were occasionally asked to give their opinion on a legal matter that had a religious dimension (such as the prosecution of a homicide), but although these opinions could be reported in court (e.g., Dem. 47.68–73), they had no official legal standing. The most significant administrative decision we hear of is the refusal of the Basileus to accept the case in Antiphon 6 (see 6.37–46).

fendant; in some cases each party then spoke again, probably in rebuttal. Since a litigant had only one or two speeches in which to present his entire case, and no issue was decided separately by a judge, all the necessary factual information and every important argument on substance or procedure, fact or law, had to be presented together. A single speech might thus combine narrative, argument, emotional appeal, and various digressions, all with the goal of obtaining a favorable verdict. Even more than today, a litigant's primary task was to control the issue—to determine which issues the jurors would consider most important and which questions they would have in their minds as they cast their votes. We only rarely have both speeches from a trial,[24] and we usually have little or no external evidence for the facts of a case or the verdict. We must thus infer both the facts and the opponent's strategy from the speech we have, and any assessment of the overall effectiveness of a speech and of the logographer's strategy is to some extent speculative.

Before a trial there were usually several preliminary hearings for presenting evidence; arbitration, public and private, was available and sometimes required. These hearings and arbitration sessions allowed each side to become familiar with the other side's case, so that discussions of "what my opponent will say" could be included in one's speech. Normally a litigant presented his own case, but he was often assisted by family or friends. If he wished (and could afford it), he could enlist the services of a logographer, who presumably gave strategic advice in addition to writing a speech. The speeches were timed to ensure an equal hearing for both sides,[25] and all trials were completed within a day. Two hundred or more jurors decided each case in the popular courts, which met in the Agora.[26] Homicide cases and certain other religious trials (e.g., Lys. 7) were heard by the Council of the Areopagus or an associated group of fifty-one Ephetae. The Areopagus was composed of all former Archons—perhaps 150–200 members at most

---

[24] The exceptions are Demosthenes 19 and Aeschines 2, Aeschines 3 and Demosthenes 18, and Lysias 6 (one of several prosecution speeches) and Andocides 1; all were written for major public cases.

[25] Timing was done by means of a water-clock, which in most cases was stopped during the reading of documents.

[26] See Boegehold 1995.

times. It met on a hill called the Areopagus ("rock of Ares") near the Acropolis.

Jurors for the regular courts were selected by lot from those citizens who registered each year and who appeared for duty that day; as with the Assembly, a small payment allowed the poor to serve. After the speakers had finished, the jurors voted immediately without any formal discussion. The side with the majority won; a tie vote decided the case for the defendant. In some cases where the penalty was not fixed, after a conviction the jurors voted again on the penalty, choosing between penalties proposed by each side. Even when we know the verdict, we cannot know which of the speaker's arguments contributed most to his success or failure. However, a logographer could probably learn from jurors which points had or had not been successful, so that arguments that are found repeatedly in speeches probably were known to be effective in most cases.

The first written laws in Athens were enacted by Draco (ca. 620) and Solon (ca. 590), and new laws were regularly added. At the end of the fifth century the existing laws were reorganized, and a new procedure for enacting laws was instituted; thereafter a group of Law-Givers (*nomothetai*) had to certify that a proposed law did not conflict with any existing laws. There was no attempt, however, to organize legislation systematically, and although Plato, Aristotle, and other philosophers wrote various works on law and law-giving, these were either theoretical or descriptive and had no apparent influence on legislation. Written statutes generally used ordinary language rather than precise legal definitions in designating offenses, and questions concerning precisely what constituted a specific offense or what was the correct interpretation of a written statute were decided (together with other issues) by the jurors in each case. A litigant might, of course, assert a certain definition or interpretation as "something you all know" or "what the lawgiver intended," but such remarks are evidently tendentious and cannot be taken as authoritative.

The result of these procedural and substantive features was that the verdict depended largely on each litigant's speech (or speeches). As one speaker puts it (Ant. 6.18), "When there are no witnesses, you (jurors) are forced to reach a verdict about the case on the basis of the prosecutor's and defendant's words alone; you must be suspicious and examine their accounts in detail, and your vote will necessarily be cast on the basis of likelihood rather than clear knowledge." Even the testimony of witnesses (usually on both sides) is rarely decisive. On the other hand, most speakers make a considerable effort to establish facts and provide legitimate arguments in conformity with established law. Plato's view of rhetoric as a clever technique for persuading an ignorant crowd that the false is true is not borne out by the speeches, and the legal system does not appear to have produced many arbitrary or clearly unjust results.

The main form of legal procedure was a *dikē* ("suit") in which the injured party (or his relatives in a case of homicide) brought suit against the offender. Suits for injuries to slaves would be brought by the slave's master, and injuries to women would be prosecuted by a male relative. Strictly speaking, a *dikē* was a private matter between individuals, though like all cases, *dikai* often had public dimensions. The other major form of procedure was a *graphē* ("writing" or "indictment") in which "anyone who wished" (i.e., any citizen) could bring a prosecution for wrongdoing. *Graphai* were instituted by Solon, probably in order to allow prosecution of offenses where the victim was unable or unlikely to bring suit himself, such as selling a dependent into slavery; but the number of areas covered by *graphai* increased to cover many types of public offenses as well as some apparently private crimes, such as *hybris*.

The system of prosecution by "anyone who wished" also extended to several other more specialized forms of prosecution, like *eisangelia* ("impeachment"), used in cases of treason. Another specialized prosecution was *apagōgē* ("summary arrest"), in which someone could arrest a common criminal (*kakourgos,* lit. "evil-doer"), or have him arrested, on the spot. The reliance on private initiative meant that Athenians never developed a system of public prosecution; rather, they presumed that everyone would keep an eye on the behavior of his political enemies and bring suit as soon as he suspected a crime, both to harm his opponents and to advance his own career. In this way all public officials would be watched by someone. There was no disgrace in admitting that a prosecution was motivated by private enmity.

By the end of the fifth century the system of prosecution by "anyone who wished" was apparently being abused by so-called sykophants (*sykophantai*), who allegedly brought or threatened to bring false suits against rich men, either to gain part of the fine that would be levied or to induce an out-of-court settlement in which the accused would pay to have the matter dropped. We cannot gauge the true extent of this problem, since speakers usually provide little evidence to support their claims that their opponents are sykophants, but the Athenians did make sykophancy a crime. They also specified that in many public procedures a plaintiff who either dropped the case or failed to obtain one-fifth of the votes would have to pay a heavy fine of 1,000 drachmas. Despite this, it appears that litigation was common in Athens and was seen by some as excessive.

Over the course of time, the Athenian legal and political systems have more often been judged negatively than positively. Philosophers and political theorists have generally followed the lead of Plato (427–347), who lived and worked in Athens his entire life while severely criticizing its system of government as well as many other aspects of its culture. For Plato, democracy amounted to the tyranny of the masses over the educated elite and was destined to collapse from its own instability. The legal system was capricious and depended entirely on the rhetorical ability of litigants with no regard for truth or justice. These criticisms have often been echoed by modern scholars, who particularly complain that law was much too closely interwoven with politics and did not have the autonomous status it achieved in Roman law and continues to have, at least in theory, in modern legal systems.

Plato's judgments are valid if one accepts the underlying presuppositions, that the aim of law is absolute truth and abstract justice and that achieving the highest good of the state requires thorough and systematic organization. Most Athenians do not seem to have subscribed to either the criticisms or the presuppositions, and most scholars now accept the long-ignored fact that despite major external disruptions in the form of wars and two short-lived coups brought about by one of these wars, the Athenian legal and political systems remained remarkably stable for almost two hundred years (508–320). Moreover, like all other Greek cities at the time, whatever their form of government, Athenian democracy was brought to an end not by internal forces but by the external power of Philip of Macedon and his son Alexander. The legal system never became autonomous, and the rich sometimes complained that they were victims of unscrupulous litigants, but there is no indication that the people wanted to yield control of the legal process to a professional class, as Plato recommended. For most Athe-

nians—Plato being an exception in this and many other matters—
one purpose of the legal system was to give everyone the opportunity
to have his case heard by other citizens and have it heard quickly and
cheaply; and in this it clearly succeeded.

Indeed, the Athenian legal system also served the interests of the
rich, even the very rich, as well as the common people, in that it provided a forum for the competition that since Homer had been an important part of aristocratic life. In this competition, the rich used the
courts as battlegrounds, though their main weapon was the rhetoric of
popular ideology, which hailed the rule of law and promoted the ideal
of moderation and restraint.[27] But those who aspired to political leadership and the honor and status that accompanied it repeatedly entered
the legal arena, bringing suit against their political enemies whenever
possible and defending themselves against suits brought by others
whenever necessary. The ultimate judges of these public competitions
were the common people, who seem to have relished the dramatic
clash of individuals and ideologies. In this respect fourth-century oratory was the cultural heir of fifth-century drama and was similarly ap-
preciated by the citizens. Despite the disapproval of intellectuals like
Plato, most Athenians legitimately considered their legal system a hallmark of their democracy and a vital presence in their culture.

THE TRANSLATION OF GREEK ORATORY

The purpose of this series is to provide students and scholars in all
fields with accurate, readable translations of all surviving classical Attic oratory, including speeches whose authenticity is disputed, as well
as the substantial surviving fragments. In keeping with the originals,
the language is for the most part nontechnical. Names of persons and
places are given in the (generally more familiar) Latinized forms, and
names of officials or legal procedures have been translated into English
equivalents, where possible. Notes are intended to provide the necessary historical and cultural background; scholarly controversies are
generally not discussed. The notes and introductions refer to scholarly
treatments in addition to those listed below, which the reader may
consult for further information.

---

[27] Ober 1989 is fundamental; see also Cohen 1995.

Cross-references to other speeches follow the standard numbering system, which is now well established except in the case of Hyperides (for whom the numbering of the Oxford Classical Text is used).[28] References are by work and section (e.g., Dem. 24.73); spurious works are not specially marked; when no author is named (e.g., 24.73), the reference is to the same author as the annotated passage.

ABBREVIATIONS

Aes.	= Aeschines
And.	= Andocides
Ant.	= Antiphon
Arist.	= Aristotle
Aristoph.	= Aristophanes
Ath. Pol.	= *The Athenian Constitution*
Dem.	= Demosthenes
Din.	= Dinarchus
Herod.	= Herodotus
Hyp.	= Hyperides
Is.	= Isaeus
Isoc.	= Isocrates
Lyc.	= Lycurgus
Lys.	= Lysias
Plut.	= Plutarch
Thuc.	= Thucydides
Xen.	= Xenophon

NOTE: The main unit of Athenian currency was the drachma; this was divided into obols and larger amounts were designated minas and talents.

1 drachma = 6 obols
1 mina = 100 drachmas
1 talent = 60 minas (6,000 drachmas)

It is impossible to give an accurate equivalence in terms of modern currency, but it may be helpful to remember that the daily wage of

---

[28] For a listing of all the orators and their works, with classifications (forensic, deliberative, epideictic) and rough dates, see Edwards 1994: 74–79.

some skilled workers was a drachma in the mid-fifth century and 2–
2½ drachmas in the later fourth century. Thus it may not be too misleading to think of a drachma as worth about $50 or £33 and a talent
as about $300,000 or £200,000 in 1997 currency.

BIBLIOGRAPHY OF WORKS CITED

Boegehold, Alan L., 1995: *The Lawcourts at Athens: Sites, Buildings,
Equipment, Procedure, and Testimonia*. Princeton.
Bonner, Robert J., 1927: *Lawyers and Litigants in Ancient Athens*.
Chicago.
Carey, Christopher, 1997: *Trials from Classical Athens*. London.
Cohen, David, 1995: *Law, Violence and Community in Classical Athens*.
Cambridge.
Cole, Thomas, 1991: *The Origins of Rhetoric in Ancient Greece*.
Baltimore.
Dover, Kenneth J., 1968: *Lysias and the Corpus Lysiacum*. Berkeley.
———, 1974: *Greek Popular Morality in the Time of Plato and Aris-
totle*. Oxford.
———, 1978: *Greek Homosexuality*. London.
———, 1994: *Marginal Comment*. London.
Edwards, Michael, 1994: *The Attic Orators*. London.
Gagarin, Michael, and Paul Woodruff, 1995: *Early Greek Political
Thought from Homer to the Sophists*. Cambridge.
Hansen, Mogens Herman, 1991: *The Athenian Democracy in the Age of
Demosthenes*. Oxford.
Jebb, Richard, 1875: *The Attic Orators,* 2 vols. London.
Kennedy, George A., 1963: *The Art of Persuasion in Greece*. Princeton.
Kerferd, G. B., 1981: *The Sophistic Movement*. Cambridge.
MacDowell, Douglas M., 1978: *The Law in Classical Athens*. London.
———, ed. 1990: *Demosthenes, Against Meidias*. Oxford.
Ober, Josiah, 1989: *Mass and Elite in Democratic Athens*. Princeton.
Rhodes, P. J., trans., 1984: *Aristotle, The Athenian Constitution*. Penguin
Books.
Sinclair, R. K., 1988: *Democracy and Participation in Athens*. Cam-
bridge.
Todd, Stephen, 1993: *The Shape of Athenian Law*. Oxford.

Trevett, Jeremy, 1992: *Apollodoros the Son of Pasion.* Oxford.

————, 1996: "Did Demosthenes Publish His Deliberative Speeches?" *Hermes* 124: 425–441.

Usher, Stephen, 1976: "Lysias and His Clients," *Greek, Roman and Byzantine Studies* 17: 31–40.

————, trans., 1974–1985: *Dionysius of Halicarnassus, Critical Essays.* 2 vols. Loeb Classical Library. Cambridge, MA.

————, 1999: *Greek Oratory: Tradition and Originality.* Oxford.

Wooten, Cecil W., trans., 1987: *Hermogenes' On Types of Style.* Chapel Hill, NC.

Worthington, Ian, 1994: "The Canon of the Ten Attic Orators," in *Persuasion: Greek Rhetoric in Action,* ed. Ian Worthington. London: 244–263.

Yunis, Harvey, 1996: *Taming Democracy: Models of Political Rhetoric in Classical Athens.* Ithaca, NY.

DEMOSTHENES, SPEECHES 18 AND 19

INTRODUCTION TO DEMOSTHENES

❖❖

By Michael Gagarin

Since antiquity Demosthenes (384–322 BC) has usually been judged the greatest of the Attic orators. Although the patriotic and nationalistic tenor of his message has been more highly regarded in some periods of history than in others, he is unique in his mastery of so many different rhetorical styles and his ability to blend them into a powerful ensemble.

LIFE

Demosthenes was born into an old wealthy Athenian family. His father Demosthenes owned workshops that made swords and furniture. His maternal grandfather, Gylon, had been exiled from Athens and lived in the Crimea, where his mother Cleobule was born (perhaps to a Scythian mother). When Demosthenes was seven, his father died leaving his estate in the trust of several guardians. According to Demosthenes' own account, the guardians mismanaged and defrauded the estate to the point that when he turned eighteen, the age of majority, he received almost nothing. He devoted the next several years to recovering his property, first studying forensic pleading and then bringing a series of suits against the guardians to recover his patrimony (speeches 27–31). He won the first case (27, *Against Aphobus I*), but then had to bring several more suits in order to collect the amount awarded him by the court. In the course of these trials he gained a reputation as a successful speaker, became sought after by others, and began to write speeches for a wide range of private suits, including inheritance, shipping loans, assault, and trespass. His clients included one of the richest men in Athens, the banker Phormio; the speech *For Phormio* (36) involves a dispute over twenty talents (equivalent to several million dollars today). Demosthenes' vivid characterization of the honest, hard-working Phormio and his malicious and extravagant opponent proved so convincing that the jurors reportedly refused to listen to the other side and took the highly unusual step of voting immediately for Phormio.

In 355 Demosthenes became involved in his first major public case (22, *Against Androtion*). By this time it was common for ambitious or influential citizens to bring legal charges against their political opponents on matters of public interest. Charges of proposing an illegal decree (the *graphē paranomōn*) were particularly common; these involved the indictment of the proposer of a decree on the ground that it conflicted with existing law.[1] Although these speeches addressed the specific issue of a conflict between laws, it was generally accepted that the merits of the decree, and of its proposer, were also relevant factors, and these cases formed a major arena for the ongoing political struggles between leading figures in the city.

About the same time Demosthenes also began to publish speeches on public issues which he delivered in the assembly, and after 350, although he continued from time to time to write speeches for private disputes, he turned his attention primarily to public policy, especially relations between Athens and the growing power of Macedon under King Philip. Demosthenes' strategy throughout was to increase Athens' military readiness, to oppose Philip's expansion and to support other Greek cities in their resistance to it. Most notable in support of these objectives were the three *Olynthiacs* (1–3) in 349 unsuccessfully urging support for the city of Olynthus (which soon afterwards fell to Philip) and the four *Philippics* (4, 6, 9, 10) in 351–341 urging greater opposition to Philip. But Philip continued to extend his power into Greece, and in 338 he defeated a combined Greek force (including Athens) at the battle of Chaeronea in Boeotia, north of Attica. This battle

---

[1] One might compare the U.S. procedure of challenging the constitutionality of a law in court. Differences include the fact that today no charge is brought against the proposer of the law and that the case is heard by a small panel of professional judges, not the hundreds of untrained jurors who would have heard the case in Athens.

is usually taken to mark the end of the Greek cities' struggle to remain independent.

After Chaeronea Demosthenes continued to urge resistance to Philip, but his efforts were largely ineffectual and his successes and failures are more a matter of internal Athenian politics. His most prominent opponent during this period was Aeschines, who had been acquitted earlier (343) when Demosthenes brought a suit against him in connection with a delegation to Philip on which both men had served (19, cf. Aeschines 2). After Chaeronea, when a minor ally of Demosthenes named Ctesiphon proposed a decree awarding a crown to Demosthenes in recognition of his service to the city, Aeschines brought a *graphē paranomōn* against Ctesiphon (Aeschines 3). The suit, which was not tried until 330, raised legal objections to the proposed decree but also attacked the person and career of Demosthenes at considerable length. Demosthenes responded with his most famous speech *On the Crown* (18), often known by its Latin name *De Corona*. The verdict was so one-sided that Aeschines was fined for not receiving one-fifth of the votes and went into exile. This was Demosthenes' greatest triumph. The last years of his life, however, resulted in notable defeats, first in the rather shadowy Harpalus affair (324–323), from which no speech of his survives (but see Dinarchus 1). Shortly afterwards he was condemned to death at the instigation of pro-Macedonian forces and committed suicide.

WORKS

Sixty-one speeches and some miscellaneous works, including a collection of letters, have come down to us under Demosthenes' name. The authenticity of many of these has been challenged, often because of the allegedly poor quality of the work; but this reason is less often accepted today, and most of the public speeches and many of the private speeches are now thought to be authentic. Among the main exceptions are a group of private speeches (45, 46, 49, 50, 52, 53, 59 and possibly 47 and 51) that were delivered by Apollodorus and are now commonly thought to have been composed by him (Trevett 1992).

Apart from a funeral oration (60) and collections of proems and letters, Demosthenes' works fall into two groups, the assembly speeches (1–17) and the court speeches (18–59); the latter can be further divided into public and private speeches, though these are not formal legal categories. Notable among the public forensic speeches are *Against Meidias* (21), which has recently drawn attention for its pronouncements on Athenian public values, and his last surviving speech, *On the Crown* (18), generally recognized as his masterpiece. In this speech he uses his entire repertory of rhetorical strategies to defend his life and political career. He treats the legal issues of the case briefly, as being of minor concern, and then defends his conduct during the past three decades of Athenian history, arguing that even when his policy did not succeed, on each occasion it was the best policy for the city, in contrast to Aeschines' policies, which, when he ventured to propose any, were disastrous. Demosthenes' extensive personal attack on Aeschines' life and family may be too harsh for modern taste, but the blending of facts, innuendoes, sarcasm, rhetorical questions, and other devices is undeniably effective.

Demosthenes' private speeches have recently begun to attract more interest from scholars, who draw from them insight into Athenian social, political, and economic life. Only the speeches concerned with recovering his inheritance (27–31) were delivered by Demosthenes himself; the rest were written for delivery by other litigants. We have already noted *For Phormio*, which is one of several having to do with banking. *Against Conon* (54) alleges an assault by several young rowdies spurred on by their father, and *Against Neaera* (59), delivered and probably written by Apollodorus, recounts the life of a former slave woman and her affairs with different Athenian men.

STYLE

Demosthenes is a master of Greek prose style; he paid careful attention to style, and to the oral delivery of his speeches. His Roman counterpart, Cicero, modeled his oratorical style (and some other features of his work) in part on Demosthenes' Greek. Although Demosthenes' style varied considerably over the course of time and among the different types of speeches, later assessments of his style are based primarily on the public forensic speeches, and especially the last of these, *On the Crown*. Long and sometimes elaborate sentences are one feature of his style, but Demosthenes' true greatness is his ability to write in many styles and to vary his style, mixing different features together both to suit the topic and to give variety and vigor to his speeches. The final product required great skill and practice to deliver effectively, and the stories about Demosthenes' rigorous training in delivery (see in general Plutarch, *Life of Demosthenes* 6–7), even if not literally true, accurately reflect his priorities. Indeed, only by reading aloud sections of *On the Crown* in Greek can one truly appreciate the power and authority of his prose.

SIGNIFICANCE

Demosthenes played a vital role in Athenian public affairs for some thirty years. His advocacy of the vigilant defense of Greece against foreign invaders, though ultimately unsuccessful in preserving Greek freedom, inspired his fellow Athenians with patriotic loyalty, and has similarly inspired many others in later times. In recent times political rhetoric has not been so widely admired as in the past, and Demosthenes is less read today than he used to be. But he still represents the greatest achievement of Greek oratory and stands as one of the greatest orators of any age.

INTRODUCTION TO THIS VOLUME

〰〰〰

By Harvey Yunis

THE PREDICAMENT OF DEMOSTHENES' GENERATION AND THE SPEECHES AGAINST AESCHINES

When Demosthenes (384–322) ventured into Athenian politics in the 350s, Athens was still the largest, wealthiest, and most powerful Greek polis. The territory of Attica had been peaceful and secure for nearly two generations following the upheavals of defeat in the Peloponnesian War. Athens' institutions of democratic government were stable to an extent that was previously unequaled. Yet the Athenians were falling ever further behind in their ceaseless attempt to rebuild their great fifth-century empire and to equal, thereby, the wealth, power, and prestige of their forebears. Even at its height in the 370s, the naval alliance that the fourth-century Athenians arduously constructed was a pale imitation of the fifth-century empire. It kept Athens engaged throughout the Aegean and in much of the Greek world, yet by mid century, Athens' largest allies had defected, and its hold on the rest of its overseas assets had begun to weaken. Nevertheless, fourth-century Athenians never abandoned the claim to panhellenic leadership which their forebears first staked out during the Persian Wars and maintained as sacred tradition ever since.[1]

Philip II ascended the Macedonian throne in 359 and quickly secured his position as king and unified the Macedonian homeland. Acquiring resources in money and manpower, he expanded and reorganized the Macedonian army, turning it into the largest and

---

[1] See Badian 1995 on Athens' foreign policy in the fourth century.

most powerful force in the Mediterranean world. He began attacking neighboring territories, not least the Greeks directly to the south and southeast of Macedonia. The threat posed by Philip was unlike any the Greeks had encountered before. In the early fifth century, Greek cities led by Athens and Sparta allied to defeat the Persians in several decisive battles, which chased the invaders back to their distant homeland. In the fifth century the Athenian empire kept the Persians at a distance; in the fourth the Persian Kings were less able to intervene in Greece, and shifting but workable arrangements of coexistence were negotiated with the leading Greek cities. But the Macedonians were too close to be chased away. As a commander, Philip was tireless, fearless, enterprising, shrewd. For him, conquest was not an end in itself but a step towards entrenched dominion through puppet regimes, dynastic marriages, established institutions. Unlike the Persians, the Macedonian royal family had been hellenized for several generations. As a young man, Philip had spent several years as a hostage in Thebes. His knowledge of Greek affairs was deep.[2]

If Greek states were to cooperate to check Macedonian expansion, Athens had both the incentive and the burden to lead. Because Athens had allies and interests in the north of Greece, it suffered the consequences of Philip's conquests from the beginning, but during the first decade of his reign, Athenian resistance was inconsistent and ineffective. In 352, Philip advanced on Thermopylae (the gateway to central and southern Greece), a move that threatened Attica. The Athenians dispatched an emergency expedition to hold the place against him, a successful but makeshift operation. When Philip conquered Chalcidice in 348 and Athens saw its ally Olynthus enslaved and its own citizens captured, fighting there against Philip, the need for concerted action became palpable. Yet the Greeks were riven by conflicting interests, allegiances, and agendas both between the various cities and within them. Neither Athens nor any other Greek city, nor any individual or clique, was in a position to organize the sort of cooperation that might have made resistance, or some other response, effective. Unity of purpose and action had to be built up city by city,

---

[2] See Griffith 1979 on Philip's reign and conquests.

and within cities, faction by faction. That, in essence, is the predicament that faced Demosthenes' generation of Athenians.

To respond to this predicament, the Athenians relied on their regular democratic procedures, which required politicians to argue against each other for the support and approval of the people, who alone decided what was to be done.[3] This took place not only in the Assembly but in the courts as well, which provided the forum for the speeches in this volume. There existed a range of charges that citizens could legitimately use to challenge in court their opponents' political standing and the soundness of their opponents' policies. Beyond treason (prosecuted by *eisangelia*), politicians were liable to attack for misconduct in an office they may have held (*euthynai*, as in Dem. 19) or for breaches of more technical aspects of public procedure (e.g., *graphē paranomōn*, as in Dem. 18).[4] In such contests, political matters were debated alongside, and sometimes in preference to, matters of law.

There being no judicial authority to interpret and impose standards of relevance, advocates could defend themselves and attack their opponents within their allotted time with any argument whose relevance they could establish in the minds of the jurors. In practice everything that the litigants had ever done, or could plausibly be said to have done, was fair game. So too were their social status, family background, personal habits, and, most importantly, their motives: litigants in Athenian political trials constantly upheld their loyalty to the people and accused their opponents of corruption.[5] From the people's point of view, such contests made sense. The people had the oppor-

---

[3] See the Series Introduction for a discussion of Athens' democratic institutions and procedures.

[4] See Hansen 1991: 203–224 on the charges and procedures of political trials in Athens' courts. See the Introductions to the speeches in this volume for explanations of the particular charge used in each case.

[5] Bribery and corruption were facts of life in Greek politics and the ancient Mediterranean world; there is nothing absurd in the charge itself. But the ubiquity of the charge in the speeches of Demosthenes and Aeschines, the prevalence of innuendo, and the absence of proof indicate that in these speeches, at least, the charge of corruption was often employed for rhetorical purposes with little regard for the truth.

tunity to reconsider their decisions and reassess their leaders. By fighting among themselves for the approval of the people, using words rather than arms, the politicians were obliged to acknowledge the supremacy of the people. Because Athenian democracy possessed little in the way of political parties or advocacy groups, policies had no viability apart from the particular politicians who advanced them. Endorsing and discarding those politicians was in itself a primary means of establishing policy.[6]

Thus Athenian democracy always provided a stage for lively public argument. But when Macedon's threat to Athens' leading role in Greece, and possibly to its security too, could no longer be avoided, the stakes were raised. Debate intensified beyond the norm. As was the case with the Persians a century and a half earlier, the danger that threatened was equaled by the glory, and the reward, of dispatching it. Demosthenes was competing with Aeschines, a fellow-citizen and political rival whose speeches in response also survive.[7] Both men sought the same thing: to have the people endorse him and repudiate his opponent. Both were experienced politicians, savvy in the language and practices of Athenian democracy. Both fought tooth and nail. With regard to the historical record, in 343 Demosthenes narrowly failed to defeat Aeschines, but he attained his political objective nonetheless (*On the Dishonest Embassy*); in 330 Demosthenes' victory was overwhelming (*On the Crown*).[8] On these occasions Demosthenes generated a war of words so intense and absolute that his two speeches are among the liveliest, most extraordinary examples of combative political argument ever produced. Of the two, *On the Crown* is the more

---

[6] See Ober 1989 on the function and conventions of political discourse in Athenian democracy. Aristophanes' *Knights* is the classic satire of politicians who vie for the favor of the people.

[7] For Aeschines' speeches, see the translation in this series by Chris Carey, *Aeschines* (Austin, 2000). Aes. 2, *On the Embassy,* is the defense against Dem. 19, *On the Dishonest Embassy.* Aes. 3, *Against Ctesiphon,* is the prosecution speech to which Dem. 18, *On the Crown,* responds. On Aeschines' career, see Harris 1995.

[8] For the historical background and basic argument of these speeches, see the Introductions to the individual speeches. Dem. 19 is also known as *On the False Embassy.* See also App. 2: Timeline for important events and dates.

compelling: Demosthenes delivered it in his own defense with his career on the line, and it is his most effective statement of opposition to Macedon.

THE HALLMARKS OF DEMOSTHENES' CAREER AND LEGACY

Demosthenes' career is marked above all by the two features that became his legacy: opposition to the Macedonian kings Philip and Alexander and rhetorical art. The latter had its roots in Demosthenes' career before politics but found its true calling when it was put in service of the former.

Demosthenes was born into a wealthy and probably aristocratic Athenian family, a typical background for a political career.[9] He never sought prestige in military command, which was common for political leaders of fourth-century Athens. Demosthenes' ancient biographers show great interest in his rhetorical training before entering public life. They mention teachers (Plato, Isaeus, contemporary actors) and record colorful anecdotes—practicing with pebbles in his mouth, speaking against the roar of the waves, and many more.[10] These and similar claims are unreliable; their authors, all of whom lived later than Demosthenes, most several hundred years later, had little or no access to the facts, and there was a tradition of using legend to fill in the lives of great men.

Yet Demosthenes' earliest speeches (27–31), composed in his early twenties to prosecute his former guardians for squandering his patrimony, are such refined productions that they imply the best rhetorical training. Demosthenes then pursued a successful career as a *logographos,* a professional speechwriter who, in return for compensation, composed speeches for others to deliver in court. Preserved speeches from the mid 350s to the early 340s attest this activity, on behalf of both clients involved in private suits and citizens prosecuting high-

---

[9] On Demosthenes' background and early career, see Badian 2000. The best full biography of Demosthenes is Carlier 1990; the best in English remains Pickard-Cambridge 1914.

[10] The most accessible sources are Plut., *Life of Demosthenes* 5–11; Pseudo-Plut., *Lives of the Ten Orators* 844b–845d.

profile political cases.[11] These are first-rate productions and demonstrate the rhetorical virtuosity that reached its full powers later on.[12]

Demosthenes' conspicuous background in rhetoric and speechwriting must have been inconvenient for a political career. Though all politicians in Athens had to speak effectively to the mass audiences of the Assembly and courts, there existed a popular prejudice against certain activities, such as rhetorical training, speechwriting, and publishing written texts, that were associated in the public mind with sophists. Such activities were held to indicate a potentially dangerous abuse of public discourse, and politicians tended to shun them.[13] Nevertheless, Demosthenes launched his career in politics in the mid 350s by addressing the Assembly on various topics and prosecuting political cases on his own.[14] To overcome the popular prejudice, he relied on sheer talent and energy, and he fastened on the menace posed by Philip and made it his crusade.

A series of speeches delivered from 351 to 341, known in antiquity as *Philippics,* reveals Demosthenes' vehement, persistent opposition to Philip, though the earliest in this series are more noteworthy for their rhetorical brilliance than for their effect on Athenian policy.[15] Demosthenes broke through to prominence in 346 in connection with the Peace of Philocrates. But it was the speech of 343, *On the Dishonest Embassy,* that positioned him in Athens' public sphere as the strongest advocate for creating a Greek alliance to stop Macedonian ex-

---

[11] Private cases (*dikai*): Dem. 32, 36, 37, 38, 39, 41, 45, 51, 54, 55, 57; political cases (*graphai*): Dem. 22, 23, 24.

[12] See Mirhady 2000 for a discussion of the artistry of these speeches. For a review of Demosthenes' rhetorical career, see Kennedy 1994: 68–80.

[13] On the popular prejudice against sophistic and rhetorical expertise, see Ober 1989: 165–182. Aeschines exploits this prejudice against Demosthenes: see Aes. 3.173; Dem. 18.276n, 19.246n. On the publication of Demosthenes' speeches, see Yunis 1996: 241–247. Speechwriters before Demosthenes published their speeches, but none of them ventured a career in politics.

[14] Dem. 13–16 to the Assembly, Dem. 20 to a court.

[15] Dem. 1–6, 8–10, of which the earliest are 4, delivered in 351, and 1–3, delivered in 349. Nowadays, the term *Philippics* is usually reserved just for speeches 4, 6, 9, 10. See Ryder 2000 for Demosthenes' policy of opposition to Philip.

pansion by force.[16] From that point Demosthenes became Athens' leading politician and the architect of the policy that put Athens at the head of a Greek alliance against Philip. Philip's defeat of the Greeks at Chaeronea in 338 brought Demosthenes' policy to a crushing end, yet Demosthenes' career outlived the defeat, which reveals the depth of popular support he enjoyed.[17] Under Macedonian hegemony, Demosthenes remained a staunch opponent of Philip and then of Alexander and sought the means to oppose them. But that hegemony ensured that Demosthenes could no longer harangue the people to resist as he had before Chaeronea, when Athens, as he put it, "was still in a position to choose the best policy" (18.320).[18]

On the Crown immortalized both the purposes behind Chaeronea and Demosthenes' own moment of glory as Athens' leader in the clash with Philip. In the next generation, to symbolize Athens' continued aspirations towards independence as Macedonian hegemony wore on, the Athenians erected a statue of Demosthenes in the center of the city and honored his descendants.[19] The image of Demosthenes as the hero of Greek freedom became fixed in later Greek culture through the influence of his speeches, which were collected and incorporated into the body of prized and closely studied literary documents of clas-

---

[16] Demosthenes' speech earlier in 343 against Pytho of Byzantium, Philip's representative on a mission to Athens, must also have contributed to Demosthenes' newly successful public stance against Philip; see 18.136. The speech does not survive.

[17] On Demosthenes' career and historical events from the Peace of Philocrates to the defeat at Chaeronea, see Sealey 1993: 160–198. These events are summarized in the introductions to the individual speeches in this volume. See also Appendix 2: Timeline.

[18] *On the Crown* itself is the most significant evidence for Demosthenes' policy after Chaeronea; for the underlying political message of the speech, see the Introduction to the speech, and 18.89n, 18.323–324. Demosthenes was included among the hostages demanded by Alexander in 335 following the destruction of Thebes; see 18.41n. For Demosthenes' career after Chaeronea until his death in 322, see Worthington 2000.

[19] Plut., *Life of Demosthenes* 30; Pseudo-Plut., *Lives of the Ten Orators* 847c–e, 850f–851f.

sical Athens. Demosthenes' speeches, with pride of place given to those against Philip and those against Aeschines, now spoke from the written page and found a second life as a model of language at its most powerful and engaging. Demosthenes became the single most important author in the rhetorical world of later antiquity (first century BCE–fourth century CE), and, especially in *On the Crown*, was emulated and studied alongside Homer, Sappho, and Plato as representing the best in Greek literature.[20] Demosthenes was a central figure in the revival of classical learning in modern Europe. Since then, Demosthenes' fortunes have been mixed, reflecting both changing attitudes towards classical rhetoric and the shifting climate of political opinion. Recently he has been perceived less as a hero of democratic freedom than as a foolhardy opponent of historical necessity. Both perceptions reduce the man and his work.[21] As *On the Crown* reveals, Demosthenes was an energetic politician, devoted to his city, and a speaker and writer of astonishing imagination.

DISCOVERING DEMOSTHENES' ART

Demosthenes' art, so concentrated that it infuses with the author's purpose the whole and all the parts, is agonistic rather than epideictic; that is, form serves strictly the purpose at hand, which is to defend himself and destroy his opponent, and is not elaborated for its own sake or for any other reason. Features of Demosthenes' art that depend on the particular order or choice of words in Greek are inevitably lost or at best approximated in translation. These include prose rhythm,

---

[20] On the rhetorical world of late antiquity, see Kennedy 1994: 201–256. For Demosthenes' reputation and influence in late antiquity, see Adams 1927: 97–130; Rutherford 1998: 61–63; Yunis 2000: 99–100. Hermogenes, *On Types of Style* (second century CE) is the best ancient treatise on Demosthenes and demonstrates how Demosthenes was studied; see Wooten 1987 for an annotated translation. See also the rhetorical works of Dionysius of Halicarnassus (late first century BCE), especially *On Demosthenes* and *On Thucydides*. For the most striking judgment on Demosthenes as a writer and the comparison to the other classical authors mentioned above, see the treatise *On the Sublime*, attributed to Longinus.

[21] On the modern reception and influence of Demosthenes, see Adams 1927: 131–174; Harding 2000; Yunis 2000.

wordplay, and certain figures of speech (artful arrangements of words that maintain their natural meanings). More important for the engaging character of Demosthenes' speeches are his figures of thought— ways of making a point so as to cast it in a certain light, regardless of the particular order or choice of words—and these can be translated directly. A few examples, mainly from *On the Crown*, are offered below to indicate the phenomenon and to encourage the reader to take notice of the form in which Demosthenes casts his thought.[22]

Amplification, a hallmark of Demosthenes' style, is the use of two words in place of one ("chosen and preferred," 18.2); it makes the thought seem important without complicating it. The impression of spontaneity, which enhances sincerity, is created by parenthesis (19.125), by breaking off a thought (18.3) or sentence (18.126), by correcting oneself (18.130). Strong emotion is conveyed by repeating words (18.208) and by exclamations and oaths, which are frequent. Demosthenes uses second-person pronouns to address his opponent or the audience (*apostrophē*), directing, as it were, a three-cornered dialogue that isolates Aeschines as it forces the audience to pay heed (18.124–125).[23] Vocatives, frequent and strategically placed, add intensity to *apostrophē* (18.143, 243). Demosthenes peppers the speeches with questions (18.282–283), for example, to suggest outrage (18.139) or to hammer home a point ("what should the city have done?" 18.62– 72). A brief, artificial dialogue of objections and answers (*hypophora*) occurs in numerous forms (18.24, 101, 180, 19.158). Demosthenes recreates monologues, such as his address to the people (18.174–178), Philip's to his allies (18.40).

Demosthenes' invective, sometimes cast in set pieces (18.126–131, 258–262), ridicules Aeschines in order to render him unworthy of the audience's confidence. These passages call attention to themselves and can hardly be missed. More subtle is Demosthenes' irony. It expresses—indirectly, for such is the means of irony—Demosthenes' Olympian self-assurance, the view that Aeschines' attempt to impugn his illustrious record of public achievement is the transparently futile

---

[22] See Vickers 1988: 294–339 on the expressive function of rhetorical figures. See Rowe 1967 on Demosthenes' artful use of language in *On the Crown*.

[23] See Classen 1991.

exertion of a contemptible, self-deluded charlatan. Irony surfaces, for instance, when Demosthenes shifts suddenly from Athens' grandeur to Aeschines' abjection (18.180, 209). Demosthenes mocks Aeschines for *pretending* to have enjoyed the hospitality of the Macedonian kings and then incites the audience to mock Aeschines along with him (18.51–52). Aeschines' trained voice and career as an actor provide Demosthenes with a rich lode (18.242, 259, 267, 313). Demosthenes' irony provides one of the greatest pleasures in reading the speech and must have proved decisive in keeping the original audiences keenly engaged.[24]

In both speeches, Demosthenes' argument derives its punch from the quasi-historical narrative of events in which it is embedded. Quasi-historical, because while the narrative comprehends a core of indisputable, commonly accepted facts, Demosthenes aims not at objectivity or disinterested truth but at compelling the audience to draw strong moral inferences. By depicting the protagonists in action — Aeschines colluding, Demosthenes resisting — Demosthenes supplies the basis for his fiercely expressed judgments condemning the traitor and defending himself.[25] Since everything Demosthenes says about the conflict with Macedon is subordinated to his polemical purpose, he distorts the facts where he can, casts them in a light favorable to his case where necessary, and otherwise omits them if they are inconvenient. He thereby builds up a story of absolute good versus absolute evil, in which he and his audience are the heroes who, even in defeat, nobly faced down Philip, Aeschines, and the rest of the Greek traitors.

NOTE ON THE TEXT

The text used for the translation of *On the Crown* is that printed in the Cambridge Greek and Latin Classics edition.[26] Major commentaries on the speech *On the Crown* include Fox 1880, Weil 1883, Goodwin 1901, Blass and Fuhr 1910, Wankel 1976, Usher 1993, and Yunis

---

[24] Demosthenes' irony is occasionally indicated in the notes, especially where it might go unnoticed.

[25] See Pearson 1976 on Demosthenes' narrative art.

[26] Yunis 2001.

2001. The spurious documents preserved in the manuscript tradition of *On the Crown* have been excerpted and translated in Appendix 1. The text used for the translation of *On the Dishonest Embassy* is that printed in the Teubner edition,[27] though I have consulted and profited from the commentary of Paulsen 1999 and the text and commentary of MacDowell 2000.[28] Other important commentaries on the speech *On the Dishonest Embassy* include Shilleto 1874 and Weil 1883.

---

[27] Fuhr 1914.

[28] In the following places I have departed from Fuhr's text and followed Mac-Dowell's: 19.112, 123, 136, 141, 149, 253, 272.

DEMOSTHENES, SPEECHES 18 AND 19

〰〰〰〰〰〰〰〰〰〰〰〰〰〰〰〰〰〰〰〰〰〰〰〰〰〰〰〰〰〰〰

Translated by Harvey Yunis

18. IN DEFENSE OF CTESIPHON
ON THE CROWN

〰〰

INTRODUCTION

Background

Following his nearly victorious prosecution of Aeschines in 343 for misconduct on the Second Embassy (Dem. 19), Demosthenes was in a strong position.[1] He continued his career on the premise that rapprochement with Philip was unachievable and that support against Philip should be sought from all quarters within and outside Greece. This policy began to pay off, for Athens and Demosthenes, after 343. With the peace still nominally in force, the Athenians increased support for their cause among the Greeks and at moments of crisis successfully deployed forces in Megara, Euboea, and Acarnania to stem the growth of Philip's influence within Greece. In 340 Demosthenes was reaching the height of his influence in Athens as Philip set his sights on the Hellespont and the Bosporus, which were vital for Athenian security and long pervaded with an Athenian presence. While laying siege to Byzantium and contending among Athenian, Persian, and local Greek forces, Philip seized an Athenian grain convoy in the Bosporus. The Athenians responded, on Demosthenes' motion, by pulling down the inscribed stone that bore the Peace of Philocrates and declaring their intentions to prosecute war vigorously.

United now behind Demosthenes' leadership, the Athenians reformed the financing of their navy, suspended regular civic expendi-

---

[1] For events up to 343 and the speech *On the Dishonest Embassy,* see the Introduction to Dem. 19. For the history of this period, see Sealey 1993.

tures in favor of military preparations, and sought allies to take the field with them against Philip. Ostensibly waging sacred war on behalf of the Delphic Amphictyony against Amphissa, Philip brought his army into central Greece in late 339 to settle matters. Bypassing Thermopylae, which Thebes had recently retaken, he seized the Phocian town of Elatea by surprise and thereby put both Thebes and Athens under the threat of immediate invasion. At that moment Demosthenes achieved his greatest diplomatic coup, bringing the two largest cities of central Greece, erstwhile enemies, into cooperation at the head of a formidable alliance against Philip. Skirmishes lasted several months before a showdown occurred in the summer of 338 near Chaeronea, a Boeotian town on the border with Phocis. The two sides were well matched; it was not impossible to suppose that Philip would withdraw, as he did in 340 at Byzantium, rather than risk a battle whose outcome was unclear. But Philip fought, his victory was decisive, and Athenian losses were severe.

In the immediate aftermath, Demosthenes took the lead in organizing emergency measures to withstand a siege, which Philip, however, chose not to attempt. Instead, he imposed generous terms: Athens survived intact, was not occupied, and was permitted to retain a measure of its former autonomy. But Athens was co-opted into Philip's overall settlement of Greek affairs, known as the League of Corinth, which enabled Philip, and later Alexander, to maintain control over Greece. The Athenians were free to settle among themselves the question of responsibility for their subjection to Macedon, and they had to ponder anew how they would respond to the Macedonian power that now encompassed them and virtually the entire Greek mainland. Lysicles, for example, one of the Athenian generals in the field at Chaeronea, bore the brunt of military responsibility; he was prosecuted, convicted, and sentenced to death for his role in the battle.

As the natural target of political recrimination, Demosthenes was subjected to a wave of prosecutions at the hands of various opponents, though he emerged unscathed. His public standing received a boost in the winter of 338/7, when the people elected him to deliver the funeral oration for the dead of Chaeronea. Thus in the initial aftermath of Chaeronea, Demosthenes was weakened but still viable as a politician even though his policy of confronting Philip had backfired disastrously. Aeschines, however, had yet to be heard from.

In the spring of 336, a citizen named Ctesiphon moved a decree that the people should bestow a golden crown on Demosthenes in a formal ceremony in the theater of Dionysus. The wording of the motion has not survived, but it can be inferred from the surviving speeches that Ctesiphon praised Demosthenes both for his repair of certain fortifications of which he had charge, including a contribution towards that work out of his own funds, and for his "merit and rectitude" generally, claiming that Demosthenes "continually advises and acts in the best interests of the people." [2] In itself, the motion was not unusual. Decrees honoring public benefactors with crowns were a regular part of Athenian political life. In the period after Chaeronea, when civic defense needed particular attention, they were especially common.

Once the Council of Five Hundred approved Ctesiphon's motion, it was up to the Assembly to decide whether the crown would be conferred and Demosthenes' public standing rehabilitated further. At that moment Aeschines acted, giving official notice that he was lodging a *graphē paranomōn* against Ctesiphon, that is, indicting him for moving a decree in conflict with statute law. The *graphē paranomōn* was formally a review of the legal fitness of either a motion officially before the Assembly (*probouleuma*) or a decree that had been approved by the Assembly (*psēphisma*). On the established principle that a decree of the Assembly had less authority than statute law (*nomos*), the *graphē paranomōn* enabled the court to examine a decree or motion for its compatibility with the existing code of statute laws, in regard to both procedure and substance. A decree or motion which the court found to be in conflict with one or more statutes was nullified and its proposer liable to punishment. With regard to the law, Ctesiphon, the proposer of the decree, was the defendant and liable party in Aeschines' indictment, while Demosthenes was an innocent third party with no ostensible role in the dispute.

Yet Aeschines' purpose was transparent from the beginning, and it had nothing to do with Ctesiphon. By the procedural rules in force, the very act of lodging the indictment removed Ctesiphon's motion from consideration by the Assembly pending the outcome of a trial.

---

[2] See 18.57; Aes. 3.49, 101, 237.

Aeschines became obliged to argue against the decree in court, and that task, in spite of the judicial setting and the question of the decree's legal fitness, was a political matter far more than a legal one. The *graphē paranomōn* provided the citizens sitting as jurors the opportunity to review a decree or motion for its political merit while they simultaneously reviewed its legal status. In addition to arguing that the indicted decree was in conflict with statute law, the prosecutor of a *graphē paranomōn* also argued that the decree was inexpedient for the *polis*, and if the indicted decree concerned a grant of honors or citizenship, the prosecutor argued that the nominee was undeserving of the grant. The defendant had the burden of rebutting these claims.

Given this breadth of argument, it does not surprise that the *graphē paranomōn* became one of the chief judicial processes through which Athenian politicians attacked each other in the incessant, ruthless pursuit of advantage. While indicating the statutes that Ctesiphon's decree supposedly violated, Aeschines also rejected Ctesiphon's claim that Demosthenes "continually advises and acts in the best interests of the people." That, he proposed to argue, could not truthfully be said of the man who led the Athenians to Chaeronea.[3] If Aeschines could persuade the people to deny Demosthenes the crown on the merits of the case, he would destroy his rival's career and resurrect his own.

But the trial was postponed as a series of epoch-making events abroad overtook the struggles of domestic Athenian politics. Philip was assassinated in the late summer of 336, soon after Aeschines lodged the indictment. Alexander emerged as the successor and established himself in the positions of power that his father Philip had used to control Greece. In 335 a rumor of the new king's death emboldened the Thebans to revolt. The Athenians were debating whether to join their former allies when Alexander crushed the rebellion, razed the city, and dispersed the survivors. The Athenians did not fail to get the message. In 334 Alexander invaded Asia; his unprecedented string of conquests stunned the Greeks, though many, regardless of their loyalties, nevertheless expected the Macedonian juggernaut to run aground eventually against the massive Persian empire.

---

[3] Aes. 3.49–50.

By 330, however, Macedonian hegemony was beginning to look permanent. In the spring of that year, Antipater, Alexander's general in Greece, crushed the revolt in the Peloponnese led by Agis III of Sparta. At Gaugamela in the fall of 331, Alexander delivered the decisive blow to Darius, the Persian King. During the first half of 330, the Athenians were steadily getting more information about the extent of the Macedonian victory and the demise of the Persian empire. No longer able to hope for assistance from Thebes, Sparta, or Persia, the only potential allies that previously had remained, Athens had virtually no prospect of emerging from its subjugation to Macedon.

That was the situation when the dispute over Demosthenes' crown went to trial in the late summer of 330. One can only speculate who revived the case and for what reason. Since Aeschines had not been a major politician since the 340s, Demosthenes would have had nothing to gain and much to lose by reviving it. Yet if Aeschines sought an opportunity to unleash the anger and disaffection of the Athenian people against his old enemy, this was the moment: at precisely that time the consequences of Chaeronea appeared more dire and unalterable than ever before.

In spite of the misgivings potentially evoked by the use of an advocate, Ctesiphon, the defendant, handed over his time to Demosthenes. It was both predictable and appropriate that Ctesiphon should allow Demosthenes to defend his own record against his own enemy.[4] Six years after the honorary decree was proposed and the indictment lodged, both Aeschines and Demosthenes argue as if the lapse of time made no difference to Ctesiphon's personal liability and more generally to the importance and immediacy of the question at issue, whether or not Demosthenes deserves to be crowned by the people. Demosthenes defeated his opponent soundly, taking more than four-fifths of the votes. Penalized for frivolous prosecution and disgraced by the lopsided loss, Aeschines had no political future in Athens, left the city, and ended up on Rhodes as a teacher of rhetoric. Demosthenes continued his career in Athens, fortified by the crown that he was awarded before a solemn convocation of fellow citizens and other Greeks.

---

[4] See 18.5n.

Demosthenes' Argument[5]

Aeschines based his argument on Demosthenes' career, which, as Aeschines reports it, brought about Athens' steady and needless decline from imperial power to its present condition of weakness and dependency. Aeschines portrays his opponent as recklessly provoking war with Philip, criminally incompetent in politics and diplomacy, and corruptly serving the interests of Philip, Persia, and sundry Greek tyrants. Beyond the central narrative, Aeschines reveals defects in the legal status of Ctesiphon's decree, portrays Demosthenes as an enemy of the people, and taunts Demosthenes relentlessly as a coward and ill-fated plague on Athens. Aeschines' speech is effective, though nothing in the prosecution approaches the intensity, grandeur, or pitiless irony of Demosthenes' reply. Aeschines' strongest argument was the one based on the simple, undeniable facts: it would be criminal and utterly disgraceful for Athens to bestow the highest public honor on the citizen who brought about the disaster at Chaeronea and undisputed Macedonian hegemony.[6] Athenian jurors, effectively representing the citizen body, were notoriously capable of responding vindictively to politicians whose policies turned out badly.[7]

In defense, Demosthenes both attacks his opponent and defends himself. In sections of narrative distributed through the speech, he casts Aeschines, as he did in the speech *On the Dishonest Embassy,* as a corrupt traitor, bribed by Philip to thwart Athens, and responsible for every important Athenian loss and Macedonian gain since the disastrous Peace of Philocrates. This part of the argument culminates in the claim that Aeschines paved Philip's way into central Greece in 339 (18.139–159), whereby the Theban alliance and the battle of Chaeronea become the emergency response to this unspeakable act of treason. This vilifying narrative is supported with irony and invective even sharper than that displayed in speech 19; in addition to abrupt, stinging attacks scattered throughout, two set pieces (18.126–131, 258–262) hilariously deride Aeschines' lack of education, disreputable parent-

---

[5] See Yunis 2000 for a fuller account of Demosthenes' argument in *On the Crown.*

[6] See especially Aes. 3.152–158.

[7] See Roberts 1982; Todd 1993: 305–306.

age, poverty, and mean upbringing, all obviously false or grossly exaggerated charges that nevertheless puncture Aeschines' claim to the elite status that was vital for Athenian politicians.

To defend himself, Demosthenes insists that his policy of confronting Philip was the right one. He rejects outcome as the measure of success and portrays himself as a hero deserving public honor even though the Athenians failed to defeat Philip. This part of the argument, which flew in the face of conventional notions of political accountability, is established on the basis of three distinct claims.

First, Demosthenes correctly perceived that Philip was an insatiable tyrant aiming at total domination over Athens and Greece. Resistance was the only conceivable policy if Athens and Greece were to survive at all: apart from outright surrender, no accommodation with Philip or third alternative was possible (18.60–72). Had Athens not followed Demosthenes' policy, allied with Thebes, and fought at Chaeronea, its fate would have been far worse.

Second, Demosthenes implemented his anti-Philip policy flawlessly and proved it correct in the years and months leading up to Chaeronea, when Athens made significant gains at Philip's expense (18.79–94, 211–243). By the best human reckoning, even in hindsight, success ought to have followed, as until then it had under Demosthenes' leadership. But the gods or inscrutable chance opposed them (18.192–194, 270–275).

Third, a "paradoxical," "extreme" claim—even if the Athenians knew the outcome of Chaeronea in advance, "not even in those circumstances should the city have abandoned its policy, if indeed it valued its reputation or its forebears or future ages" (18.199). To risk all for Greek freedom, and thereby win glory, is the burden of the Athenian past, and it inspires Demosthenes' most powerful rhetoric. As a politician *in Athens,* conscious of Athens' heritage as the defender of Greek freedom against barbarian tyranny, Demosthenes claims that he had no choice but to recommend aggressive resistance to Philip; likewise, the people, who were reminded of that heritage daily by civic monuments and patriotic occasions, also had no choice but to act accordingly (18.66–68). How could Demosthenes' policy have been misguided if the dead of Chaeronea were emulating the ancestors who fought at Marathon and Salamis? No matter that the Athenians lost the battle with Philip: the civic impulse was one and the same in both triumph and defeat, a principle that the Athenians already implicitly recognize when they bestow public burial on all Athenian soldiers who die in battle, regardless of whether they won or were defeated (18.208).

This rhetorical move presents Demosthenes' intentions, his decisive fidelity to Athenian tradition at a moment of crisis, as his lasting, successful contribution to Athens. Thus Demosthenes does not argue for the crown on the basis of law or justice. Rather, in typical Athenian fashion, he argues that it is the very superior interests of the community that should encourage the jurors to crown him, as a public statement that in Athens, questions of self-interest are still subordinated to questions of honor, as they always have been in the Athenian tradition (18.207, 210).

In 330 the Athenians were weak, subjugated, in no position to revolt, yet also unwilling to accept defeat. Demosthenes offered his audience a noble version of their reasons for adopting his advice, reasons that were compelling in the face of a failure they were forced to reckon with but not prepared to accept as final.[8] While presenting himself as a hero, Demosthenes takes meticulous care to present his audience simultaneously as true-born Athenian heroes like the fighters of Marathon. If he was heroic and true to Athenian tradition for leading them to Chaeronea, they were equally heroic and true to that tradition for choosing to follow him there. If they could not defeat Philip, at least they could save their reputation and their purpose, which is what Demosthenes managed for them while preserving his career. And—equally important—he did so without openly inciting them to revolt.

Synopsis

1–16: Prooemium: prayer, plea for a fair hearing, the illegitimacy of the prosecution

---

[8] In addition to Demosthenes' victory in this trial, the mood of the post-Chaeronea years is revealed most clearly, perhaps, in the events of 323: When Alexander died suddenly, the Athenians revolted immediately and with massive force, putting at sea the largest fleet ever in their history. They had been waiting and preparing for the moment, but having had no battle experience in sixteen years, they were no match for the battle-tested Macedonians.

18. ON THE CROWN

[1] To begin, Athenians, I pray to all the gods and goddesses that during this trial you have as much concern for my welfare as I have always had for yours and the city's, and further—a matter of the greatest importance to you, to your piety, and to your reputation—that the gods inspire you not to accept my opponent's advice on how you

should listen to me, for that would be cruel, [2] and instead to heed the laws and your oath, for beyond all your other obligations, you have specifically sworn to listen to both sides equally.⁹ That means not only to decide nothing beforehand and to be impartial but also to allow every litigant to use the order of argument and method of defense that he has chosen and preferred.

[3] In many respects, Aeschines has me at a disadvantage in this trial, though two points, Athenians, are especially important, the first being that my stake in the matter is not equal to his. It is not the same thing for me to be deprived of your goodwill and for him to fail to win his case, since if I—but I'll omit any inauspicious words as I begin the speech.¹⁰ Nevertheless, as prosecutor he enjoys an advantage. The second point is simply a matter of human nature: people listen with delight to insults and accusations but are annoyed by those who praise themselves. [4] He gets the part that provides enjoyment, while it is left to me to annoy practically everyone. But if I am too cautious on this score and fail to speak about my achievements, I do not see how I can acquit myself of the charges and show why I deserve the honor. But if I talk about what I have done in general and specifically as a politician, I will often be forced to talk about myself. I will try to do it as modestly as possible, but whatever this predicament forces me to say, by rights he should be blamed for it, since he is the one who instigated this trial.¹¹

---

⁹ Aes. 3.202–206 argued that Demosthenes was obliged to use the same order of arguments in defense as that used by Aeschines in prosecution, viz. first the legal arguments, then the political ones. Since Demosthenes minimizes the legal arguments (see 18.110n) and puts the onus of his case on his political record, he must first deflect Aeschines' attempt to prejudice the jurors against his mode of defense. The oath in question is the Heliastic Oath taken by all Athenian jurors: it bound them to listen impartially. Other requirements of the Heliastic Oath are mentioned in 19.179.

¹⁰ Demosthenes stops himself before uttering out loud the thought that he might lose the case.

¹¹ One of Demosthenes' chief rhetorical problems of the speech is praising himself without giving offense. He succeeds by mixing praise of himself with praise of the audience, by diminishing his own role at crucial moments, and by limiting the self-praise at a point that makes it acceptable. The pinnacle of his

[5] I think you would all agree, Athenians, that this trial is a matter of common concern to me and Ctesiphon, and it deserves no less effort on my part.[12] To be robbed of anything is painful and hard, especially if it happens at the hands of an enemy; yet even more painful is to be robbed of your goodwill and devotion, just as gaining these is most important. [6] Since that is what's at stake in this trial, I charge and beseech all of you alike to listen to me fairly as I make my defense against the allegations, just as the laws demand. Solon,[13] who first established these laws, was well disposed to you and favored democracy. He believed that the laws would have authority not only if they were written down but also if those who pass judgment swore an oath to uphold them. [7] Solon did not distrust you, in my view, but he saw that there is only one way for the defendant to overcome the slanderous charges which strengthen the prosecutor's case because he speaks first: each of you sitting in judgment must preserve your piety before the gods by generously admitting the just claims of the second speaker, and you must render a decision on every point only after making yourselves fair and impartial auditors of both sides.

[8] Since I am now about to give an account of virtually my entire life as well as my public accomplishments, I wish to invoke the gods once more, and in your presence I pray, first, that in this trial you have as much concern for my welfare as I have always had for yours and the city's, and second, that the gods inspire you to decide this case in a manner that will foster both our common reputation and the piety of every individual.

[9] Now if Aeschines had restricted his accusations just to the issues under prosecution, I too would begin my defense with the prelimi-

---

career—the alliance that faced Philip at Chaeronea—was in obvious respects a failure. The pathos defuses resentment.

[12] Ctesiphon, not Demosthenes, was officially the defendant (see the Introduction), and so Demosthenes justifies his speaking as an advocate (*synēgoros*) in Ctesiphon's place. Aes. 3.202, 242 sought to impugn Demosthenes on this basis, since defendants in Athens were expected to speak on their own behalf. In fact, advocates were not uncommon; see Rubinstein 2000.

[13] Athenian reformer of the early sixth century BCE, Solon was viewed by fourth-century Athenians as the founder of their democracy and the author of their legislation.

nary decree.[14] But since he spent most of his speech discussing other matters and mainly told lies about me, I think it necessary as well as just, Athenians, first to say a few words on these points so that none of you will be guided by irrelevant arguments or listen with any less favor to what I have to say about the indictment.[15]

[10] Consider how simply and fairly I can answer all the outrageous slanders he devised about my personal life. If you know me to be the kind of person he has alleged—and I have not lived anywhere else except among you—do not allow me to go on, not even if my entire public career has been exemplary, but stand up and convict me now. But if you supposed and still recognize that I am far better and better born than he, that I and my family are no worse than average (I don't wish to say anything offensive), then do not trust him in any other matter—for clearly he's invented everything in the same way—and grant me now the same consideration that you showed me in many previous trials.[16] [11] Though you are a malicious person, Aeschines, you conceived this perfectly foolish idea that I would abandon all discussion of my actions and policies and turn instead to the abuse that you emitted. I will not do that. I am not so stupid. Rather, I will examine your slanderous distortions of my public record and only later, if it please the court, will I take up the derision that has gone unchecked.

[12] He has leveled many accusations, and for some of them, the laws prescribe significant and even extreme penalties. But the very fact that he chose to bring the present legal action[17] reveals an enemy's malice and insolence and revilement and vilification and everything

---

[14] "Preliminary decree" (*probouleuma*) is a technical term, referring to a proposal that had passed the Council but was awaiting treatment by the Assembly. Ctesiphon's motion to honor Demosthenes had precisely this status when Aeschines lodged the indictment.

[15] Athenian rhetoric utilized the notions of pertinent and extraneous arguments and censured the latter for the obvious reasons. Nevertheless, arguments that were plainly extraneous were routine in Athenian law; it was a question of how best to use them. Demosthenes was a master.

[16] See 18.249–250 for Demosthenes' account of his previous trials, in all of which he was successful.

[17] I.e., the *graphē paranomōn,* or indictment of an illegal proposal, which was directed at Ctesiphon, not at Demosthenes; see the Introduction.

else of that kind. If the stated charges and accusations were true, there is no way the city could exact fitting punishment or anything close to it. [13] To be sure, it is not acceptable to try to rob someone of access to the people and the opportunity to address them and especially to do that out of spite and malice—it's not right, by god, nor, Athenians, is it just or in accord with civic practice. But if he saw me committing such prodigious crimes against the city, as he has now been recounting for us in that tragic voice of his,[18] he ought to have pursued the prescribed penalties when the crimes occurred, bringing a charge of treason (*eisangelia*) against me and placing that decision before you if he saw me committing treasonable offenses, or indicting me for an illegal proposal if he saw me committing that offense. For it surely cannot be that he means to prosecute Ctesiphon in order to attack me, yet would not have indicted me if he thought he would convict me.[19]

[14] Further, there are laws and penalties for every other crime that he may have seen me commit against you, those he has falsely accused me of today and any others whatsoever; the trials and judgments entail significant, severe penalties, all of which he might have pursued; and had it ever been plain that he acted in this way and dealt with me thus, his accusation today would agree with his deeds. [15] But in fact he turned aside from the straight and just road and refused to present evidence at the time of the events. Now, long afterwards, he has gathered a heap of derisive and abusive charges and puts on a show. What's more, he accuses me but puts Ctesiphon on trial. He makes his feud with me the foremost issue of the entire lawsuit, but, although he has never challenged me directly, he seems bent on depriving another man of his rights. [16] Yet beyond everything else one might mention on Ctesiphon's behalf, Athenians, one point strikes me as particularly reasonable: Aeschines and I ought rightly to put our feud to the test by ourselves and not seek someone else we can harm while avoiding fighting each other. That is excessively unjust.

[17] From this one can see that all the charges he has brought are

---

[18] Throughout the speech Demosthenes mocks Aeschines for his former career as a tragic actor and his trained voice; see 18.127, 180, 242, 262, 267, 280.

[19] Ironic: since Ctesiphon was the liable party in Aeschines' prosecution, the prosecution could not legally touch Demosthenes and was, as Demosthenes puts it, unfairly directed at an innocent third party.

likewise unfair and have no foundation in truth. Yet I wish to examine each of them individually, in particular his fabrications concerning the peace and the embassy, for he ascribed to me the actions that he took in concert with Philocrates.[20] It is necessary, Athenians, and perhaps appropriate, to remind you how matters stood at that time in order that you consider each point in relation to the relevant circumstances.

[18] When the Phocian War broke out[21]—not my doing since I was not yet active in public life—your position at first was that you supported security for the Phocians though you were aware of their transgressions, and you would have been pleased by whatever the Thebans suffered, since your anger against them was reasonable and justified. They had grown arrogant as a result of their victory at Leuctra.[22] Further, the entire Peloponnese was in discord: the Spartans' opponents were not strong enough to destroy them, and those who previously held power through the Spartans' influence were not in control of their cities; among them and everyone else a deadlock prevailed, with strife and confusion.[23] [19] Philip saw this situation, which in fact was obvious, and by bribing the traitors within each faction he set them against each other and increased the confusion among them. Then, while the other Greeks were blundering and behaving foolishly, he strengthened his position and grew in power at the expense of all. The length of the war sapped the once proud but now hapless Thebans, and everyone recognized that they would be forced to turn to you for protection. To prevent that and forestall an alliance between our cities, Philip offered you peace and them relief. [20] What abetted him as you were almost voluntarily deceived into putting yourself in his hands? Call it whatever you wish, cowardice or

---

[20] See the Introduction to Dem. 19 on Philocrates, the Peace of Philocrates, and the Second Embassy.

[21] Also known as the Third Sacred War, it began in 356 and ended in 346 as a result of the Peace of Philocrates. Phocis is in central Greece, not far from Delphi.

[22] This Theban victory over Sparta in 371 initiated a decade-long period of Theban hegemony in Greece.

[23] The latter part of this sentence, describing the confusion in the Peloponnese, is a reminiscence of Xen., *Hellenica* 7.5.27, the penultimate sentence of the work.

ignorance or both, the other Greeks gave you no support whatsoever in money or manpower or anything else, though you were fighting a long, uninterrupted war and, as events have made clear, doing it for the benefit of all Greece. Justifiably enraged at this situation, you readily listened to Philip.

It was these events and not, as Aeschines maliciously claimed, my actions that brought about the peace we reached at that time. And anyone who fairly inquires will find that the current state of affairs has its origin in the crimes and corruption of these men[24] during the peace. [21] Out of regard for the truth I will furnish a precise explanation of all these points. For whatever criminal activity was involved, surely that has nothing to do with me. The first to speak up for peace was the actor Aristodemus.[25] After him, the man who formally proposed the motion and joined him in selling his services to achieve it was Philocrates of Hagnus—your partner, Aeschines, not mine, even if you split apart from lying—and for whatever reason, which I'll pass over for the moment, their supporters were Eubulus and Cephisophon.[26] I had no part in any of it.

[22] Nevertheless, in the face of these facts as established by the truth itself, Aeschines was so shameless as to dare to assert that not only was I responsible for the peace, but I am also supposed to have prevented the city from extending it at a general convention of the Greeks. You—but what word can one use to address you properly! Was there ever a time when you were troubled because you personally saw me rob the city of a venture or alliance as important as you now claim, or when you came forward to inform the public of the deeds you now accuse me of? [23] If Philip had paid me to obstruct a common Greek alliance, it was your job not to be silent but to cry out, to protest, to inform the people. The fact is you never did that, and no one ever heard that voice of yours. At the time there was no delegation

---

[24] Here and throughout the speech, Demosthenes uses the phrase "these men" to refer to Aeschines and his unnamed cronies.

[25] See 19.12n.

[26] Eubulus, extremely influential in the 350s–340s, especially through his administration of Athens' finances, supported Aeschines in the trial on the Second Embassy (Aes. 2.184; Dem. 19.290), but Demosthenes had no reason to criticize Eubulus in 330 when he was dead. Little is known of Cephisophon.

abroad to any of the Greeks, since they had all been asked long before,[27] nor is anything that Aeschines said about this matter reliable. [24] But apart from that, his lies slander the city above all. If you were urging the Greeks towards war and at the same time sending envoys to Philip to discuss peace, you were acting in a manner worthy of Eurybatus,[28] not in a way that suits a real city or honest men. But these things are not true, they are not true. For what reason would you have for summoning the Greeks at that point? For peace? But everyone had that. For war? But you were making plans for peace yourselves. Thus, it is clear that I was neither the main proponent of peace in the beginning nor responsible for bringing it about, and it is evident that none of the other lies he told about me is true either.

[25] Consider what each of us proposed to do after the city made peace; that will tell you who was helping Philip and who was acting on your behalf and pursuing the city's best interests. As a member of the Council I formally proposed that the envoys should find out where Philip might be, sail to that spot as soon as possible, and receive his oath.[29] But they were unwilling to do that even after I made the proposal. [26] What was the point of that, Athenians? I will explain. It was in Philip's interest to delay his oath as long as possible, while it was in your interest to minimize the time. Why? Because you ceased all military activity not merely from the day on which you swore your oath but from when you expected that there would be peace. That was Philip's strategy all along. He believed, rightly as it turned out, that he would securely hold all the territory that he seized from us before he gave his oath, since no one would abrogate peace for the sake of that territory. [27] I anticipated this, Athenians, and took it into account when I made the aforementioned proposal, that we should sail to the spot where Philip might be and exact his oath as soon as possible. If he were to swear the oath while your Thracian allies still held Serrium, Myrtenum, and Ergisce, the very places that Aeschines was just now

---

[27] Whether or not they wished to join the peace agreement with Philip.

[28] Eurybatus, a Greek who betrayed Croesus and went over to the Persians (mid sixth century), became proverbial for a traitor.

[29] This was the Second Embassy, whose purpose was to receive from Philip the oath that would ratify the Peace of Philocrates on his part.

ridiculing,[30] and not after he had seized the strategic positions and made himself master of Thrace, he would not gain possession of abundant wealth and manpower and thereby easily set to work on his next endeavors.

[28] Well, Aeschines did not read that proposal of mine in court today or have the clerk read it out. Instead, he attacked me for urging the Council to bring Philip's envoys before the Assembly.[31] What was I to do? Move that the envoys who came here precisely to negotiate with you should not be introduced? Order the theater manager not to give them a spot in the theater? Without my motion they would have sat in the two-obol seats![32] Was I obliged to save the city trivial sums while selling off everything important to it, as these men have done? Of course not. Clerk, take the decree that Aeschines obviously omitted on purpose and please read it.[33]

[29] [DEMOSTHENES' DECREE][34]

[30] Such was my proposal at the time, undertaken to advance our city's interests, not Philip's. Meanwhile these worthy envoys paid no heed, sitting in Macedon for three whole months until Philip returned from Thrace in control of the entire territory. We could have been at the Hellespont in ten days or even three or four, and by exacting the oath before he conquered the place, we could have saved it.[35] For he would not have laid a hand on them had we been there, or

---

[30] Aes. 3.82. These were three small fortified cities in Thrace.

[31] See 19.234–236 for Demosthenes' earlier attempt to defend this part of his record.

[32] These are the cheap unreserved seats, open to anyone. It was impossible to imagine that the Athenians could have allowed Philip's envoys, including Antipater and Parmenion, two of his closest associates, to plunge into the thronging people. Aes. 3.76 attacks Demosthenes for his supposedly fawning treatment of Philip's envoys.

[33] Demosthenes' proposal to have the envoys sail to Philip as quickly as possible (18.25–27).

[34] For this and the other spurious documents that are found in the medieval manuscripts, see App. I below.

[35] Because it is unlikely that a few Athenian envoys could have stopped Philip's military progress, this is a doubtful assertion. It is typical of the manner in which

else we would not have taken his oath, in which case he would have forfeited the peace and not had both things, namely, the peace and the territory.

[31] Thus Philip's first act of fraud during this mission was likewise the first occasion these immoral men were corrupted, which, I admit, is the reason that I then was, still am, and always will be at war and at odds with them. Now consider their next unscrupulous deed, even more serious than the previous one. [32] After their defiance of my proposal had allowed Philip to take possession of Thrace before ratifying the peace, he bribed them again in order to delay our departure from Macedon until the forces he had trained on the Phocians were ready to move. He hoped that if we did not inform you that he was intending, indeed, preparing to march, you would not march forth either, and you would not send triremes around to Thermopylae to close it off as happened once before.[36] His goal was to be inside Thermopylae by the time you heard this news from us, and there would then be nothing you could do. [33] Yet even if he successfully took this place, Philip was filled with such dread and consternation at the prospect of failing to secure his aims if you voted to aid the Phocians before he destroyed them that he hired this contemptible man,[37] no longer in league with the other envoys but alone and on his own, to report matters to you in such a way that total destruction ensued.

[34] Now I ask and entreat you, Athenians, to keep this fact in mind during the entire trial: had Aeschines made no charges extraneous to the indictment, I would not discuss anything outside it either; but since he resorted to all manner of vilification and defamation, I must answer each of his charges briefly.

[35] What words did he utter then that led to total destruction?[38]

Demosthenes, like his opponent and all advocates in Athenian courts, portrays the facts to suit his case.

[36] When in 352 the Athenians mobilized quickly in aid of the Phocians to prevent Philip from seizing Thermopylae, Philip backed down. This episode is contrasted with Athens' failure to do anything to challenge Philip's seizure of Thermopylae in 346, for which Aeschines is blamed.

[37] Uttered with a gesture towards Aeschines.

[38] Demosthenes refers to Aeschines' report to the Assembly following the Second Embassy, which was one of the strongest elements of his case against Aeschines in 346; see 19.19–24.

That there was no reason to be upset because Philip had passed Thermopylae, since everything would be as you wished, provided you made no move; and that you would hear within two or three days that Philip has become a friend of those who greeted him as an enemy and likewise he has become an enemy of those who greeted him as a friend.[39] For alliances are strengthened, he claimed, not because of names,[40] which he pronounced with great solemnity, but through conformity of interests; and the interests of everyone alike—Philip's, the Phocians', yours—lie in being freed from the ruthless oppression of the Thebans.[41] [36] Some welcomed what they heard, since at the time the Thebans were thoroughly hated. But what happened immediately afterwards, not a long time later? The Phocians fell, and their cities were demolished, and you, under the influence of Aeschines, did nothing, though when you were shortly transporting your goods in from the countryside,[42] Aeschines was taking his money. And on top of all this, our city earned the hatred of the Thebans and Thessalians, while Philip earned goodwill for what he did.[43] [37] To show that these claims are true, clerk, please read Callisthenes' decree[44] and Philip's letter, which together will establish all these points. Read.

[DECREE]

[38] Was this what you hoped for when you made the peace treaty? Was this what this hireling promised you?

---

[39] The Phocians and the Thebans respectively. The reversal of alliances with Philip that Aeschines is here said to have predicted was, certainly in 330 if not in 346 too, patently absurd.

[40] I.e., "friend" and "enemy."

[41] Demosthenes portrays Aeschines as a consistent opponent of the Thebans, who, in Demosthenes' view, were Athens' natural allies against Philip (see 18.161–168, 19.85n).

[42] Fearing invasion by Philip, the Athenians took refuge behind the walls of their city and harbor.

[43] By settling the Phocian or Third Sacred War in Thebes' favor, Philip won over the Thebans as allies against Athens.

[44] This decree authorized the emergency measures against a possible invasion by Philip in 346.

[39] Now, clerk, read the letter that came from Philip afterwards.

[LETTER]

[40] See how Philip's letter to you contains a clear and specific message to his allies, as if he were saying, "I accomplished my goals though the Athenians objected and paid dearly. So you, Thebans and Thessalians, if you are wise, will consider them your enemy and put your confidence in me." That was his meaning even if he didn't use those words. Then he was off, having established such control over the Thebans and Thessalians that they did not anticipate or even notice what happened later but allowed him to take charge of everything. As a result, those wretched cities still cope with fresh disasters.[45] [41] Yet the man who aided and abetted Philip in winning their confidence, who gave false information here and cheated you, is this very man who now bewails the anguish of the Thebans and proclaims their misery.[46] He is responsible for those events, for what the Phocians suffered, and for all the other troubles that befell the Greeks. Naturally you're pained by these events, Aeschines, and you feel pity for the Thebans, since you own property in Boeotia and farm their land, but I'm delighted, since the author of the crime immediately demanded my surrender.[47]

[42] Yet I've stumbled onto a topic that will perhaps be more fitting later on. Let me return to my argument that the crimes committed by these men brought about the present situation.

After you had been tricked by Philip when he bribed your envoys to bring you false information, and the poor Phocians had also been tricked and their cities destroyed, what happened then? [43] The despicable Thessalians and the obtuse Thebans viewed Philip as friend, benefactor, savior.[48] He was everything to them, and if some-

---

[45] A reference to the Thebans, whose city was razed by Alexander in 335 as punishment for insurrection.

[46] Aes. 3.156–157.

[47] Behind this sarcasm is the fact that Demosthenes was one of ten Athenians whom Alexander, after putting down the Theban revolt, demanded as hostages. The demand was later rescinded. Demosthenes also implies that Aeschines' property in Boeotia came to him from Philip in return for services rendered.

[48] Standard terms used in public expressions of gratitude, but Demosthenes' irony suggests that such gratitude to Philip was a colossal delusion.

one wished to say otherwise, they wouldn't hear a word of it. You regarded the situation warily and felt anxious, but you kept the peace anyway since there was nothing else you could do. The rest of the Greeks were, like you, duped and cheated of their hopes, and even though in some fashion war had been waged against them for some time, they too were content to keep the peace. [44] Continually moving about, Philip conquered Illyrians, Triballians, and some Greeks too, thereby acquiring significant forces. Citizens of various cities were taking advantage of the peace to travel to Macedon, where they, like this man here, were corrupted. By that time all who were the object of Philip's designs were under attack. If they did not understand it, that's another matter and has nothing to do with me. [45] I repeatedly warned and protested, both here in Athens and wherever I was dispatched. But the other Greek cities were hurting: the politicians and influential citizens were taking bribes and seeking money for their services; among the mass of private citizens, some did not see the problem coming, others were seduced by the calm and easy pace of daily life; all suffered this same experience: they thought that the danger would strike anyone but themselves and that the risks incurred by others would allow them to preserve their own property at will. [46] As a result, I suppose, abundant and ill-timed complacency cost the masses their freedom, while the leaders, under the impression that they were selling everything but themselves, realized that they had sold themselves first. In place of what they were called when they were taking bribes—Philip's friend or Philip's guest—now they are known as bootlickers, enemies of the gods, and other fitting terms.

[47] Indeed, Athenians, no one spends his own money to advance a traitor's interests, and no one who has got what he paid for has any further use for a traitor's advice. If they did, no one would be better off than a traitor; but that's not how things are. How could it be? Far from it! When a would-be tyrant takes control of a government, he also gains control over those who sold it to him, and then, precisely then, knowing their viciousness, he despises them, suspects them, and scorns them. [48] Reflect on this, for even though timely action is no longer possible, it is always timely for prudent citizens to understand such matters. Lasthenes was considered a friend until he betrayed Olynthus. So too was Timolas until he destroyed Thebes, and Eudicus and Simus of Larissa until they delivered Thessaly to Philip. The

world is full of such people—banished, humiliated, what haven't they
suffered? What about Aristratus in Sicyon and Perilas in Megara?
Were they not thrown out?[49] **[49]** These examples show clearly that
the very citizen who takes the lead in defending his country and opposing such men furnishes you and your friends, Aeschines—the traitors and hirelings—with the opportunity to take your bribes. Indeed,
you are alive and take your pay because of the many men present
here[50] who resist your plots. Left to your own devices, you would have
perished long ago.

[50] There remains a great deal that could be said about the events
of that time, but I suppose what I've said so far is more than enough.
Yet it was Aeschines' fault, since he covered me with the stale dregs, as
it were, of his own depravity and crimes. I had to clear myself before
those of you too young to remember the events, while those of you
who knew his venality even before I said a word were probably already
annoyed. **[51]** Yet Aeschines prefers terms like "friendship" and "hospitality" and just now mentioned somewhere in his speech "the person who reproaches me for being Alexander's guest."[51] I reproach you
for being Alexander's guest? How did you acquire that status? What
did you do to deserve it? I wouldn't say that you were Philip's guest or
Alexander's friend—I'm not that crazy!—unless by Zeus we also have
to call farm hands and other hired workers the friends and guests of
those who hired them! **[52]** But I do call you a hireling, formerly of
Philip, now of Alexander, and all these men call you the same. If you
don't believe me, ask them yourself or, rather, I'll do it for you. Do you
think, Athenians, that Aeschines is Alexander's hired hand or his
guest? You hear what they say.[52]

---

[49] This brief list of Greek traitors is amplified below, 18.295. On Lasthenes, see
19.265, 342.

[50] I.e., the audience, whom Demosthenes flatters by portraying them as stal-
wart patriots (see 18.89n).

[51] Demosthenes is citing Aes. 3.66, which he is able to use against Aeschines.

[52] As it stands, the text implies a response from the audience to Demosthenes'
question. What if anything did Demosthenes do to ensure the desired response?
Was the tactic too bold to risk before a live audience, in which case the passage
would have been contrived for publication after delivery? Ancient scholars devised
ingenious but improbable answers. Most likely Demosthenes was sure either of

[53] I wish now to reply to the indictment itself and to describe my accomplishments so that Aeschines may hear, though he already knows it, on what basis I assert that I deserve to obtain the honors enumerated in the decree and even much greater ones. Clerk, take the indictment and please read it.

[54–55] [INDICTMENT]

[56] These are the specific points in the decree that he has chosen to prosecute, Athenians, and starting from these same points, I expect to show you that my entire defense will be fair. I am going to take up the points of the indictment in the same order as he has done, address them all in succession one by one, and do my best to omit nothing.[53]

[57] Now, according to the decree, I always acted and spoke in the best interests of the people, and I was always eager to do whatever good was in my power, and for these reasons I was to be commended. The key to deciding these matters lies, I take it, in my public acts, for by examining them we can discover whether the claims made about me in Ctesiphon's decree are true and fitting or whether they are false.

[58] Regarding two further issues—that Ctesiphon urged the crown without insisting that I first submit to an audit (*euthynai*) and that he assigned the formal ceremony to the theater[54]—I believe that the question whether or not I merit the crown and a ceremony before the citizens also pertains to my public record. I recognize, however, that the laws that permit Ctesiphon to formulate the decree in this way must indeed be specified. Thus I am satisfied, Athenians, that my defense is fair and straightforward, and I shall move on to my public acts.

---

his audience or of his ability to manipulate their response to his advantage. Eliciting vocal response from the audience was a crucial part of Athenian oratory.

[53] Unlike Aeschines' speech of prosecution, in which the legal charges were treated first, then the political ones, in the indictment of 336 Aeschines apparently listed his political charge first, then the legal one. That offers Demosthenes an amusing irony at Aeschines' expense, since the latter placed so much emphasis on requiring Demosthenes to respond to the charges in the same order as he, the prosecutor, set them out; see 18.2n.

[54] These are the points in which Aeschines argued that Ctesiphon's decree was formally incompatible with statute law; see 18.110n. Demosthenes responds to them below, 18.110–121.

[59] But no one should suppose that my speech strays from the charges if I enter into a discussion of Greek affairs. By prosecuting the decree for its claim that in word and deed I advanced your best interests and by designating the falsity of this point as the basis of his indictment,[55] it is Aeschines who has made a discussion of all my public acts germane and essential to the case. Further, since public life offers many avenues of activity and I chose Greek affairs as mine, I am entitled to draw my arguments from that realm.

[60] I will not speak about the places that Philip took and occupied before I entered politics and began to address the people; such matters have nothing to do with me. Rather, I will discuss and present an account of the actions that thwarted Philip from the very day I turned my attention to politics,[56] though I begin with this preliminary remark. Philip had, Athenians, a great advantage. [61] For among the Greeks—not just some, but all alike—there arose so huge a crop of treacherous, corrupt, and loathsome men that no one could recall its like ever before. Philip took them on as accomplices and helpers, and though the Greeks were already ill-disposed to one another and rent with faction, he made things worse; some he tricked, some he bought, others he thoroughly corrupted. Thus, he divided Greece into many blocs though one policy was advantageous for all: to prevent his becoming powerful.

[62] Since all Greeks were in this situation, still ignorant of the gathering, growing evil, you need to consider, Athenians, what were the policies and actions that the city ought to have chosen, and you need to hear an explanation of these matters from me. For I am the

---

[55] In addition to the legal arguments that buttressed his case, Aeschines' main argument was that Demosthenes' public record was such that he did not deserve the crown.

[56] In what follows, Demosthenes speaks as if he entered politics in the mid 340s, when Athens began to recover from the disastrous Peace of Philocrates. It would be truer to say that at that time, Demosthenes began to take the leading role in determining Athenian policy. Since the decade leading up to the Peace of Philocrates (356–346) was generally a bad one for Athens' foreign policy, Demosthenes wants to minimize the extent to which he could even be associated with that period.

one who took up that post[57] in the city. [63] Ought the city, Aeschines, to have dispensed with its pride and the esteem in which it is held and to have taken up its post alongside Thessalians and Dolopians,[58] thereby helping Philip acquire his empire over Greece and erasing the noble and just achievements of our forebears? Or was the city right not to have done that—it would have been truly horrible—and should we instead merely have watched events develop even though we perceived them, it seems, in advance and saw they would take place if no one prevented them? [64] Even now I would gladly put the question to the severest critic of our policy: which side does he wish the city had joined? Those who share the blame for the evil, disgraceful outcome that befell the Greeks, among whom one could mention the Thessalians and their allies? Or those who looked on as events transpired in the hope of some profit for themselves, in which group I would put the Arcadians, the Messenians, and the Argives? [65] But many of these cities, indeed all of them, fared worse than we did! For if after his victory[59] Philip straightaway up and left and then kept to himself, bringing grief neither to any of his allies nor to any other Greeks, then one could blame and disparage those who opposed his actions. But since he stripped from all alike their reputation, their power, and their freedom, and, from as many as he could, even their very form of government, how is it that your decision to follow my advice was not absolutely commendable?

[66] But I return to my previous point. What, Aeschines, should the city have done when it saw Philip building towards empire and tyranny over the Greeks? And what was an adviser in Athens—for that makes all the difference—obliged to say and propose? During all my time until the day I myself stepped onto the speaker's platform, I knew that our country always fought for the first prize in honor and glory and had expended more money and men in pursuit of honor and the common good than all the other Greeks had expended on their own behalf. [67] Yet I also saw that in pursuit of power and dom-

---

[57] Demosthenes' "post" was to be an adviser on foreign policy ("Greek affairs," 18.59).

[58] Greek allies of Philip.

[59] At Chaeronea in 338.

ination, Philip, our opponent in the struggle, had his eye knocked out, his collarbone broken, his hand and leg maimed, in fact that he readily sacrificed any part of his body that fortune might take so that afterwards he might live in honor and glory.[60] [68] Indeed, no one would have dared assert that a man raised in Pella, a small, obscure place at the time,[61] would become so bold as to desire rule over the Greeks and to make that his purpose, or that you—Athenians!—who every day behold reminders of the valor of your forebears in all manner of speeches and monuments, would be so cowardly as to surrender your freedom to Philip voluntarily. No one would say that.

[69] Surely the only remaining course of action, indeed the necessary course, was to oppose on the side of right everything that he did to wrong you. That is what you did from the beginning, reasonably and appropriately, while I moved the decrees and argued the case for as long as I have been active as a politician. I admit it. What should I have done? I ask you that now, putting aside all other matters—Amphipolis, Pydna, Potidaea, Halonnesus—I exclude all of them. [70] As for Serrium, Doriscus, the sack of Peparethus, and all the other crimes inflicted on the city, I take no notice of their existence.[62] But you claimed, Aeschines, that by talking of these matters I incited the citizens to hostility, even though Eubulus, Aristophon, and Diopeithes moved the decrees,[63] not I— O Aeschines, you casually say whatever you like. Nor will I say anything about those matters

---

[60] Philip was famous for the wounds he acquired in battle. The fullest preserved ancient account is in Didymus, *On Demosthenes* 12.40–13.12.

[61] Demosthenes exaggerates Pella's insignificance before Philip. At the time, Pella, Philip's capital, was a large city, having been built up by Macedonian kings since the late fifth century.

[62] These places and those mentioned in the previous sentences exemplify Philip's aggressive strikes at Athens' expense during the two decades leading up to Chaeronea. Philip took Amphipolis, Pydna, and Potidaea, all in northern Greece, in 357–356. Serrium and Doriscus were Thracian cities seized by Philip during the peace negotiations of 346 (see 18.27n). The Aegean islands of Halonnesus and Peparethus were formerly under Athenian domination. Having been taken by Philip probably in the 350s, Halonnesus became a pawn in failed negotiations between Philip and Athens in 342. Philip sacked Peparethus in 340.

[63] See 18.75n on these politicians.

now. [71] But when Philip was expropriating Euboea and turning it into a fortress against Attica, when he was plotting against Megara, when he was taking over Oreus and leveling Porthmus, when he set up Philistides as tyrant in Oreus and Clitarchus in Eretria, when he took control of the Hellespont and besieged Byzantium, when he razed various Greek cities and restored exiles to others—when he did all these things did he act unjustly and contravene the accord and break the peace or not?[64] Was it necessary that some Greek step forward who would stop his doing these things or not? [72] For if that was not necessary, but it had to be revealed that Greece was "Mysian plunder," as the saying goes,[65] even though Athens was still alive and well, then my labor in speaking about these matters has been wasted, and your labor in heeding my advice has been wasted too. Let everything the city has done count as my crimes and my mistakes. But if there was a need for someone to step forward to stop these things, who should have done it but the Athenian people? That, in fact, was my policy, and when I saw him enslaving all mankind I opposed him, and I constantly proclaimed and advised that people should not surrender. [73] Yet our city did not violate the peace, Aeschines, Philip did, when he seized our merchant ships.[66]

Clerk, take the decrees and Philip's letter and read them one after the other. These documents will make clear who is responsible for what.

[74] [DECREE]

[75] This decree was moved by Eubulus, not by me. Then Aristophon moved a decree, then Hegesippus, then Aristophon again, then

---

[64] Philip's actions in the places named in this sentence, all in the period 343–340, represent an intensification of his aggression against Athens and determined the Athenians for war.

[65] Meaning an easy victim; see Arist., *Rhetoric* 1372b31–33.

[66] During his siege of Byzantium in 340, Philip seized a grain fleet in the Bosporus, which outraged the Athenians and led them, on Demosthenes' initiative, officially to renounce the peace. In this passage, Demosthenes omits his own role in renouncing the Peace of Philocrates in order to put all the blame for the breakdown of peace on Philip.

Philocrates, then Cephisophon, then all of them.[67] I made no motion on these matters. Clerk, read.

[DECREES]

[76] These are the decrees that I exhibit; now you, Aeschines, exhibit any decree that I moved that makes me responsible for the war. You cannot, for if you could, there is nothing you would have shown us sooner. In fact, not even Philip holds me responsible for the war; he blames others. Clerk, read the letter from Philip.

[77–78] [LETTER]

[79] Nowhere in the letter does Philip mention Demosthenes or cast any blame on me. Why does he denounce others and not mention my actions? Because he would thereby have mentioned his own crimes! For I fastened on them and opposed them. First, I proposed the diplomatic mission to the Peloponnese when he first stole into the Peloponnese, then the mission to Euboea when he tried to seize Euboea, then the expedition to Oreus—military, not diplomatic—and another to Eretria after he established tyrants in those cities.[68] [80] Next, I dispatched all the naval expeditions that saved the Chersonese, Byzantium, and all our allies in that region. For you the outcome was excellent: praise, glory, honor, crowns, gratitude from the beneficiaries. Among the victims, those who heeded you gained their safety, while those who scorned you can often recall your predictions and consider you to be not only well disposed towards them but also prudent, even prophetic people. For everything turned out as you predicted.

[81] Yet everyone knows that Philistides would have given much money to hold Oreus, Clitarchus would have given much to hold Eretria,[69] and Philip himself would have given much to use these places against you as well as to avoid detection in other matters and escape

---

[67] These are prominent politicians from across the spectrum of Athenian politics, from the esteemed Eubulus to the traitor Philocrates. According to Demosthenes, they all viewed Philip as responsible for violating the peace.

[68] These operations and those mentioned in the next sentence took place in 341–340.

[69] Philistides and Clitarchus were tyrants established by Philip in their respective cities (18.79).

an inquiry into his unjust actions everywhere. You, Aeschines, know this better than anyone, [82] since the envoys who kept arriving here from Clitarchus and Philistides stayed in your house, and you represented them.[70] The city sent them away because they were enemies who proposed unjust, harmful measures, but they were your friends. However, none of those things was accomplished, Aeschines, you who slander me by saying that I keep silent when I've taken and scream when I've spent.[71] But you are different: you scream even when you have[72] and you will not stop unless these men stop you by disenfranchising you today.[73]

[83] Anyway, when you conferred a crown on me for that episode, and Aristonicus, the proposer, said the same thing, word for word, as has Ctesiphon in his decree, and the crown was announced in the theater,[74] Aeschines, though present, neither objected nor indicted the proposer. Clerk, please take that decree and read it.

[84] [DECREE]

[85] Is anyone aware that the city was somehow humiliated because of this decree, or mocked or ridiculed, which is the outcome that Aeschines is now predicting if I receive the crown?[75] In fact, when a policy is recent and familiar to everybody, if it works out well, one is thanked, if otherwise, punished. Well, it is clear that I was thanked at that time, not censured or punished. [86] Therefore, up to the time when these achievements took place, it was recognized that in every respect I advanced the city's best interests: my advice and proposals triumphed when you met in the Assembly; that which I proposed was carried out and led to crowns for the city, for me, and for everyone;

---

[70] Aeschines was the official representative (*proxenos*) of Oreus and Eretria; hence, it was appropriate for envoys from those cities to stay at his house.

[71] The reference is to money from bribes. Aeschines (3.218) charged Demosthenes with taking bribes (in secret, of course) and enjoying the money while seeking a prominent role in politics (hence "scream").

[72] I.e., all the time, again referring to money from bribes.

[73] If Aeschines failed to receive the minimum number of votes to avoid a fine for frivolous prosecution (see 18.103n), he would be in danger of falling into public indebtedness and thus losing his citizen status.

[74] In spring 340. The wording used in honorary decrees was largely formulaic.

[75] Aes. 3.155–156, 247.

and in recognition of this favorable outcome you held sacrifices to the gods and processions in their honor.

[87] Then, when we drove Philip from Euboea,[76] you through force of arms, and I—even if some may burst denying it—through political strategy and decrees, he began to look for another stronghold against the city. Noticing that we consume more imported grain than anyone else, he wished to take control of the grain shipments and went to Thrace.[77] First, he demanded that the Byzantians, his allies, join his war against you, and when they refused and denied that they had made the alliance for that purpose, which was true, he built up a palisade against the city, erected engines, and besieged them. [88] I will not ask what you were obliged to do while that was going on— that's obvious to everyone. But who was it who helped the Byzantians and saved them? Who was it who prevented the Hellespont from falling into foreign hands at that time? It was you, Athenians, and when I say you, I mean the city. And who was it who addressed the city, moved decrees, took action, and in truth devoted himself unsparingly to the situation? It was I. [89] But you do not need a report to teach you how much everyone benefited; you lived through the actual events. Besides bringing you glory, the war that then broke out provided you with a way of life in all respects more plentiful and cheaper than the current peace,[78] which, to the detriment of our country, these worthy gentlemen watch over in hopes of future gain. May they fail in their hopes; may they have no share in that which you, the true patriots, ask of the gods; and may they not confer on you what they prefer for themselves.[79] Clerk, read them the crown decrees of the

---

[76] In 343–342.

[77] Athens had been reliant on grain imported from the Black Sea since at least the mid fifth century; the Bosporus and the Hellespont were the choke points. This vulnerability was well understood by both the Athenians and potential enemies and thus became a focus of military strategy. Philip tried to take control of the Hellespont in 340.

[78] Since the establishment of Macedonian hegemony after Chaeronea and Athens' consequent inability to control the importation of grain, there were periodic grain shortages and sharp rises in grain prices in Attica.

[79] Demosthenes comments obliquely on Athenian political factions at the time of the trial. The ironically named "worthy gentlemen" seek to maintain Macedonian hegemony. The audience, flatteringly addressed as "the true patriots"

Byzantians and the Perinthians, in which they bestowed crowns on the city because of these events.

[90–91] [DECREE OF THE BYZANTIANS, DECREE OF THE PERINTHIANS]

[92] Read the crown decree from the citizens of the Chersonese too.

[DECREE OF THE CHERSONESIANS]

[93] Thus, the policy that I devised not only saved the Chersonese and Byzantium, prevented Philip from taking over the Hellespont at that time, and brought the city honors for these actions, it also displayed to all mankind the city's magnanimity and Philip's treachery. Though he was the Byzantians' ally, everyone saw that he besieged them. What could be more shameful or abominable than that? [94] And though you might reasonably have brought many well-founded complaints against the Byzantians because they had treated you unfairly on a previous occasion,[80] you demonstrated that you not only do not hold grudges or abandon those who are mistreated but in fact save people in that condition, which won you fame and goodwill everywhere. Moreover, everyone knows that before now you have bestowed crowns on many politicians. Yet no one could assert that any other single person apart from me—I mean among advisers and politicians—has won crowns for the city.

[95] Next, I intend to show that when Aeschines slandered the Euboeans and Byzantians by recalling whether they had ever mistreated you, he was trying to cause mischief. Not only were his claims false, as I think you already know, but even if they were entirely true, it was to our advantage to handle the situation as I handled it. To that end, I wish to discuss briefly one or two of the noble acts done by the city during your lifetime. Both individual citizens and the city as a whole must ever strive to act in accord with the noblest standards of our tradition.

(lit. "those who desire the best [sc. for the city]"), desire freedom from Macedon. See 18.323.

[80] Byzantium seceded from the Second Athenian League in the late 360s and supported the rebelling states in the Social War of 357–355.

[96] When the Spartans ruled sea and land, Athenians, and held the territories round Attica with garrisons and military governors— Euboea, Tanagra, all Boeotia, Megara, Aegina, Ceos, the other islands —when the city still possessed no ships and no walls, you marched out to Haliartus and then again not many days later to Corinth,[81] even though the Athenians of that day could well have borne a grudge against the Corinthians and Thebans for their actions during the Decelean War.[82] But they did not come close to doing that. [97] It was not that they performed these two actions in aid of benefactors, Aeschines, or failed to see the dangers. But that was not reason for them to abandon those who sought help from them. Rather, they were ready to submit to mortal danger for the sake of glory and honor, which was the right and noble decision. Indeed, since all men find the limit of life in death—even one who has shut himself in a closet and watches—good men must always venture all noble acts with good hope as their shield and worthily endure whatever god gives them.[83]

[98] That is how your ancestors acted, and that is how you older men acted when the Thebans defeated the Spartans at Leuctra and tried to destroy them.[84] You prevented it, though the Spartans were neither friends nor benefactors and had inflicted many grievous injuries on our city. You did not fear the power and reputation of the Thebans at that time, nor did you stop to consider how the people for whose sake you were about to risk your lives had behaved. [99] So in this case too you showed all Greeks that when someone wrongs you in

---

[81] In the aftermath of the Peloponnesian War, beyond controlling the territories named here, Sparta placed severe restrictions on Athenian military power. Athenian resurgence began in the 390s, as demonstrated by the battle at Haliartus (in Boeotia) in fall 395, when Athens aided Thebes against Sparta, and then in spring 394, when Athens helped defend Corinth against the Spartans.

[82] I.e., the last decade of the Peloponnesian War (413–404), so named from a Spartan fort established at Decelea in Attica. During the Peloponnesian War, Thebes and Corinth were allied with Sparta against Athens.

[83] This moralistic statement anticipates Demosthenes' argument with regard to the defeat at Chaeronea; see 18.208.

[84] After the Thebans defeated the Spartans at Leuctra in 371, they threatened Sparta itself. In 369 the Athenians sent a force to aid the Spartan defense against the Thebans.

any way, though you generally get angry, you neither bear a grudge nor let it affect your judgment when their safety or freedom is somehow endangered. That was your disposition not only then but also when the Thebans were trying to take over Euboea. You did not sit by idly or recall the injuries that Themison and Theodorus inflicted on you for the sake of Oropus, but you sent help even to them.⁸⁵ That was the first occasion on which the city used volunteer trierarchs, of which I was one;⁸⁶ but more about that later. [100] You performed a noble act just to save the island, yet it was still nobler, while holding power over the cities and their inhabitants, to give them back, as fairness required, to the people who had wronged you and to allow none of the wrongs you had suffered to influence the trust that they placed in you. I pass over countless other examples I might mention, engagements at sea and on land, both long ago and during our own day, all of which the city undertook for the freedom and safety of the rest of Greece.

[101] Since I had seen so many instances of this kind where the city was ready to fight for the interests of others, what was I to urge the city to do, what was I to advise, when the question essentially concerned its own interests? That we should bear a grudge, by Zeus, against those who wished to be saved and that we should seek excuses for giving up completely.⁸⁷ Who would not have been right to kill me had I endeavored to shame the city's noble tradition just by making a proposal to that effect? That you would not actually have done it, I know perfectly well. For had you wanted to, what prevented it? Was it not possible? Were not these men on hand advising you to do it?

[102] I wish to turn now to the next achievement in my political career. In this matter too, consider once more what was best for the city. I saw, Athenians, that your fleet was falling apart, that while small payments left the wealthy practically untaxed, citizens of moderate

---

⁸⁵ In 366 Themison of Eretria helped Thebes take Oropus from Athens. Nonetheless, in 357 in response to a request from Themison, the Athenians sent a force that successfully resisted a Theban attempt to control Euboea.

⁸⁶ A trierarch undertook the responsibility and expense of maintaining a publicly owned warship (trireme) for one year. To meet the needs of the emergency expedition to Euboea of summer 357, the Athenians began the practice of seeking out and recognizing official "volunteers" to assume this task.

⁸⁷ Uttered with irony.

and small means were losing their property, and further, that the situation was causing the city to miss opportunities. I proposed a law through which I compelled some, the rich, to assume their fair burden, stopped the unjust treatment of the poor, and brought about what the city most needed—armed forces ready for action.[88] [103] I was indicted, came before you to stand trial on this issue, and was acquitted, the prosecutor failing to win even his minimum share of the votes.[89] Yet how much money do you think I was offered by the heads of the taxation-groups, as well as by the citizens in the second and third ranks, to refrain from bringing the law forward or, failing that, to let it drop in the event of an indictment?[90] So much, Athenians, that I hesitate to tell you. [104] They had good reason to act this way. Under the previous law, they could perform their public service in groups of sixteen, which allowed them to ruin the needy citizens while paying little or nothing themselves. Under my law, each citizen was obliged to pay his share as determined by his property, whereby a citizen who previously was one of sixteen contributors to one ship now became the trierarch of two. They called themselves no longer trierarchs but contributors! In fact, there is nothing they didn't offer to have this law nullified and to avoid having to assume their fair burden. [105] Clerk, please read, first, the decree that brought the case to trial,

---

[88] In 340 Demosthenes initiated legislation to reform the trierarchy, the system whereby the Athenians raised money from wealthy citizens to supply the city with triremes (see 18.99n). The reform increased the burden on the wealthiest citizens and lessened the burden on citizens of more moderate means; see Gabrielsen 1994.

[89] In Athenian law, a prosecutor had to win at least one-fifth of the votes cast by the jurors or face a penalty for frivolous prosecution. The penalty could be severe enough to effectively deprive the person of his citizen rights through failure to pay (see 18.82, 266, 312n). Demosthenes was indicted for moving an inexpedient law (*graphē nomon mē epitēdeion theinai*), a legal action similar to the *graphē paranomōn,* which was directed against decrees.

[90] The taxation-groups (*symmoriai*) were groups of wealthy and less wealthy citizens formed to pay financial obligations to the state. The "heads" of these taxation-groups, together with the citizens of the second and third ranks, made up the so-called Three Hundred, the wealthiest citizens of Athens who traditionally assumed the heaviest public financial obligations. The Three Hundred had much to lose if Demosthenes' attempt to reform the trierarchy succeeded.

then the trierarch-registers, both the one drafted under the previous law and that drafted under mine. Read.

[DECREE]

[106] Bring forward the magnificent[91] register of trierarchs.

[REGISTER]

Now bring forward the register of trierarchs drafted under my law, and place it beside the first one.

[REGISTER]

[107] Does it seem that I helped the poor citizens among you only a little, or that the wealthy would have spent little to avoid doing what was right? I take pride not only in not compromising and being acquitted after I was indicted but also in passing a law that was beneficial, as experience proved. During the entire war the naval forces were organized on the basis of my law, yet not a single trierarch laid a suppliant's branch at your feet because he was treated unfairly;[92] none occupied the temple in Munichia;[93] none was imprisoned by the naval magistrates; no trireme was abandoned abroad and lost to the city; none was left behind here, unable to put to sea. [108] But all these things did happen under the previous laws, because the obligation to fund the ships fell on the poor, which led to many impossible situations. I transferred the trierarchies from the poor to the rich; then everything that was necessary followed.[94] Thus, I merit praise for this reason too: I devised all the policies that enabled the city to acquire glory, honor, and power at once. No policy of mine was ever malicious or vindictive or mean; none was trivial or unworthy of the city.

---

[91] Ironic: this is the register of trierarchs drafted under the old law.

[92] A trierarch who could not meet his obligation could, as a last resort, supplicate the people for relief.

[93] To seek asylum. The temple belonged to Artemis; Munichia was in Piraeus.

[94] Demosthenes exaggerates by speaking of the citizens of moderate means who contributed towards trierarchies as "poor." To portray himself as the reliever of oppression, he exaggerates the oppression. However, the problem he mentions did occur under the old trierarchy system.

[109] It's clear, then, that my character is the same in both domestic policy and general Greek affairs. Within the city I did not prefer the gratitude of the rich to the just claims of the masses. So too in Greek affairs I did not covet Philip's gifts and hospitality in preference to the common interests of all Greece.

[110] I believe it now remains for me to speak about the proclamation of the crown and the audit,[95] for I think what I have said thus far demonstrates that I acted in the city's best interests and have always been public spirited and eager to help you. Indeed, I leave aside my most important political achievements, because, first, I owe you a discussion of the issue of illegality in its proper place, and, second, even if I say nothing about the rest of my public acts, each of you is, I trust, nevertheless aware of them.

[111] Seeing how Aeschines thoroughly jumbled his arguments regarding the conflicts with statutory law,[96] I don't imagine, by god, that you understood much of it, nor could I make sense of it either. I will discuss the legal issues simply and straightforwardly. Far from claiming that I was exempt from an audit,[97] as he maliciously asserts,

---

[95] Demosthenes now responds to Aeschines' two legal arguments (3.9–48) against Ctesiphon's decree: a statute forbade the proclamation of crowns in the theater of Dionysus; a statute forbade a magistrate from receiving a crown before he had successfully completed the mandatory audit (*euthynai*) at the end of his term of office. See the Introduction on the *graphē paranomōn*. Demosthenes' legal arguments seem weak and focus more on attacking Aeschines than on responding to his legal arguments (see Yunis 2001: 174–175 for details and references; Harris 1994 finds Demosthenes' legal arguments compelling). The main question before the court was whether or not Demosthenes deserved the crown, and that would be answered not by interpreting the laws but by assessing his career as a politician. The legal arguments of both advocates were of minor importance and served primarily to bolster their standing as defenders of the law in the eyes of the audience.

[96] The purpose of the legal argument in a *graphē paranomōn* was to demonstrate that the decree (*psēphisma*) under indictment was in conflict with one or more statutes (*nomoi*).

[97] Every citizen who held an office that involved the use of public funds was obliged to undergo a two-stage audit (*euthynai*) when he completed the office; see the Introduction to Dem. 19.

I submit that my whole life long I am subject to audit by you for whatever public funds I have handled and for whatever public business I have undertaken. [112] However, I claim that I am not subject to an audit on any day for any private funds that I have openly declared as a gift to the people—are you listening, Aeschines?—and that holds for every citizen, even the Nine Archons.[98] For what law is so unfair and loaded with resentment that it would deny gratitude to the citizen who has made a donation from his private resources and performed a considerate, generous act, haul him before the *sykophants*, and force him to submit his accounts to them?[99] There is no such law. If Aeschines says there is, let him disclose it, and I'll be satisfied and shut up. [113] But there is no such law, Athenians. Rather, he invents the specious charge that I made a private donation while still treasurer of the Public Festival Fund (*to theōrikon*) and claims: "Ctesiphon proposed public commendation of Demosthenes while he was subject to an audit," though the proposal did not concern anything for which I was subject to an audit, but only my private donations, you *sykophant*. "But you were also a commissioner for repairing the city walls." Indeed, for that reason too it was right to commend me, since I donated the expenditures and did not charge them to the public account. Charges to the public account require audits and citizens to examine them. Gifts merit thanks and commendation, which is the very reason that Ctesiphon proposed the measure on my behalf.

[114] Many examples make it abundantly clear that this principle is based not only on the laws, Athenians, but also on your values. First, you bestowed several crowns on Nausicles for voluntary contributions from private resources while he was general.[100] Then Diotimus received a crown for a donation of shields, as did Charidemus. And Neoptolemus, right here, was publicly honored for private contribu-

---

[98] The highest civic magistrates, including the Archon, the Basileus, the Polemarch, and the six Thesmothetae (see Arist., *Ath. Pol.* 55–59).

[99] *Sykophants* were citizens who engaged in malicious political attacks or prosecutions for pay or extortion; thus, to be accused of *sykophancy* was a grievous insult (see the Series Introduction). Here Demosthenes speaks of *sykophants* in place of *logistai*, the duly appointed public accountants.

[100] Nausicles and the others mentioned in the following sentences were public benefactors and contributed resources to the fight against Macedon.

tions while in charge of several public tasks. It would be appalling if while holding some office, a citizen cannot give his own money to the city because of that office or else must undergo an audit for his gifts rather than receive thanks. [115] To verify these statements, clerk, take the decrees that honored these men and please read them. Read.

[DECREE]

[116] [SECOND DECREE]

[117] Each of these citizens, Aeschines, was subject to an audit for the office that he held, but not subject to an audit for the deeds that won him the crown. Therefore, neither am I, for surely justice requires that I be treated in the same way as others in the same circumstances. I made private donations; I am being commended for that, and I am not subject to an audit for those donations. I held public offices; accordingly, I submitted to an audit for those offices, not for my private donations. But, by Zeus, I was delinquent in office. Well then, Aeschines, you were there when the accountants (*logistai*) heard my case. Why did you not accuse me then?

[118] Clerk, now take the decree proposed in my honor and read it through so that you citizens can see that Aeschines himself provides evidence that I was honored for deeds for which I was not subject to audit. For those parts of the original decree that he elected not to mention in his indictment will expose as malicious fabrications the charges that he is prosecuting. Read.

[DECREE]

[119] My private donations are precisely what you did not indict, Aeschines, while that which the Council decrees I am to get in return for them is precisely what you are prosecuting.[101] So you concede that it is legal to accept the gifts, but you indict as illegal the expression of

<hr>

[101] That which Demosthenes is to get in return is the crown. The "Council decrees" because Ctesiphon's proposal was approved by the Council before Aeschines indicted him.

gratitude for them. By god, what kind of person perfectly exemplifies an unscrupulous, loathsome, and truly malicious human being? Is it not this kind?

[120] The next point concerns the theater as the place of proclamation.[102] I leave aside the fact that thousands of people on thousands of occasions have received their crowns in the theater, as I myself have done on several previous occasions. Yet, by god, Aeschines, are you so stupid and obtuse as to be unable to comprehend that the crown brings the recipient the same admiration wherever it is announced, but it is proclaimed in the theater because that is to the advantage of those who bestow it? All those in attendance are motivated to do the city some good, and they praise those who display gratitude more than they do the honoree. For that reason, the city instituted the following law. Clerk, take the law and please read it.

[LAW]

[121] Do you hear the clear voice of the law, Aeschines: "except any whom the People or the Council specify in a decree: these are to be proclaimed by the herald"?[103] Why do you prosecute on false premises, you wretch? Why do you make up lies? Why don't you take some hellebore for your trouble?[104] But you're not ashamed to bring suit out of envy rather than for an actual offense and to rewrite laws or snip off parts of them, even though citizens sworn to render judgment according to the laws should hear them in their entirety.[105] [122] That's how you act, and yet you tell us what attributes must belong to a politician who supports the people,[106] acting like someone who has

---

[102] According to Aes. 3.32–48, statute law required that crowns bestowed by the Council be proclaimed in the Council and those bestowed by the Assembly be proclaimed in the Assembly and nowhere else.

[103] Demosthenes claims that this clause of the relevant statute, which would exonerate Ctesiphon, was omitted by Aeschines.

[104] Hellebore was a popular remedy for madness.

[105] The Heliastic Oath sworn by the jurors required them to give judgment according to the laws; see 18.2n, 19.179.

[106] Aes. 3.168–170 enumerated five qualities that must belong to a "supporter-of-the-people." Of course, Aeschines found Demosthenes deficient.

commissioned a statue according to a contract but then takes possession of something that departs from the contract, or as if one could
recognize supporters of the people from a description of them and not
by their acts and policies. You scream all kinds of names at me, decent
and indecent, as though from the wagon,[107] though they suit you and
your family, not me.

[123] Consider this point too, Athenians. Accusation, I would say,
differs from abuse in that accusation presupposes an offense punish-
able by law, but abuse entails insults of the kind that enemies naturally
direct at each other. I assume that our ancestors founded this court
of law not so that we litigants could gather you together and then
hurl the proscribed slurs[108] at each other for personal reasons but to
convict someone who may have committed a crime against the city.
[124] Aeschines knows this as well as I, yet rather than accuse, he has
chosen to abuse. Yet he ought not to get off with any less himself!
I'll come to that in a moment. First this question: would you rather,
Aeschines, be considered the city's enemy or mine? Mine, of course.
Yet when you had opportunities to act on behalf of these men[109] and,
if I committed some offense, to punish me as the laws prescribe—in
audits, in public trials, in other judicial decisions—you let them pass.
[125] But on an occasion when every consideration makes me not liable—the laws, the passage of time, the statute of limitations, the fact
that I've already been tried many times on all these questions, that I've
never yet been convicted of wronging you citizens in any way—and
when the city necessarily has some stake, whether large or small, in the
esteem that results from the actions undertaken by the people,[110] then
you have taken me on? Watch out that you don't turn out to be the enemy of these men while pretending to be mine.

[126] Since it has been demonstrated to all how piety and justice require you to vote, since, despite my reluctance to defame, the slanders
he uttered virtually compel me to reveal the most basic facts about

---

[107] During a procession that formed part of the Anthesteria festival of Dionysus, men engaged in ritual insults while being conveyed in wagons.

[108] The use of specific denunciations, such as parricide, matricide, deserter,
could make a citizen liable to a suit for libel (*kakēgoria*).

[109] Referring to the audience.

[110] I.e., fighting Philip at Chaeronea.

him while exposing his many lies, and since I must explain the identity and origin of the person who so casually launches abuse and ridicules my choice of words[111]—though what normal person would not have recoiled from uttering the words he used?[112] [127] If the prosecutor were Aeacus or Rhadamanthys or Minos[113] and not a sponger, a common scoundrel, a damned clerk, I don't believe he would have spoken that way or produced such repulsive expressions, bellowing as if on the tragic stage, "O earth and sun and virtue" and such like, or appealing to "understanding and education, through which we distinguish noble from base." You did hear him utter those words![114] [128] But what do you or yours, you piece of filth, have to do with virtue? How can you tell the difference between what is noble and what is not? How did you come by that ability? How are you worthy of it? And what gives you the right to talk about education? No truly educated person would ever say such things about himself, but he'd blush just to hear someone else say them. When people like you, who lack education but pretend to it, open their mouths, their stupidity ends up inflicting pain on the audience and fails to produce the desired impression.

[129] I have no difficulty finding things to say about you and your family, but it is difficult to decide where I should start. With your father Tromes, who as slave to Elpias, the schoolteacher in the temple of Theseus, wore heavy fetters and a wooden collar?[115] Or with your

---

[111] Aes. 3.72, 166–167 ridiculed various metaphors and similes that Demosthenes supposedly used, though none of them are present in the surviving speeches; see 18.232n.

[112] Demosthenes' passion leads him to break up the sentence and pursue a new idea. Such apparently spontaneous passion gives the appearance of sincerity.

[113] Virtuous judges of the underworld.

[114] In Aeschines' peroration, 3.260. What Demosthenes faults in Aeschines' words is their pomposity.

[115] Demosthenes begins a series of assaults on Aeschines' background, many of which are obviously false or greatly exaggerated; see also 18.259–265. For instance, Aeschines' father, though perhaps of humble origin, was not a slave (on the father's name, see 18.130n). Such attacks were common in Attic oratory; the purpose was to puncture the opponent's claim to elite status by exposing him to ridicule.

mother, who engaged in midday matrimonies in a shed[116] by the shrine of the hero Calamites and raised her pretty doll and consummate bit-part actor,[117] namely, you? Everyone knows these things without my having to mention them. Or with Phormio, flautist-stroke to the rowers,[118] slave of Dion of Phrearrii, who raised her up from this noble trade? But by Zeus and the gods, I worry that by using the appropriate terms to describe you I might seem to choose terms that are inappropriate for me to utter. [130] So I'll leave that aside and begin from the life he has led himself. He abandoned the station to which he chanced to belong and enlisted among those whom the people curse.[119] At some time recently—do I say recently? —rather, it was yesterday or the day before that he became an Athenian citizen and politician. He turned his father Tromes into Atrometus by adding two syllables,[120] and he made his mother into the very dignified Glaucothea, though everyone knows she was called Empusa, a name she obviously got because she would do anything and allow anything to be done to her.[121] How else would she have gotten it? [131] You are naturally so ungrateful and vile that even though these men brought you from servitude to freedom and from destitution to wealth, not only do you show no gratitude but you hire yourself out to conduct the city's business against their interests. I leave aside in-

---

[116] Demosthenes intensifies the standard insult "your mother is a whore" by turning Aeschines' mother into a cheap whore and one who is so depraved as to ply her trade by day rather than in the obscurity of night.

[117] A gibe at the limited success of Aeschines' career on stage. Demosthenes' word for "bit-part actor," *tritagōnistēs,* literally "third actor," refers to the third and lowest in rank of the three actors who would play a tragedy. It may not have been the standard term but a pejorative coinage by Demosthenes.

[118] Phormio played the *aulos,* a wind instrument like a pipe. He must have been a poor *aulos* player to take a position giving the stroke aboard ship.

[119] At the opening of every meeting of the Assembly and Council, a herald, speaking in the name of the people, pronounced a curse on traitors.

[120] Tromes = trembler; Atrometus = intrepid.

[121] Glaucothea = gray goddess. Empusa, a shadowy female monster of the underworld, capable of changing shape (Aristoph., *Frogs* 288–293), is typical of the names borne by prostitutes. Demosthenes' quip about the origin of Aeschines' mother's nickname refers to sexual versatility.

stances where there may be some question whether he actually spoke in the interest of the city; but I shall recall instances where it has been clearly established that he acted on behalf of the enemy.

[132] Who among you does not know about the Antiphon who had been disenfranchised but returned to the city after informing Philip that he would burn down our dockyard? I caught him hiding in Piraeus and brought him before the Assembly, but that malicious Aeschines shouted and shrieked that in a democracy it was intolerable for me to assault hapless citizens and enter their homes without a decree,[122] and thus he had him released. [133] Had not the Areopagus Council understood the situation and seen the danger arising from the Assembly's untimely mistake, had it not reopened the investigation, arrested the man, and hauled him back to face you, this venerable speaker here would have snatched the fellow away and spirited him off without his paying the penalty. As things turned out, you put the man on the rack and executed him, which you ought to have done to Aeschines too. [134] Clearly the Areopagus Council was aware of Aeschines' role in this episode when, because of the same blindness that often caused you to mismanage public affairs, you elected him to plead our case regarding the temple on Delos.[123] For once you invited the Council into the affair and ceded to it the power of decision, it immediately dismissed him as a traitor and assigned Hyperides the job of advocacy. It rendered its decision by a vote from the altar, and this scoundrel received not a single vote.[124] [135] To prove the truth of this statement, clerk, call the witnesses who will attest it.

---

[122] This Antiphon, otherwise unknown, lost his citizenship during a review of the citizen rolls in 346/5, but Aeschines insisted that Demosthenes violated Antiphon's rights, which could only be the case if Antiphon were a citizen. Hence, below, Demosthenes trumpets that the Assembly ultimately put Antiphon on the rack, a punishment reserved for noncitizens.

[123] Athens was party to an arbitration with Delos over control of the temple and treasury of Apollo on Delos.

[124] For the well-known politician and orator Hyperides, see the volume in this series *Dinarchus, Hyperides, and Lycurgus*, trans. I. Worthington, C. Cooper, and E. M. Harris (Austin, 2001). Quotations from Hyperides' *Delian Speech* survive (ibid., pp. 141–142). Casting the votes from the altar increased the solemnity of the action.

[WITNESSES]

By dismissing Aeschines as he was about to speak and assigning the task to another, the Areopagus Council thereby declared him a traitor and public enemy.[125]

[136] That's one example of the political conduct of this youngster. Quite similar, is it not, to what he accuses me of? Recall another instance. When Philip dispatched Pytho of Byzantium together with delegates from all his other allies to humiliate the city and prove that we were at fault, as Pytho grew brazen and poured forth a flood of accusations against you, I did not retreat.[126] I stood up, spoke against him, and did not forsake the just claims of the city; in fact, so clearly did I prove Philip to be at fault that even his allies stood up and agreed. But Aeschines supported Pytho and gave testimony against his country, false testimony at that.

[137] Even that was not enough, but some time later Aeschines was apprehended meeting the spy Anaxinus at the house of Thraso. Now, anyone who privately met and discussed matters with a representative of the enemy is himself a spy by nature and an enemy of his country.[127] To prove the truth of this statement, clerk, please call the witnesses who will attest it.

[WITNESSES]

[138] There are countless other things that I could say about him, but I leave them aside. The problem essentially is this: though I could

---

[125] Demosthenes plays on the word "declared." In addition to its ordinary sense, this word refers to a legal action taken by the Areopagus Council known as "declaration" (*apophasis*), i.e., to the Assembly, in which the Areopagus Council officially instigated proceedings against a suspected traitor. So far as we know, Aeschines was never subject to the legal procedure of declaration, but in this passage, Demosthenes leaves the impression that he was.

[126] In early 343 Pytho visited Athens as Philip's representative in an attempt to salvage the crumbling Peace of Philocrates. The negotiations failed. Demosthenes says nothing about the substance of the negotiations and emphasizes only his defense of Athens' honor against Pytho's supposed attempt to impugn it.

[127] According to Aes. 3.223–224, while Anaxinus of Oreus was in Athens just to do some shopping for Olympias, Philip's wife, Demosthenes arrested him, tortured him, and had him put to death, all of which is held to be especially abominable because Demosthenes had once enjoyed the man's hospitality.

point out many instances during this time when he was found aiding the enemy and plaguing me, you do not remember them accurately or feel the appropriate degree of anger in response. Instead, you have a bad habit of granting anyone who wishes abundant opportunity to trip up and harass a speaker who advocates your best interests. You give up the city's advantage in return for amusement and the pleasure of vituperation. For this reason, it is always easier and safer to seek employment in the service of the enemy than to take up a post in defense of your interests and to conduct politics from there.

[139] That Aeschines supported Philip before war broke out is deplorable, O earth and gods—how could it not be?—and against his own country! But allow him that, if you wish, allow it. Yet after it was clear that the merchant ships had been seized, that the Chersonese was being pillaged, that the man [128] was marching on Attica, when there was no longer any doubt that a state of war prevailed, this malicious devourer of insults [129] could point to nothing that he ever did for your sake, nor does there exist a single decree, large or small, that was proposed by Aeschines to advance the city's interests. If he claims that one does exist, let him show it to us now during my allotted time. But there isn't any. He had only two options: either to make no counterproposals because he could find no fault with my policy at the time or to bring forward no proposals better than mine because he was devoted to the cause of our enemies.

[140] Did Aeschines also fail to speak, as he indeed failed to make proposals, when there was opportunity to do harm? Why, no one else could take the floor. Though the city could endure much else, as it seems, and Aeschines could do it without attracting attention, nevertheless, Athenians, he committed one additional deed that surpassed his entire previous record. Although he expended many words discussing the Amphissian decrees in an attempt to distort the truth, [130]

---

[128] Philip.

[129] Lit. "devourer of iambs." Iambic verse was the traditional mode of invective. Demosthenes is adept at such coinages, which quickly pin a ridiculous image on Aeschines and are then past before any further thought is given. Cf. "deformed little clerk" (18.209), "a real ape on the tragic stage" (18.242).

[130] Aes. 3.107–129. The Amphissian decrees were the decisions of the Delphic Amphictyony that led to the Sacred War against Amphissa and ultimately to Philip's invasion of central Greece in 339 (18.143n).

it is not the kind of thing that one can conceal. How could it be? Never will you wash from yourself what you did there, Aeschines. You couldn't talk so much.

[141] In your presence, Athenians, I summon all the gods and goddesses who guard the territory of Attica, and Pythian Apollo who is the divine father of this city.[131] I pray to them all: if I speak the truth to you and spoke it also then in the Assembly as soon as I saw this scoundrel latching on to this affair—for I knew it, I knew it right away—grant me good fortune and security, but if I charge him falsely from enmity or out of jealousy, render me bereft of all good things.

[142] Why have I uttered this curse, and why did I express myself so vehemently? Though documents available in the public archive will enable me to prove my case decisively and though I know that you recollect the events, I nonetheless fear that Aeschines might be considered too insignificant for the disasters he brought about (which happened before, when he caused the destruction of the poor Phocians by reporting false information).[132] [143] For the war in Amphissa, which brought Philip to Elatea and led to his election as leader of the Amphictyons, which entirely upset Greek affairs, was brought about by this very man, the one person responsible for all our greatest troubles.[133] At the time I immediately protested and cried out in the As-

---

[131] Pythian Apollo, singled out because of the upcoming discussion of the Delphic Amphictyony, was connected to Apollo the "divine father," worshiped by every Athenian citizen in his home or phratry, through the myth of Ion, Apollo's son and ancestor of the Ionians. The story provides the plot of Euripides' *Ion*.

[132] A reference to Demosthenes' prosecution of Aeschines in 343 (Dem. 19), in which Aeschines was narrowly acquitted. Demosthenes presented his view of the Phocian episode in 18.32–41.

[133] The Pylaeo-Delphic Amphictyony (to use the full name) was a league of Greek states responsible for the sanctuary of Demeter in Anthela (near Thermopylae) and the sanctuary of Apollo in Delphi. In 339, the Amphictyony initiated a Sacred War against Amphissa, a traditional ally of Thebes, for cultivating sacred land (18.149n). Philip, who largely controlled the Amphictyony since the defeat of Phocis in 346, was eventually asked to lead the war against Amphissa, which led to his invasion of central Greece in the fall of 339. Demosthenes blames Aeschines for engineering Philip's intervention, which led first to the fall of Elatea, then to the defeat at Chaeronea.

sembly, "You are bringing war into Attica, Aeschines, Amphictyonic war." But a section of the audience he had packed would not let me speak, while other citizens, amazed, supposed that my protest was unfounded and motivated by private enmity. [144] Hear now, Athenians, since you were prevented from hearing me then, what the idea behind this scheme was, for what reason it was conceived, and how it was executed. You will see that the scheme was well contrived, you will be well served with regard to understanding public affairs, and you will observe how much cleverness resided in Philip.

[145] Philip could not end his war against you or get free of it unless he turned the Thebans and Thessalians against the city. Though your generals were miserably inept in their operations against him, he was nevertheless suffering considerable losses from both the war itself and pirates. He was not exporting any agricultural produce nor importing what he needed; [146] he was at the time neither stronger than you at sea nor able to march on Attica unless the Thessalians joined him and the Thebans granted passage; and though he defeated in battle any generals you dispatched—I leave that matter aside—his situation was such that the very location of his territory and the assets of both sides caused him distress. [147] Now, if Philip were to declare his own enmity in order to persuade either Thessalians or Thebans to march against you, he did not suppose that they would show the slightest interest. But were he to espouse motives shared by them and be chosen their leader on that basis, he expected that he would more easily mislead or persuade them, as circumstances required. What happened then? He tried—and look how well he did it!—to incite war among the Amphictyons and to create discord at their meeting, for they would immediately call on him, he assumed, to handle those problems. [148] Nevertheless, Philip realized, if this move were initiated by one of the Sacred Delegates[134] sent by him or his allies, both Thebans and Thessalians would suspect it, and everyone would be on their guard, but if the instigator should be an Athenian, sent by you, his enemies, his own role would easily pass unnoticed. Which is precisely what happened.

---

[134] Sacred Delegates (*hieromnēmones*), two from each of twelve Greek tribes, were the regular, voting members of the Amphictyonic Council.

[149] How did Philip do it? He hired this man here. Since no one, I suppose, foresaw the plan or took precautions—the kind of thing that happens here often—Aeschines was put forward to serve as Accompanying Delegate[135] and was proclaimed elected when three or four citizens voted for him. He arrived at the Amphictyons' meeting draped in the prestige of the city and straightaway cast aside and neglected everything else to execute the task for which he had been hired: he composed fine-sounding arguments together with his stories about the consecration of the Cirrhaean plain and delivered them before delegates who had no experience of rhetoric and no insight into what was coming.[136] [150] Thus, he persuaded them to vote for a survey of the territory. The Amphissians claimed that the land they were farming was their own, whereas Aeschines alleged that it was consecrated ground, though the Locrians[137] were not engaged in bringing any legal action against us, which he now falsely gives as his excuse.[138] You will know this to be true from the following: the Locrians obviously could not carry out legal action against the city without issuing a summons. Who issued the summons? Before what magistrate were we summoned? Tell us who knows these facts, Aeschines, produce the person. But you cannot do it. You're just making what use you can of that empty, lying pretext.

[151] To resume: as the Amphictyons were out surveying the land in accord with Aeschines' directive, the Locrians attacked, hitting nearly all of them with their javelins and also seizing a few. This im-

---

[135] Accompanying Delegates (*pylagoroi*) accompanied the Sacred Delegates (*hieromnēmones*) to the meetings of the Amphictyonic Council and had the right to speak.

[136] Amphissa, the largest city of west Locris, cultivated territory in the plain of Cirrha, southwest of Delphi. At the meeting of the Amphictyonic Council in spring 339, other member states of the Amphictyonic League, urged on by Aeschines and backed by Philip, claimed that the territory was sacred and did not belong to Amphissa. This dispute was the basis of the Sacred War against Amphissa (18.143n).

[137] I.e., the Amphissians.

[138] Aes. 3.115–117 claimed that his condemnation of Amphissa was in response to their attempt to fine Athens for rededicating spoils from the Persian Wars.

mediately gave rise to complaints, and war was stirred up against the Amphissians, with Cottyphus[139] leading the forces raised from the Amphictyons themselves. But when some failed to appear, and those who appeared accomplished nothing, certain notoriously corrupt citizens of Thessaly and the other cities who were organized in advance began to arrange for Philip to take over as leader at the next Amphictyonic meeting.[140] [152] They seized on an attractive argument: either the Amphictyons themselves would have to raise funds, maintain a mercenary force, and fine those who would not contribute, or they could elect Philip. What need to say more? He was elected leader for that reason. The next move was quick: gathering his forces and marching as if to attack Cirrha, he bids a fond farewell to the Cirrhaeans and Locrians and seizes Elatea. [153] Had the Thebans not changed their minds and joined us as soon as they saw this, the whole affair would have descended on the city like a swollen torrent. In fact, they checked him for the moment, chiefly, Athenians, because some god was kind to you but also, insofar as it depended on any one man, because of me. Clerk, please hand over the Amphictyonic decrees and the dates for each of these events so that you understand what serious troubles this rotten creature set in motion without being punished. [154] Clerk, please read the decrees.

[AMPHICTYONIC DECREES]

[155] Clerk, now read the dates when these events took place. They occurred when Aeschines served as Accompanying Delegate. Read.

[DATES]

[156] Clerk, now hand over the letter that Philip sent his Peloponnesian allies when the Thebans defected. From this document too you will see clearly that Philip was hiding the true motive of his policy, which was directed against Greece, the Thebans, and you. He was only pretending to achieve what had been resolved in common with the Amphictyons. But the one who gave Philip the opportunity and the pretext was Aeschines. Clerk, read.

---

[139] Of Pharsalus in Thessaly.
[140] In fall 339.

[157] [LETTER]

[158] You see how Philip shrinks from his own motives and seeks shelter in the pretext afforded by the Amphictyons. Who assisted him in this matter? Who supplied him with the pretext? Who is most responsible for the troubles that ensued? Is it not this man? Do not, Athenians, go around saying that disaster befell Greece because of one individual.[141] Not because of one, but because of many corrupt people from all over, O earth and gods, [159] and among them is this man here, whom I at least, if the truth must be uttered freely, would not hesitate to call a universal villain who caused all the ensuing destruction of people, places, cities. For he who sows the seed is responsible for the evils that sprout. I wonder that you did not turn away as soon as you saw him. But a great deal of darkness, it seems, hangs about you, screening off the truth.

[160] Having touched upon Aeschines' actions against the interests of our country, I now come to the policies that I devised to counter them. There are many reasons why you would be wise to listen, one above all: if I undertook the labor of the actual deeds for your sake, it would be disgraceful of you not to endure listening to an account of them. [161] Now, I saw that because of supporters of Philip and corrupt citizens in both cities, the Thebans and perhaps you too were overlooking that which threatened danger to both and required much vigilance, namely, the unchecked growth of Philip's power, and were not taking any precautions at all; on the contrary, the two cities were disposed to mutual hostility and a head-on collision, which I was ever watchful to prevent. Not only did I conclude on my own that that was the expedient policy [162] but I also knew that Aristophon and Eubulus[142] too always wished to foster that friendship, and though frequently at odds on other issues, they were always of the same mind on this one. These men, you fox, whom you flattered and trailed when they were alive, you unwittingly condemn now that they're dead. For by denouncing my Theban policy you condemn them far more

---

[141] Philip.

[142] The dominant Athenian politicians of the previous generation. Aristophon, politically active from 403 until the late 340s, opposed the abandonment of Amphipolis in the Peace of Philocrates. On Eubulus, see 18.21n.

than you do me, since they recommended that alliance before I did. [163] But to return to the point: it was after Aeschines provoked the war in Amphissa and the other accomplices joined him in fomenting ill will towards the Thebans that Philip marched against us. That was precisely what those who were agitating the cities against each other had been aiming at. Had we not barely preempted them, we would not have been able to recover, so far along had they carried matters. Hear these decrees and the responses to them and you will know how you and the Thebans stood towards each other at the time. Clerk, please take them and read.

[164–165] [DECREES]

[166] Now read the responses too.

[167] [RESPONSES]

[168] Such were the relations between the two cities that Philip engineered with the aid of his accomplices. Encouraged by these decrees and responses, he marched here with his army and seized Elatea, believing that no matter what happened, we and the Thebans would not reconcile. All of you know about the turmoil that struck the city then; but listen to just a few of the most important points.

[169] It was evening, and a messenger reached the Presiding Officers with the news that Elatea had been taken.[143] Immediately they got up from dinner, some to clear the stalls in the marketplace and set the scaffolding alight, others to summon the generals and call out the trumpeter.[144] The city was full of turmoil. At break of dawn the next

---

[143] The Presiding Officers (*prytaneis*) were those members of the Council of Five Hundred who, for an assigned period, were responsible for civic security and administration. They were on call twenty-four hours a day and dined together. From Elatea, which Philip seized in fall 339, the road to Thebes, and from there to Athens, was open. Hence the alarm. Demosthenes' account of this moment was famous in antiquity for its intensity, clarity, and the way it slowly moves the focus to Demosthenes himself, rising to save Athens at the moment of need (18.173).

[144] The scaffolding, which supported the stalls, was lit to begin a series of fire signals that, like the trumpeter, would summon rural Athenians to the city for the Assembly in the morning.

day, the Presiding Officers called the Council to the Council-house while you proceeded to the Assembly, and before the Council could deliberate and endorse a proposal, the entire citizen body was seated up there.[145] [170] After this, the Council entered and the Presiding Officers announced the news they had received, and they produced the messenger to give his report. Then the herald asked, "Who wishes to speak?" but no one came forward. The herald asked many times but to no avail. No one rose, though all the generals were present and all the politicians too, and the country was calling for a speaker to save it. For the voice of the herald lawfully discharging his task is rightly considered the common voice of the country. [171] If those who desired the city's safety were asked to come forward, all of you and all other Athenians would have risen and advanced to the platform, for all of you, I know, desired the city to be safe; if the richest were asked, it would have been the Three Hundred;[146] if those who possessed both attributes, devotion to the city and wealth, it would have been those who conferred the large donations afterwards,[147] for their devotion and wealth led them to do that.

[172] But it seems that that moment and that day called for a man who not only was devoted and wealthy but had also followed events from the beginning and figured out correctly what Philip was aiming at and what his intentions were in taking the action he did. Someone who did not know these things and had not studied the situation for a long time, even if he was devoted and even if he was wealthy, would not be better informed about what had to be done or be able to advise you. [173] The one who emerged as the right man on that day was I. I stepped forward and addressed you, and for two reasons listen carefully to what I said. First, you should know that I alone of the speak-

---

[145] On the hill called Pnyx, where the Assembly met. It would have been visible from the court. The "entire" citizen body never attended any single Assembly, but this one must have been packed. The Council of Five Hundred normally met before the Assembly to prepare the agenda.

[146] The wealthiest property class in Athens, who opposed Demosthenes during his reform of the trierarchy (18.103n).

[147] I.e., after Chaeronea, when certain citizens made extraordinary donations to meet the public emergency.

ers and politicians did not abandon my post of civic concern at the moment of danger but rather proved to be the one who in the very midst of the horrors both advised and proposed the necessary measures for your sake. Second, in a short time you will gain much experience regarding all aspects of your future political life.[148]

[174] I spoke as follows: "Some people are extremely distraught, believing that the Thebans stand with Philip, but in my view they misunderstand the current situation. If that were the case, the news, I am sure, would be that Philip is not in Elatea but on our border. However, I know for a fact that his purpose in coming is to prepare the ground in Thebes. Now hear," I said, "what is going on there. [175] Philip already has on his side all the Thebans whom he could either bribe or deceive, but he has no chance of swaying those who resisted from the beginning and still oppose him. What then does he want, and with what purpose did he seize Elatea? By displaying his power and deploying his forces nearby, he wishes both to bolster his friends and make them confident and to terrify his opponents so that they either yield out of fear or be forced to yield, which they now refuse to do. [176] Thus," I said, "if we choose to recall at this moment anything unpleasant that the Thebans ever did to us and to distrust them for being in the ranks of our enemies, first, we will bring about just what Philip would pray for. Second, I fear that if those who now resist Philip welcome him, and their entire citizen body unanimously joins his camp, both parties—Philip and the Thebans—might invade Attica. But if you heed me and apply yourselves to considering what I say instead of quarreling with it, you will realize, I believe, that what I propose is necessary and that I will dispel the danger hanging over the city.

[177] "What then in my view must be done? First, rid yourselves of the general fear. Next, change your point of view and let everyone be

---

[148] The following account of Demosthenes' Assembly speech after the fall of Elatea in 339 preserves touches of the original setting, but it is a reminiscence of remarkable swiftness and concision. Its purpose is to display Demosthenes in supreme control and to remind the audience in a palpable way (many of them would have been in the Assembly that morning) why they followed Demosthenes' recommendation and decided to pursue the alliance with Thebes.

alarmed for the Thebans, since they are much closer to the terrible events than we, and the danger threatens them first. Next, let the cavalry and men of military age travel to Eleusis[149] and show the world that you are under arms yourselves, which would give your allies in Thebes equal footing to speak out for their just cause. They would see that even as those who would sell their country to Philip have a force to help them in Elatea, so those who choose to vie for freedom have you ready and willing to assist if anyone should move against them. [178] Next, I urge you to elect ten envoys and to empower them in concert with the generals to decide both when to move our forces there and how to conduct the expedition. How do I suggest the matter should be handled once the envoys have arrived in Thebes? Pay close attention, please, to this point. Ask nothing of the Thebans—it is entirely the wrong occasion. Rather, since they are in the direst straits, and we take a longer view of things than they do, announce that we will respond to a request for help. If they find our offer acceptable and agree to it, we will thereby have attained what we wanted and done so for a reason worthy of the city. But if the plan fails to materialize, they would have themselves to blame should they falter in any way, and we will have done nothing shameful or mean."

[179] Having spoken these words and others to the same effect, I stepped down. Everyone approved, and no one said a word in opposition. I did not deliver the speech without moving a proposal, nor did I move a proposal without serving as envoy, nor did I serve as envoy without winning over the Thebans.[150] I persevered from beginning to end and for your sake applied myself entirely to the dangers encircling the city. Please produce the decree that was passed then.

[180] And yet, Aeschines, how would you like me to describe your performance that day, and how would you like me to describe mine? Would you have me assign myself the role of Battalus,[151] as you like to

---

[149] From Eleusis, west of Athens in Attica, the army could move easily into Boeotia.

[150] The account of the Assembly is completed with this sentence impressively formulated as a *climax* ("ladder"), the most famous example in ancient literature.

[151] This is Demosthenes' childhood nickname, which meant "lisper" but which Aeschines on earlier occasions used against him in an obscene sense (1.131, 164, 2.99).

call me with your insulting ridicule, and you the role of not just any hero but one of those stage heroes such as Cresphontes or Creon or the Oenomaus whom you once horribly savaged at Collytus?[152] So be it: on that occasion at the moment of crisis I, Battalus of Paeania, showed myself to be more valuable to our country than did you, Oenomaus of Cothocidae.[153] But then you never did anything useful on any occasion, while I did everything that one would expect of a good citizen. Clerk, please read the decree.

[181–187] [DEMOSTHENES' DECREE]

[188] This was the start and first step of the rapprochement between us and Thebes; previously these men had pushed the cities into enmity, hatred, and distrust. This decree caused the danger then encompassing the city to pass by like a cloud. An honorable citizen would have let everyone know then if he had a better plan instead of criticizing now. [189] Though an adviser and a *sykophant* are in no respect similar, they differ most of all in this: the one discloses his view before things develop and makes himself answerable to those who are persuaded, to fortune, to the occasion, to anyone who wishes; the other is silent when there is need for speech and then maligns if anything unpleasant happens. [190] So, as I said, that occasion called for a public-spirited citizen to speak out honorably. And I will go so far as to admit my culpability if anyone can now produce a better plan or if some other plan beyond what I advanced was even possible. If there is anything that someone has now perceived that would have been expedient had we undertaken it then, I agree that I should have known about it. But if there neither is nor was such a thing, and if no one even today is able to say what it might be, what was an adviser to do? Was it not to choose the best course from the possibilities that presented themselves? [191] That, in fact, is what I did, since the herald was asking, Aeschines, "Who wishes to speak?" not "Who wishes to

---

[152] A comment on both the quality of Aeschines' acting and the role of Oenomaus (mythical king of Olympia) he played not at the prestigious Greater Dionysia held in the theater of Dionysus in the city center but in less important Rural Dionysia held in the deme Collytus (even though this deme was actually located within the city).

[153] Demosthenes was from the deme Paeania; Aeschines, from Cothocidae.

lay blame for the past?" or "Who wishes to offer guarantees for the future?"[154] While you sat speechless during the assemblies of those days, I was coming forward and speaking. Well then, since you disclosed nothing then, do it now! Tell us what plan I ought to have had ready or what opportunity I missed that was expedient for the city. What other alliance, what other course of action should I have urged these men to adopt instead?

[192] And yet, people always put the past aside, and no one ever makes it a subject for debate, but the future and the present call for the adviser at his post. At the time in question, the terrible events were partly in the future, as it seemed; partly, however, already at hand.[155] Examine my choice of policy in that situation, and do not use what followed to make frivolous charges, for all things end up as god determines, but the adviser's intention is clear only from his policy. [193] Therefore, do not consider it my fault that Philip happened to prevail in the battle, since the outcome of that event lay in god's hands, not mine. Rather, that I failed to pursue all possible contingencies disclosed by human calculation and failed to execute them honorably, carefully, and with exertion surpassing my strength, or that I failed to establish a policy that was noble and worthy of the city as well as necessary—show me that, and then go ahead and accuse me. [194] If the thunderbolt that struck overpowered not only us but also all the rest of Greece, what is to be done? Suppose a shipowner were blamed for a shipwreck though he took every precaution and fitted the ship with every conceivable device to insure safety, but a storm came up and the rigging strained and then snapped completely. "I was not at the helm," he would say—as indeed I was not in command in the field—"and I did not control fortune, but fortune controlled everything."

[195] Take note of the following point, Aeschines, and consider it. If it was our lot to suffer this fate while fighting with the Thebans, what ought we to have expected had we not had them as allies but they had joined Philip, a goal he pursued with all his powers of persuasion? And if so much danger and fear assailed the city when the actual battle

---

[154] The herald opened debate in the Assembly with the cry, "Who wishes to speak?" (see 18.170).

[155] Chaeronea and Elatea respectively.

took place at a distance of three days' march from Attica,[156] what ought we to have expected had the same disaster struck somewhere within our territory? Do you understand that as it happened, the one day and the two days and the three days allowed the city to stop, to come together, to catch its breath, to undertake many protective measures, but otherwise[157]—best not to mention what we did not have to face because some god was kind and the city was protected by the alliance that you, Aeschines, denounced.

[196] I intend this entire long discussion for your benefit, jurors, as well as for that of the surrounding audience,[158] since for this contemptible man a short, simple statement suffices. If what was going to happen was clear in advance to you alone, Aeschines, you were obliged to speak out then, when the city was debating it. But if you did not know in advance, you are answerable for the same ignorance as anyone else, so why should you censure me for this more than I you? [197] I am a better citizen than you for the following reason (speaking with regard just to the point at issue since I'm not yet discussing the rest): while I devoted myself to the policy decided by all as expedient and did not hesitate or even consider any risk to myself, you neither proposed a policy better than mine (otherwise mine would not have been adopted) nor played any useful role to support it. Instead, it is now confirmed that afterwards you committed an act worthy of the meanest, most treacherous citizen: while Aristratus on Naxos and Aristoleus on Thasos—both of them our declared enemies —are putting Athenian sympathizers on trial, Aeschines is at the same time accusing Demosthenes in Athens.[159] [198] Assuredly, one who hoarded Greek misfortune to gain glory for himself ought by rights to die rather than to accuse another, and one who profited from the same circumstances as did the city's enemies cannot be devoted to his coun-

---

[156] At Chaeronea; see 18.230n.

[157] I.e., if the battle had taken place in Attica.

[158] A ring of interested spectators stood just outside the court proper, observing the proceedings. This case attracted a large crowd (Aes. 3.56).

[159] Aristratus and Aristoleus are otherwise unknown, but Demosthenes implies that as supporters of Macedon, they used the opportunity afforded by Macedonian hegemony to punish partisans of Athens.

try. You make that clear, Aeschines, by how you live, act, engage in politics, and likewise do not engage in politics. Something is about to happen that apparently benefits you: Aeschines is speechless. Something has thwarted you, and what ought not to have happened has: there is Aeschines, just as ruptures and sprains break out when the body suffers an injury.

[199] Since Aeschines insists vehemently on how things have turned out, I wish to say something rather paradoxical. No one, by Zeus and the gods, should be astonished if my argument is extreme; rather, it should be examined sympathetically. If what was going to happen was clear to all in advance, and all knew in advance, and if you, Aeschines, spoke out in advance and shouted and shrieked in protest, you who uttered not even a sound, not even in those circumstances should the city have abandoned its policy, if indeed it valued its reputation or its forebears or future ages. [200] True, the city seems to have failed in its objectives, which is the common lot of all mankind when god so decides. But if it claimed to be the leader of the rest of Greece and then abandoned that claim to Philip, it would have been guilty of betraying all Greeks. For if the city chose to surrender without a fight the position that our forefathers faced every danger to acquire, who would not have spat on—you?[160] Not, indeed, on the city, nor on me! [201] With what expression, by Zeus, would we look upon visitors to the city if events turned out as they have, and Philip was elected leader and master of all, but others, without us, had undertaken the struggle to prevent that outcome, even though up to that time the city had never yet chosen inconspicuous safety in preference to the risk of fighting for a noble cause? [202] What Greek, what barbarian does not know that the Thebans, the Spartans (who dominated before the Thebans), and the Persian King too would have graciously and gladly allowed the city to take what it wanted and retain what it had so long as it followed orders and surrendered to another the leadership of Greece?[161]

---

[160] For rhetorical effect, in place of the expected "us" Demosthenes substitutes this reference to Aeschines.

[161] The Persians, the ultimate basis of Demosthenes' argument for fighting at Chaeronea (18.208), yet thus far kept in reserve, are introduced with a reference to an episode narrated by Herodotus (8.136, 140–143, 9.4–5): the Athenians re-

[203] But that was not part of the Athenians' heritage; it was intolerable and not in their nature. Since the beginning of time, no one has ever been able to persuade the city to side with the powerful but unjust and to find safety in servitude. Rather, in every age, despite the danger, the city constantly fought for the first prize in honor and glory. [204] You consider that principle so important and intrinsic to your character that you praise most those ancestors who demonstrated it in action. With good reason, for who could fail to admire the courage of those citizens who, to avoid having to follow orders, dared to leave land and city behind and took to the ships? Themistocles, who proposed that course,[162] they elected general, while Cyrsilus, who advised submission, they stoned to death, and not only him, but your wives did the same to his wife. [205] Those Athenians did not look for a politician or general to lead them into a prosperous slavery; they thought life not worth living unless they could do it in freedom. Each one of them saw himself as the child not only of his father and mother but of his country as well. What does that matter? He who considers himself born to his parents alone awaits the natural death allotted him by fate, but he who considers himself born to his country too will prefer to die than to see it enslaved. He will regard the insults and humiliations that one must bear when his city is enslaved as more terrible than death.

[206] Were it my intention to argue that I moved you to aspire to the standards of your forebears, everyone would chastise me with good reason. But my point, in fact, is that you made that choice yourselves, and I have been demonstrating that the city aspired to those standards even before my time; I do claim, however, to have been of service in bringing about particular achievements. [207] This man, on the other hand, denounces the whole enterprise and urges you to despise me for putting the city in terrible danger, and though he yearns to deprive me of an honor for the present, he is trying to steal from you the praises of all future time. For if you convict Ctesiphon because my policy was

jected an offer from Xerxes to keep their territory, autonomy, and their temples in return for the use of their fleet against the rest of Greece.

[162] In 480 the Athenians abandoned Attica to the Persian army and put all their resources into resistance at sea, where they were victorious in the battle of Salamis. On Themistocles' decree, see 19.303n.

not the best one, you will make it appear that you were wrong, not that subsequent events befell you by fortune's cruelty. [208] But you were not wrong, no, you were not, Athenians, to take on danger for the sake of the freedom and safety of all—I swear by your forefathers who led the fight at Marathon, by those who stood in the ranks at Plataea, by those who fought aboard ship at Salamis and Artemisium,[163] and by the many other brave men who lie in the public tombs, all of whom the city buried, deeming them all equally worthy of the same honor, Aeschines, not just those among them who were successful or victorious.[164] Rightly so, for they all performed the task required of brave men, and they each met with the fortune conferred on them by god.

[209] And yet, you abominable, deformed little clerk, in your eagerness to deprive me of the honor and goodwill of these men, you discoursed on victory monuments, battles, and great deeds of long ago.[165] But which of them is pertinent to the case at issue right now? I, the city's adviser in the pursuit of the first prize, ask you, you third-rate actor: what attitude was I to adopt as I was about to step up to the speaker's platform? That of a citizen who would propose measures unworthy of those achievements? [210] In that case, I would have truly deserved to die.[166] Because you too, Athenians, should not judge legal disputes among individuals and those that concern the whole citizen body from the same point of view. To judge the transactions of daily life, you should consider your own laws and practices, but to judge

---

[163] The most powerful and famous passage of the speech, establishing the claim that the Athenians were right to confront Philip at Chaeronea without regard for consequences. Demosthenes swears by those who fought in Athens' great battles of the Persian Wars (Marathon in 490, the others in 480–479), according those revered ancestors the place that would normally be accorded to gods.

[164] The state cemetery, reserved for those who died in battle, was an impressive series of monuments and the site of the funeral orations (see 18.285n). "Brave men" (*agathoi andres*) is the particular designation of those who died in battle, bestowed in the funeral orations precisely because they chose to risk death in battle. This choice is the fundamental link between the Athenians of the Persian Wars and those who fought at Chaeronea.

[165] Aes. 3.181–190.

[166] Like Cyrsilus (18.204).

public policy you should look to the standards of your forebears. Each of you must realize that when you come into court to decide a case of public import, you bear along with the staff and token of your office[167] the aspirations of the city—if, in fact, you think you ought to act worthily of your forebears.

[211] My discussion of your ancestors' achievements has led me to pass over certain decrees and accomplishments. So I wish to return now to where I left off.[168]

When we reached Thebes, we found delegates from Philip, the Thessalians, and the rest of their allies already there. Our supporters were terrified; Philip's were confident. To prove that I am not saying this merely to help my case, please read the letter that we envoys sent at just that time. [212] The malice of this man's prosecution is so outrageous that he credits the occasion, not me, for any positive achievement, but blames me and my fortune for everything that turned out otherwise. It's clear, then, that in his eyes I, adviser and speaker, deserve no credit at all for anything that was achieved through speaking and advising but am solely responsible for the disasters in the army and among the generals. Could there be a more impudent, a more reprehensible *sykophant?* Clerk, read the letter.

[LETTER]

[213] When the Thebans convened their assembly, they introduced our adversaries first since they were officially their allies.[169] Coming forward to address the people, they had much to applaud in Philip and much to accuse you of, since they recalled every action you ever took against the Thebans. In short, they insisted that the Thebans reciprocate the favors that Philip had bestowed on them and exact retribution

---

[167] Implements of the juror's office: the color-coded staff directed him to the assigned court; the token may have been used for seating or voting.

[168] Demosthenes resumes the narrative interrupted at 18.179, when the Athenians voted to follow Demosthenes' advice and seek alliance with Thebes.

[169] In spite of their sympathies with Amphissa in the Fourth Sacred War (18.143n) and their recent seizure of the stronghold at Nicaea overlooking Thermopylae, which had been garrisoned by Macedon (Philochorus, *FGrHist* 328 F 56b = Harding 1985: 97), the Thebans had not yet formally broken off the alliance with Philip that stemmed from the Third Sacred War (18.18n).

for the crimes inflicted by you, offering the Thebans a choice: either to grant the Macedonians passage for an attack on you or to join the invasion of Attica. They also showed, as they saw it, that following their advice would mean a flow of Athenian livestock, slaves, and other goods into Boeotia, but following the plan they said we would propose would cause Boeotia to be plundered by war. They said a good bit more, but it all led to the same conclusion. [214] As for what we said in response, I would give my entire life to relate it in detail, but since the moment has passed, and you may feel as if a cataclysm has overtaken the political world, I fear that the speeches on this subject would seem pointless and tedious. But hear what we persuaded them to do and how they answered us. Clerk, take the document and read it.

[RESPONSE OF THE THEBANS]

[215] The Thebans then appealed to you and asked you to come. You marched, you brought aid—I skip over the ensuing details— they received you so hospitably that when the hoplites and cavalry were outside the walls, they took your army into their city and homes among their children and wives and most precious possessions. By their actions on that day the Thebans extolled you before all mankind for three qualities that inspire supreme admiration: the first is courage; the second, justice; the third, moderation. By choosing to fight with you rather than against you, they deemed you braver than Philip and your offer more just than his; and by putting within your reach the things that they, indeed that all men guard most carefully, children and wives, they showed that they trusted in your moderation. [216] Throughout the whole affair, Athenians, it was made evident that, insofar as it lay in your power, they judged aright. When your army came inside the city, no one registered a single complaint against you, not even an unfair one, so moderate was your conduct. On two occasions in the first battles that you joined, that by the river and the winter battle,[170] you proved yourselves not just flawless but remarkable in your discipline, readiness, and morale. For that reason, the other Greeks acclaimed you and you paid honor to the gods with sacrificial feasts and processions. [217] I would gladly ask Aeschines

---

[170] Skirmishes in early 338 preceding the battle of Chaeronea.

whether he took part in the festival and shared the general rejoicing when these things were going on and the city was full of ardor, joy, and acclamations, or did he sit at home grieving, mourning, and resentful of the public success? If in fact he did join in and did take his place among the community, how is his present conduct not appalling, or rather, even sacrilegious—that he himself declared before the gods that my policy was best, but he now asks you, who are under oath to the gods, to vote to condemn that policy as not the best?[171] Yet if he did not join in, how does he not deserve to die many times over—for being distressed to see events that gladdened everyone else? Clerk, please read these decrees too.

[DECREES PROCLAIMING SACRIFICES]

[218] So at that time we were occupied with festivals and the The-bans with the thought that we had saved them. Thus it transpired that we, who had seemed to need help because of the plots of these men, were ultimately the ones to help others through the measures that you adopted on my advice. You will see from Philip's letters to the Pelo-ponnese what line he took in public at that time and what kind of trouble these events caused him. Clerk, please take the letters and read them. You need to understand what was accomplished by my tenac-ity, my going from place to place, my toils, and my many decrees that this man was just now ridiculing.

[219] Before me, Athenians, you have had many great and illustri-ous politicians: the eminent Callistratus, Aristophon, Cephalus, Thra-sybulus, scores of others.[172] Yet none of them on any occasion ever de-

---

[171] Aeschines would have "declared before the gods" that Demosthenes' pol-icy was best by participating in the celebrations thanking the gods for the success of the policy. The judges are "under oath to the gods" because of the Heliastic Oath (18.2n).

[172] Demosthenes would not boast that he surpassed Athens' legendary fifth-century leaders (18.314–319); those mentioned here were active during the fourth century. Hence, this Thrasybulus is not the hero of Phyle (403) of the deme Steiria but his younger namesake of the deme Collytus, who made his reputation in the decades after the Peloponnesian War. Cephalus was a leading politician in the 380s, Callistratus in the 370s and 360s; the latter was remembered in later rhetori-cal tradition for having impressed the young Demosthenes when speaking on the

voted himself to the city in every way. One would move proposals without serving as envoy, while another would serve as envoy without moving proposals. Each of them thereby reserved for himself some repose as well as a way out if something happened. [220] "Well, then," someone might say, "were you so far superior in power and audacity that you could do everything yourself?" I don't say that at all; rather, I was convinced that the danger gripping the city was so great that it seemed to allow no room, or even any thought, for one's personal security. One had to be content to do what was necessary while omitting nothing. [221] As for my part in the matter, I was convinced, absurdly perhaps, but convinced nonetheless, that no one who might move proposals, who might undertake action, who might serve as envoy could do so with more energy or with greater integrity than I. For that reason I stationed myself at every post. Clerk, read Philip's letters.

[LETTERS]

[222] That is the effect my policy had on Philip, Aeschines. That was the public line Philip adopted, though previously he had directed many defiant words at our city. For this achievement I was deservedly awarded a crown by these men, and though you were there, you said nothing against it, while the citizen who did indict it, Diondas, did not capture the minimum share of the votes.[173] Clerk, please read the decrees that were vindicated in court, although Aeschines never even indicted them.

[DECREES]

[223] These decrees, Athenians, have the same language, word for word, as both the one earlier proposed by Aristonicus[174] and the one now moved by Ctesiphon here, though Aeschines neither prosecuted them himself nor lent any support to the prosecutor. Yet if his current charges against me have any merit, he would have had more reason to

---

Oropus affair of 366 (Plut., *Life of Demosthenes* 5.1–5). On Aristophon, see 18.162n.

[173] See 18.103n.

[174] See 18.83n.

prosecute the authors of these decrees, Demomeles and Hyperides, at that time than he now does to prosecute Ctesiphon. [224] Why so? Because Ctesiphon can refer to those men,[175] to the prior decisions of the courts, to the fact that Aeschines did not bring charges against them though they proposed the same honors as Ctesiphon does now, to the fact that the laws allow no further accusations in cases that have been decided, and to many other considerations. Previously, the question was subject to adjudication on its own merits without these additional factors. [225] But it was not possible to do then, I take it, what can be done now, namely, to vilify by selecting from many old dates and decrees those that no one knew about before now or believed would be mentioned today, or to give the impression of saying something consequential by mixing up dates and attaching false motives to actions in place of the true ones. [226] That was not possible then. When events were recent and your memory of them was still fresh, with the details practically at your fingertips, the entire debate would have had to be conducted on the basis of the truth. Which is why Aeschines shunned confrontation when the events occurred and comes forward only now. In my view, he thinks you intend to conduct a competition between public speakers rather than an examination of political deeds and that the decision you are about to make concerns words rather than the city's interests.

[227] Next, Aeschines made a very clever suggestion:[176] you are to disregard the opinion that you had of us when you came here from home, and, just as when you audit people for supposedly retaining surplus funds but acquit them if the figures balance and there is no surplus, so in this case too you are to concur with the evident force of the argument. Well now, look how every dishonest action turns out to be, as it were, inherently rotten. [228] Precisely as a result of this clever analogy, he has now admitted that people have come to know us, me for advancing the city's interests, him for advancing Philip's. After all, he would not be trying to change your minds unless that is how each of us, in fact, is viewed. [229] Yet I will easily demonstrate that he is wrong to demand that you change your opinion. I will not add up

---

[175] Aristonicus, Demomeles, and Hyperides.
[176] Aes. 3.59–61.

figures, which is no way to examine policy. Instead, I'll briefly recount all the particulars and use you, the audience, as both accountants (*logistai*)[177] and witnesses. My policy, which he assails, accomplished the following: in place of the Thebans' invading our territory in concert with Philip, which everyone expected would happen, they joined forces with us to check him; [230] in place of war in Attica, the battle took place on the Boeotian frontier, seven hundred stades from the city;[178] in place of depredations inflicted by pirates from Euboea, Attica was unmolested from the sea throughout the war; in place of Philip's capturing Byzantium and thereby controlling the Hellespont, the Byzantians fought on our side against him. [231] Does examining the facts seem to you, Aeschines, the same as tallying figures? Must we eliminate these facts from the record because they amount to an even exchange, or must we consider how they might be remembered for all time? And I will not add this further point: the cruelty that can be observed in places once Philip took over was left for others to experience, but the compassion that he feigned while securing the rest of his objectives was yours, through your good fortune, to cultivate and enjoy. But I'll pass over that point.

[232] I have no hesitation in making the next point. Anyone who wants to judge a politician honestly and to refrain from malicious prosecution would not level the kind of charges that you did in your speech just now, Aeschines, when you invented examples and mimicked my words and gestures[179]—for, of course, the fate of Greece rests on this (don't you agree?), whether I uttered this expression and not that one, or whether I waved my hand in this direction and not that one. [233] Rather, an honest judge would investigate on the basis of the facts alone what resources and military forces the city had at the time that I first took up politics and what I brought to it during my involvement from that time on, as well as what the enemy's situation was. Then, if my actions brought about a decline in our

---

[177] See 18.111n, 112n, Introduction to Dem. 19 on these magistrates.

[178] There are roughly 6 stades in a kilometer. Chaeronea, a Boeotian town near the border with Phocis, was 130 km. or 80 miles by foot from Athens; see 18.195n.

[179] Aes. 3.166–167 ridiculed Demosthenes' gestures; on ridicule of Demosthenes' words, see 18.126n.

forces, he would demonstrate that the fault was mine; if a significant increase, he would forego malicious prosecution. Since you shunned this course, Aeschines, I'll do it. Consider, Athenians, whether my account is a fair one.

[234] The city's power was based on the islanders, not all of them but just the weakest, since neither Chios nor Rhodes nor Corcyra was with us. Monetary contributions came to forty-five talents, and these were advance collections.[180] There was no infantry, no cavalry beyond our own. What caused us the greatest dismay and proved the greatest boon to our enemies was the contrivance of these men that all our neighbors—Megarians, Thebans, Euboeans—should regard us more as enemies than as friends. [235] That was the situation in which the city found itself, and nothing more can be said. Consider the situation of Philip, our opponent in the struggle. First, he ruled in his own person as full sovereign over subservient people, which is the most important factor of all in waging war. What's more, his people were continually under arms,[181] he was flush with money, and he did whatever he wished. He did not announce his intentions in official decrees, did not deliberate in public, was not hauled into court by *sykophants*, was not prosecuted for moving illegal proposals, was not accountable to anyone. In short, he was ruler, commander, in control of everything. [236] But I, who took up my post in direct opposition to him (and this point too deserves scrutiny), what did I control? Nothing! In the first place, the only way that I could take part was precisely by addressing the Assembly, and you granted that opportunity equally to Philip's paid agents and to me. Whenever they prevailed over me, which for various reasons happened often, you left the Assembly having made a

---

[180] Demosthenes is describing the situation in roughly 346, the time of the Peace of Philocrates. The "weakest" islanders are those who still remained in the Athenian maritime empire after the defections of the large islands during the Social War of 357–355. From these remaining states Athens took a "contribution" (*syntaxis*), euphemistically named to avoid the onerous sounding "tribute" (*phoros*) of Athens' fifth-century empire. Forty-five talents is a paltry sum, but it was diminished further: "advance collections" implies that financial straits compelled Athenian generals to collect the funds while on campaign and to spend them there, leaving little or no revenue for the city.

[181] A standing army was rare among the Greeks.

decision that benefited the enemy. [237] Starting from these disadvantages, I nevertheless forged alliances with Euboea, Achaea, Corinth, Thebes, Megara, Leucas, and Corcyra[182]—places that contributed fifteen thousand mercenaries and two thousand cavalry apart from the citizen-soldiers. I also secured the largest contribution of money that I could.

[238] If you bring up the question of fair terms with the Thebans, Aeschines, or with the Byzantians or with the Euboeans, or if today you raise the issue of equal contributions,[183] you forget, in the first place, that once before too, when that famous fleet of three hundred triremes fought on behalf of Greece, the city furnished two hundred of them.[184] The city did not suppose that a wrong had been committed, or condemn those who advocated that arrangement, or feel annoyed over the matter, which would have been a disgrace; rather, it gave thanks to the gods that when a common danger encompassed Greece, it contributed on its own twice as much as the rest to the cause of saving everyone. [239] Second, it is futile to try to ingratiate yourself with this audience by defaming me. Why do you tell us now what we should have done when you didn't propose it then, though you were in the city and in a position to speak—that is, assuming such a proposal was even possible during that critical time when we had to accept not all that we wanted but whatever the circumstances would grant us. After all, the buyer competing directly with us, who would immediately welcome anyone we drove away and would offer cash in addition, was ready to act.[185]

[240] If I currently face condemnation for what I actually did, what do you think these unregenerate persons would do, what would they say had the cities gone off and joined Philip and he taken control of

---

[182] These are the allies that joined Athens before Chaeronea.

[183] Aes. 3.106, 143 rebukes Demosthenes for allowing Athens to shoulder an unfair burden of money and men in the alliance with Thebes.

[184] At Salamis in 480. Regarding the Athenian contribution to the total number of Greek ships at Salamis, the sources vary from roughly one-half to two-thirds Athenian out of three to four hundred total. Demosthenes' numbers, two hundred Athenian ships out of three hundred total, answer Aeschines' assertion (3.143) that Demosthenes saddled Athens with two-thirds of the costs of the war and Thebes with only one-third.

[185] The "buyer" is Philip.

Euboea, Thebes, and Byzantium while I was arguing over the fine points in our terms with them? [241] Wouldn't they say, "The cities were surrendered"? Wouldn't they say, "They were driven off despite their desire to ally with us"? Or "the Byzantians have enabled Philip to take over the Hellespont and control the grain shipments to Greece, and the Thebans have inflicted on Attica a grievous invasion from a neighboring state, and pirates operating from Euboea have closed the sea"? Would they not make these charges and many others besides? [242] Every *sykophant* is a depraved character, Athenians, depraved as well as backstabbing and faultfinding at every opportunity; and this puny fellow is by nature a rogue. From the beginning he's done nothing useful or generous. He's a real ape on the tragic stage,[186] an Oenomaus of the countryside,[187] a counterfeit politician. What good, Aeschines, has your cleverness done the country? Now you talk to us about past events? [243] Just like a physician who, though he attends the sick, gives them no information at all about how they might recover, but when one of them dies and receives the customary rites, he joins the funeral procession and declares, "If the man had only done such and so, he would still be alive." Imbecile, now you tell us?

[244] Next, regarding the defeat, though you, wretch, are delighted when you should have wept, you citizens will find that it befell the city through circumstances that had nothing to do with me. Consider it in this light. Wherever I went on diplomatic missions at your behest, in no case did I ever return defeated by Philip's envoys: not from Thessaly or Ambracia, not from the Illyrians or the Thracian kings, not from Byzantium, not from any other place ever, and, finally, not from Thebes, but wherever his envoys were defeated, he attacked and conquered those places by force of arms. [245] Do you hold me responsible for that, Aeschines? Are you not ashamed to mock the cowardice of the same person whom you expect to defeat Philip's forces single-handedly, and to do it with words?[188] Why, what else was I in charge

---

[186] The image suggests atrocious overacting; see 18.139n on the ridiculous image.

[187] See 18.180n for Demosthenes' disparaging reference to Aeschines' acting in Rural Dionysia.

[188] Finally, and only when it suits his argument, Demosthenes responds to Aeschines' frequent charge (3.152, 175, 253, etc.) that Demosthenes deserted the

of? Not the heart of individuals, not the fortune of the soldiers in the line, not the military command, for which you now seek to hold me accountable. You utter fool!

[246] Undertake, Athenians, a thorough inquiry into whatever a politician is accountable for; I don't ask to be excused. What are those activities? To notice things when they first take shape, to anticipate developments, and to alert others. That is what I did. Further: to minimize ever-present procrastination, vacillation, ignorance, rivalry—problems that inevitably plague all political communities—and conversely to push towards unanimity, mutual regard, and an eagerness to do what's needed. I did every one of these things too, and, as everyone can see, omitted nothing. [247] Indeed, should anyone whatsoever be asked by what means Philip attained the vast bulk of his achievements, without exception people would reply that he did it by means of his army and by bribing and corrupting the leading politicians. I was neither commander nor in charge of the armed forces, so responsibility for events in that area also has nothing to do with me. And with regard to corruption and bribery, I proved victorious over Philip. After all, someone looking to buy conquers the man who accepts the offer when the deal is consummated, but should the man refuse the offer, he has conquered the prospective buyer. Thus, as far as it lay in my power, the city was undefeated.

[248] These and similar arguments, in addition to many others, constitute my case that Ctesiphon was right to propose the decree on my behalf. The arguments all of you have provided form the next subject of my speech. Right after the battle, when people were fully aware of my entire record and beset by the awesome terrors of the moment, it would not have been surprising if most citizens felt rather bitter towards me. Yet not only did they adopt my plan to safeguard the city and not only were all the defensive measures—the placement of the

---

ranks at Chaeronea. That charge deserves as much credence as does Demosthenes' charge that Aeschines was Philip's hired hand: both charges are vituperative and have no basis in fact. It is inconceivable that Demosthenes would have been chosen as funeral orator after the battle (18.285) had he deserted. Since Demosthenes was among neither the one thousand Athenian dead (18.264) nor the two thousand captives (Diodorus Siculus 16.86.5) but returned safely to Athens, that was sufficient ground for Aeschines to make his gibe.

sentries, the trenches, the funds for the city-walls—undertaken after I proposed them, but out of the whole citizen body, they chose me to serve as grain commissioner.[189] **[249]** Following that, the persons intent on doing me harm joined forces and subjected me to indictments, audits, trials for treason, and all the attacks of that kind, though at first they refrained from acting in their own name and tried to shield their own identity by employing others.[190] Surely you recollect that in those early days, I was brought to court daily; I was subject to every kind of attack, such as the derangement of a Sosicles, the malice of a Philocrates, and the insanity of a Diondas and a Melantes.[191] Thanks mainly to the gods but also to you and the rest of the Athenians, I survived all these cases unharmed. Rightfully so, since that judgment is based on the truth and redounds to the credit of sworn jurors acting in awareness of their oath. **[250]** Thus, when I faced trial for treason, by acquitting me and denying the prosecutors the minimum number of votes, you voted that my policy was the best. When I was acquitted of having moved an illegal proposal, my decrees and policies were publicly declared to be lawful. When you put your seal of approval on audits of my service, you acknowledged that I acted honestly and with no trace of bribery. In view of these facts, what was the fitting and just language for Ctesiphon to use in describing my activity? Was it not the language that he saw the citizen body using, that he saw the sworn jurors using, that he saw confirmed by the truth in the eyes of all?

[251] "Well and good," Aeschines says, "but Cephalus had a splendid record. He was never indicted at all." [192] It was a lucky record too, by Zeus. Yet how could it be right to find more fault with someone

---

[189] This important office was especially crucial in the months after Chaeronea, when a siege of the city was possible and grain was hoarded (see 18.87n).

[190] Demosthenes' opponents hired *sykophants* to prosecute Demosthenes for them; see 18.112n.

[191] Sosicles and Melantes are otherwise unknown. Diondas was mentioned in 18.222. The Philocrates mentioned here, from the deme Eleusis (see Pseudo-Dem. 25.44), is not Philocrates of Hagnus, who, as the author of the discredited peace agreement that bore his name (18.21), fled Athens in 343.

[192] I.e., for moving an illegal decree (*graphē paranomōn*; Aes. 3.194). Cephalus was a politician of the first half of the fourth century.

who was often indicted but never once convicted? What's more, Athenians, as far as Aeschines is concerned, you could attribute to me even Cephalus' splendid record, for Aeschines never indicted or prosecuted me, which means that you, Aeschines, have admitted that I am no worse a citizen than Cephalus.

[252] Aeschines' stupidity and rancor are evident everywhere, not least in his remarks about fortune.[193] In my view, it makes no sense at all for one human being to reproach another for the effects of fortune. A man may suppose that he enjoys the utmost prosperity and believe that he possesses unsurpassed good fortune, but he does not know if he shall still have it that evening. How then can one speak about it? How can one reproach another? But since on top of everything else, Aeschines speaks arrogantly on this subject too, observe closely, Athenians, how much more truthfully and humanely I shall speak about fortune than he does.

[253] As I see it, our city enjoys good fortune, and I note that the oracle of Zeus at Dodona told you this too. But mankind in general, as matters currently stand, is ruled by harsh, grim fortune. Which Greeks, which barbarians do not at the moment confront an abundance of troubles? [254] I count it as part of the city's good fortune that we chose the noblest course of action and enjoy better circumstances than those Greeks who expected to secure a happy future by casting us off.[194] Though the city has absorbed a blow, and we have failed to achieve all our aims, yet I view this as the share of mankind's general fortune that descends on us. [255] Now in my opinion, it is fair to examine the personal fortune allotted to me as well as that allotted to each of us with regard to our personal circumstances. That is how I judge fortune, and that seems to me and to you too, I believe, correct and fair. Yet Aeschines asserts that the fortune allotted to me personally is more powerful than the common fortune of the city, that is, the small and mean is more powerful than the honorable and great. How can this be?

[256] Now, Aeschines, if you in fact propose to examine my fortune, look at it in comparison with yours, and if you find that mine is

---

[193] Aeschines claimed that Demosthenes was cursed and brought misfortune on all with whom he came in contact (3.114, 134–136, 157–158).

[194] Such as the Greeks of the Peloponnese who tried to remain neutral (18.64).

better than yours, stop belittling it. Consider the matter right from the beginning. And no one should condemn me, by Zeus, for being harsh, since in my view there is no reason either to reproach someone for being poor or to be proud about an affluent upbringing. Yet the malicious lies of this heartless man force me to raise this topic, which, given the facts, I will present as moderately as I can.

[257] It was my lot, Aeschines, as a boy to attend the right schools and to have everything that would assure a life free of the mean behavior caused by poverty; as an adult to take up the tasks that correspond to that background, namely, providing choruses, maintaining triremes, paying property tax, and garnering every distinction in private and public life while making myself useful both to the city and to my friends; and when I decided to enter the public arena, to advocate policies that often brought me crowns both from my own country and from many other Greeks and that prevent even you, my enemies, from trying to brand what I advocated as less than noble. [258] That has been my fortune, and though I could say much more about it, I desist, reluctant to give offense by boasting about myself. But you, you pretentious and haughty man, compare my lot with that enjoyed by you: as a boy raised in that great poverty, serving at the school alongside your father, you rubbed the ink, wiped the benches, and swept the schoolroom, relegated to the status of a household slave, not that of a freeborn youth.[195] [259] Grown to manhood, you used to read aloud from books for your mother as she conducted initiation rites, and you colluded with her in other ways.[196] By night you clothed the initiates

---

[195] See 18.129 on Demosthenes' attempt to blacken Aeschines by deriding his father. Here the father is no longer the schoolteacher's slave but the teacher himself, which is, however, hardly less inappropriate for the father of a political leader.

[196] Demosthenes demeans Aeschines by casting him as a menial attendant in the initiation rites of an ecstatic cult presided over by his mother Glaucothea. Such cults aroused suspicion because they were practiced in private and outside the established religious life of the *polis*. See Parker 1996: 158–163. Glaucothea's predecessor, in fact, was sentenced to death for her activity in this cult (see 19.281). The elements of worship disparagingly enumerated by Demosthenes in the following passage were common to initiation cults of Dionysus, Orpheus, and Sabazius; see Burkert 1987. Sabazius was a god originally worshiped in Thrace and Phrygia and brought to Attica in the fifth century.

in fawn skins, plied them with wine, purified them, and scrubbed them down with clay and bran. You raised them up after purification and bade them utter, "Affliction removed, condition improved," proud of yourself because no one ever shrieked so loud. I quite agree. Don't believe that one who talks so loud does not also shriek piercingly. [260] By day you led brilliant bands of reveling worshipers through the streets. They wore crowns of fennel and white poplar as you clutched fat-headed snakes and swung them over your head. You would shout, *"Euhoi saboi,"* and dance to the beat of *"Hyes Attes Attes Hyes"*[197] as the old hags[198] would hail you as leader and guide, bearer-of-the-casket and bearer-of-the-winnow,[199] and so on. You were paid with soppy bread, twisted rolls, and flat cakes. Enjoying all this, who would not regard himself and his lot in life as truly fortunate?

[261] When you were enrolled as a citizen, however that happened (which I'll pass over)—in any case, when you were enrolled, you straightaway chose the most noble of occupations, namely, scribe and errand boy to minor officials.[200] Though you finally abandoned that line of work, in which you yourself perpetrated every transgression that you imputed to others, in the next stage of your life, by Zeus, you cast no shame on your previous career. [262] You went to work for those bellowers, the actors Simyccas and Socrates, playing bit parts, but you earned more collecting figs, grapes, and olives from other people's fields like a fruit seller than you did from the dramatic contests in which your troupe competed at mortal peril.[201] For the war between your troupe and the spectators knew no armistice and

---

[197] The rhythmic cry and dance, central to the ecstatic experience, form the climax of Aeschines' ministration.

[198] Aeschines' ministering to women, revealed only now, demeans him. The audience in court, strictly men, are invited to look on this business with a discomfort not unlike that evoked by Aristophanes' old hags who force a young man to pleasure them (*Women at the Assembly* 976–1111).

[199] The casket contained sacred objects used in the initiation rites; the winnow symbolized purification because it separated the grain from the chaff.

[200] Menial administrative tasks were incompatible with political leadership.

[201] Aeschines' career as an actor supplies the basis for these gibes. Here, in addition to being limited to the "bit parts" (see 18.129n), Aeschines is demeaned further by the quality of his senior colleagues, the implication of the agrarian setting

no truce. You incurred many wounds at their hands, so you have good reason to mock the cowardice of those who have never known such dangers.[202]

[263] But I pass over the flaws that could be blamed on poverty and turn now to charges that concern your character. When, at some point, it occurred to you to take up politics, you chose a position whereby any improvement in our country's fortune forced you to live the life of a hare, cowering, trembling, expecting a blow at any moment for crimes that you knew you had committed; yet when the fortune of the rest of the citizen body was in decline, you appeared courageous in the eyes of all. [264] How then should those who are still alive justly punish the man who grew in courage as a thousand fellow citizens died?[203] I could say much more about him, but I leave it aside. I do not think it would be appropriate to report all the disreputable, opprobrious conduct that I could point out in his record, and so I include only what I could utter without incurring shame.

[265] So examine my life and yours in comparison with each other, and do it sympathetically and without bitterness, Aeschines. Then ask each member of the audience whose fortune in life he would prefer. You taught school, I was a student; you conducted initiation rites, I was initiated;[204] you served as a public scribe, I attended the Assembly; you played bit parts on stage, I sat in the audience; you were hissed offstage, I was hissing. All your policies helped the enemy; mine helped our country. [266] I forego the rest but for this point. Right now, today, I am under scrutiny for the sake of a crown, and it has been ac-

---

that he played at Rural Dionysia (see 18.180n), and the unforgiving reaction of the audiences to whom he played; see also 19.337.

[202] An ironic response to Aeschines' attempt to brand Demosthenes a coward (see 18.245n).

[203] At Chaeronea. Diodorus Siculus 16.88.2 reports the same number of dead, a devastating figure for a citizen army of five to ten thousand and a body of adult male citizens of about thirty thousand. This is a good example of the way in which Demosthenes combines ridicule and deadly serious condemnation; so also 18.209.

[204] Discretion restrains Demosthenes from identifying the cult into which he was initiated and which contrasts with Glaucothea's despised private cult. It can only be the Eleusinian Mysteries, the established cult overseen by the *polis* and popular among Athenians.

knowledged that I am guilty of no crime whatsoever. You, however, are known as a *sykophant* and you are hovering between continuing to act in that manner and being stopped today by failing to win one-fifth of the votes.[205] So as the beneficiary of such good fortune (don't you see?), you cast aspersions on the fortune allotted to me.

[**267**] Let me read now the testimonies that affirm the liturgies I have performed.[206] Contrast that, Aeschines, with the lines you were in the habit of mutilating on stage:[207]

I come from the den of corpses and the gates of darkness,[208]

and

Know that I bring bad news, though unwillingly,[209]

and

May you, you wretch, wretchedly—

be destroyed, first of all, by the gods but also by all these people,[210] since you are a miserable citizen and a miserable bit-part actor.

Clerk, read the testimonies.

---

[205] See 18.82, 103n.

[206] Liturgies were public works financed by wealthy citizens for the benefit of the community, such as providing a chorus at a dramatic festival (18.257) or paying the expenses of a trireme (18.99).

[207] Demosthenes takes advantage of the fact that Aeschines had performed no liturgies and thus could not boast of that service to the people. The contrast consists in the public value of Demosthenes' considerable liturgies vs. the uselessness of Aeschines' bad acting.

[208] The opening line of Euripides' *Hecuba,* a popular play that the audience would have recognized and that would have put them in mind of tragedy and impending doom.

[209] A nondescript verse that could have come from any tragedy or been made up for this context. With evident mockery, Demosthenes is himself the "I" who brings bad news.

[210] The third verse evokes tragedy as it begins, but it is so hackneyed that it could just as well evoke comedy. We are meant to think that the verse originally included "by the gods," but Demosthenes breaks away from verse and into prose because he adds "by all these people." They too are entreated, by rejecting the prosecution, to destroy the wretched man, who in Demosthenes' delivery becomes, of course, Aeschines, the referent of "you."

[TESTIMONIES]

[268] That is my record in public life. If any of you are unaware that in my private life I am generous, compassionate, and helpful to the needy, I'll say nothing. I would rather not utter a word or provide any testimony about those matters, for instance, about any prisoners of war whom I ransomed from the enemy,[211] or about the daughters of any citizens whose dowry I provided, or about any similar matters. My view essentially is this: [269] I believe that the recipient of a favor should remember it for all time if he is to act honorably, and the one who conferred the favor should forget it immediately if he is to avoid mean-spiritedness. Recalling benefactions conferred in private and talking about them is nearly the same as insulting people. So I will do nothing of the kind, nor shall I be provoked into doing it, but whatever reputation I have in this regard is good enough for me.

[270] I wish to leave my private life aside and say a few more words on issues of public concern. If you, Aeschines, can point to a single man under the sun, either Greek or barbarian, who has escaped unscathed the domination imposed first by Philip, now by Alexander, so be it, I admit that my fortune or ill fortune, however you choose to name it, is responsible for everything. [271] But if many who have never even seen me and never heard my voice[212] also suffered terrible, extensive damage, not just individuals but whole cities and peoples,[213] isn't it much more honest and truthful to attribute these outcomes to the common fortune of virtually all mankind and a grievous rush of events that should not have been? [272] You dismiss that point and hold me responsible, though my political career has been conducted among these people here, and you are well aware that part of your

---

[211] Demosthenes ransomed Athenians captured by Philip in the battle for Olynthus (see 19.166–172).

[212] This responds to the notion underlying Aeschines' claim that Demosthenes was cursed (see 18.252n), namely, that the contagion was spread by personal contact or close proximity, as would happen within a *polis*.

[213] The cities and peoples of Asia, most notably the Persians, who were recently conquered by Alexander. These people, of course, never came into contact with Demosthenes.

reproach, at least, if not all of it, applies to everyone and most of all to you. Indeed, had I conceived policy on my own, with sole power to act, it would be possible for you other politicians to hold me liable. [273] But if you politicians were present at every Assembly, if the city always conducted a public discussion of our best interests, and if everyone, you above all, Aeschines, decided that that policy was the best one at the time—for surely it was not out of affection for me that you conceded the ambitions, enthusiasm, and prestige that accrued to the work I was then undertaking, but clearly you were defeated by the truth and had nothing better to propose—how then is it not a crime and an outrage for you to criticize policies now that you could not improve on then?

[274] I notice that among all the rest of mankind the following definitions and rules apply. A man commits a crime intentionally: he meets with anger and punishment. A man makes a mistake unintentionally: he is pardoned, not punished. A man commits no crime, makes no mistake, devotes himself to the policy everyone thinks is expedient but does not succeed in common with everyone else: the right thing is not to censure or berate the man but to commiserate with him. [275] Not only will our laws reveal all these principles, but nature herself established them in unwritten laws and in human customs. Yet Aeschines so exceeds all mankind in malicious cruelty that he blames me for things that he himself has described as bad fortune.[214]

[276] On top of all this, as if he himself were sincere and loyal in everything he says, he urges you to be alert and to guard against my misleading or deceiving you, and he calls me a skillful speaker, a sorcerer, a sophist, and other such names.[215] He hopes that by preemptively ascribing his own attributes to another, this description will be accepted, and the audience will not consider any further what kind of person is saying these things. But I am confident that all of you know

---

[214] Aes. 3.57.

[215] Throughout his speech Aeschines called Demosthenes these and other names intended to brand him as a skillful, untrustworthy, manipulative speaker. That was a common stratagem in Athenian oratory (see 19.246n). Demosthenes defends himself by admitting his skill in speaking, which could hardly be denied, and by arguing that it was always used on behalf of the people and never against them.

him and realize that those terms apply far more to him than they do to me. [277] Now, I know well that my skill at speaking—for so it is. Yet I observe that the audience usually is in control of the ability of the speakers. Your judgment of each speaker's message depends on how you regard the speaker and the extent to which you are favorably inclined towards him. Even if I do have some experience of this kind, you will all find that I always use it in the public domain to advance your interests and never to oppose them or in pursuit of private ends. He, on the other hand, uses his experience in speaking not only to help our enemies but also to harm anyone who has ever annoyed or crossed him; he does not use it fairly or for the benefit of the city.

[278] No worthy, upstanding citizen should ask a court convened on a matter of public concern to endorse his anger or hatred or any other such feeling, nor should he come before you with that intent. He really should not have those feelings in his nature, but when they are unavoidable, he should keep them calm and moderate. In what circumstances then should a politician or a speaker be passionate? When any of the city's vital interests is at risk and when the people are facing their enemies, that's when! That's the mark of an honorable, good citizen. [279] Yet on no occasion did Aeschines see fit to exact justice from me for any public crime, or, I might add, for any private one either, acting in defense of the city's interests or in defense of his own, but he has come into court with an elaborate indictment of a crown and a public acclamation and has squandered so many words—this is a sign of private hatred, spite, and mean-spiritedness, and nothing honorable. And his repeated refusal to prosecute me directly while coming forward now against this man here[216] reveals his complete, utter cowardice.

[280] From these points, Aeschines, I infer that you chose to have this trial to show off your eloquence and vocal dexterity, not to exact punishment for any crime. Yet the valuable thing, Aeschines, is not a politician's words or the quality of his voice, but his pursuit of the same policy as the masses and his having the same friends and enemies as his country. [281] When a person's heart is in the right place, every word he utters will be loyal. But when he fawns on those whom the city views as a threat to its interests, he is not moored at the same an-

---

[216] Ctesiphon.

chor as the masses and thus does not look for security in the same place. But—do you see?—I do! For I pursued the same goals as these men here, and I have done nothing apart from them or self-serving. [282] Have you done the same? How could that be? Immediately after the battle you went on a diplomatic mission to Philip,[217] who was responsible for the disasters that befell our country in those days. You did so even though formerly, as everyone knows, you always denied any association with him. So—who has been deceiving the city? Is it not the man who fails to say what he really thinks? Who deserves the herald's curse?[218] Is it not the man who acts in that manner? Can a politician be accused of a greater crime than saying one thing while thinking another? You, as we have discovered, are that politician. [283] And now you open your mouth? You dare look these men in the face? Perhaps you think that they don't know who you are? Or maybe they are so fast asleep and so oblivious that they don't remember the speeches you delivered to the Assembly during the war, when with oaths and imprecations you disavowed any connection to Philip and called it a false charge trumped up by me out of personal spite. [284] Yet as soon as news of the battle[219] reached home, you immediately forgot all about those prior statements, admitted the relationship, and pretended that you and Philip were bound by friendship and hospitality, substituting those terms for your wage-earning. On what reasonable or honest pretext was Philip the host, friend, or even acquaintance of Aeschines, son of Glaucothea, the drumming priestess?[220] I can't think of one. In fact, you earned wages in return for destroying the best interests of these men. And yet, although you have been plainly exposed as a traitor and afterwards provided information against yourself, you revile and reproach me for crimes that you could more easily blame on anybody else.

[285] Through me, Aeschines, the city pursued and realized many

---

[217] In the aftermath of Chaeronea, Aeschines was part of the Athenian delegation dispatched to negotiate terms with Philip.

[218] The herald's curse (see 18.130n) included those who would address the people with the intent to deceive.

[219] Chaeronea.

[220] "Drumming" because a tambourine-like instrument was used in ecstatic initiation rites (see 18.260). See 18.51–52 on Aeschines' claim of friendship with Philip.

important, noble objectives, which it has not forgotten. Consider this. At the time of those events, the people were to elect a citizen to speak at the public funeral.[221] Though you were a candidate, you were not elected, in spite of your pleasing voice. Demades was not elected, though he had just concluded the peace, and neither was Hegemon or any other of your group,[222] but I was. You and Pythocles[223] then took the cruel and shameless step, O Zeus and the gods, of coming forward and attacking me with the same reproaches that you are using now, but the city elected me by an even bigger margin. [286] You are not ignorant of the reason for this, but I'll explain it to you just the same. The people themselves knew two things: the loyalty and devotion I showed in conducting affairs and your dishonesty. For what you and your friends had denied under oath when our policy was succeeding, you then admitted when the city stumbled. So the people concluded that those who found it safe to speak their minds in the midst of communal disaster had been their enemies all along, though that fact came out only then. [287] They also deemed it inappropriate that the citizen who was to speak over the dead and to extol their courage should have shared a roof and dined with those who were arrayed against the dead in battle, or should join with the perpetrators of murder in praising the gods and celebrating Greek misfortunes[224] and then come here and receive honor, or should use his voice to perform a tearful lament for the fate of the dead rather than grieve with his soul for the common lot—this is what they saw in themselves and

---

[221] In Athens the remains of citizens killed in war were interred in common graves at a public funeral (see 18.208). One citizen was elected to deliver a common funeral oration extolling the dead and Athens itself; cf. Thucydides' famous account of Pericles' funeral oration of 430 (Thuc. 2.34–46). A speech preserved in the Demosthenic corpus (Dem. 60) purports to be the speech delivered by Demosthenes over the dead of Chaeronea, but its authenticity remains uncertain.

[222] Demades was the primary negotiator for Athens in the settlement with Philip following the defeat at Chaeronea. Almost nothing is known of this Hegemon.

[223] An enemy of Demosthenes, associate of Aeschines, and Macedonian sympathizer according to 19.225, 314, but otherwise little known.

[224] Demosthenes accuses Aeschines of having celebrated with Philip the Macedonian victory at Chaeronea, as he previously accused him of celebrating with Philip the victory over Phocis (see 19.128).

in me, but not in you. For these reasons they elected me and not you. [288] This was not just the view of the people. It was the same for those fathers and brothers of the dead whom the people chose to organize the funeral. When the funeral meal needed to be held at the house of the closest relative of the dead, as is the custom, they held it at my house. Rightly so. Though each of them had a closer familial tie to his own dead kinsman than I, no one had a closer public bond to all the dead. For the person to whom their safety and success mattered most had the greatest share of grief for all of them when they suffered what I wish they never had.[225]

[289] Clerk, read him the epitaph that the city chose to inscribe on their tomb at public expense, so that you understand, Aeschines, that in this matter too you are a vile, malicious fool. Read it.

[EPITAPH][226]

*[Here lie those who in defense of homeland arrayed themselves
for battle and dispelled the enemies' insolence.
They fought, sparing not their lives, and took Hades
as the common judge of courage and fear,
so that Greeks not wear the yoke of slavery
on their necks and meet hateful insolence on every side.
Ancestral earth holds in her lap the bodies of those
who toiled most, since this was Zeus' decision for mortals.]*

---

[225] For a brief moment the relentless champion of Athenian glory acknowledges the human cost. While avoiding formal consolation, Demosthenes achieves a consolatory effect merely by speaking of those whose return was missed and the attendant grief. Among the audience were necessarily many who lost a father, brother, or son at Chaeronea. They would not miss the gesture contained in this passage, which answers Aeschines' claim that Demosthenes had no regard for Athenian lives.

[226] Except for the ninth line that Demosthenes himself quotes in the next paragraph, this ten-line epigram is, like the other documents preserved in the speech, evidently spurious: it attributes glorious victory to the defeated Greeks (*"dispelled the enemies' insolence"*), which would make a mockery of both the fallen soldiers and Demosthenes' argument. The epigram is also overlong, unclear, and plainly lacks the polish of comparable epigrams; and it makes no mention of the place of battle, a customary feature of such poems.

Never to fail and ever to succeed belongs to the gods
[in life, and Zeus granted no escape from fate.]

[290] Do you hear, Aeschines: "Never to fail and ever to succeed belongs to the gods"? It ascribes the power to assure the combatants' success not to the politician but to the gods.[227] Why then, wretch, do you berate me for this and say things that I entreat the gods to inflict upon you and yours?

[291] Surely, Athenians, he has leveled many false accusations, but most amazing of all was when he recalled the events that befell the city at that time. His attitude was not that of a loyal and honest citizen. There were no tears, no sign that emotion stirred his soul. Rather, although he thought he was denouncing me, of course, his cheerfully raised voice and loud roars gave proof against himself that the dire events did not affect him in the same manner as the others. [292] But anyone who, like this man here, claims to care about our laws and form of government[228] ought at the very least to feel the same pain and pleasure as the people and not choose a public policy that places him in the ranks of the enemy. Yet that is clearly what you have done today by blaming me for everything and calling me the cause of the city's troubles, though you citizens began coming to the aid of Greece well before I made that my policy or advised you to do it. [293] Should you give me credit for this, namely, for causing you to oppose the empire that was building against Greece, you would give me a greater gift than all the gifts that you ever bestowed on others. But I would not claim that achievement (for I would be doing you an injustice), nor would you, of course, concede it, and if this man had acted honorably, he would not have tried to disfigure and defame your most noble achievement out of hatred for me.

[294] Why do I raise that objection when he falsely accused me of far worse? If the man accuses me, O earth and gods, of joining Philip's side, what would he not say? By Heracles and all the gods, if you had to eliminate the lies and malicious statements and to examine truth-

---

[227] Taken by itself, the verse seems to mean that the gods alone, i.e., and not mortals, always succeed and never fail, an unexceptional statement. Demosthenes interprets it to mean that the gods decide which mortals succeed and which fail, an interpretation that suits his argument.

[228] Aes. 3.1–8.

fully who the people really are whom everyone, with reason and justice, would hold responsible for what happened, in every city you would find people like him, not like me. [295] When Philip was weak and had very little power indeed, and we were continually warning, exhorting, and explaining the best policy, they were sacrificing the common good to their own base pursuit of greed, eventually reducing their own fellow citizens to slavery through deception and subversion. In Thessaly it was Daochus, Cineas, Thrasydaus; in Arcadia, Cercidas, Hieronymus, Eucampidas; in Argos, Myrtis, Teledamus, Mnaseas; in Elis, Euxitheus, Cleotimus, Aristaechmus; in Messenia, Neon and Thrasylochus, sons of the fiend Philiades; in Sicyon, Aristratus, Epichares; in Corinth, Dinarchus, Demaretus; in Megara, Ptoeodorus, Helixus, Perilas; in Thebes, Timolas, Theogiton, Anemoetas; in Euboea, Hipparchus, Clitarchus, Sosistratus.[229] [296] The day will give out before I finish reciting the traitors' names. All of them, Athenians, have the same designs on their own countries as these men have on you—foul men, bootlickers, evil demons; each of them hacked off the limbs of his own country, handed freedom on a platter first to Philip, now to Alexander, measured happiness with his stomach and basest impulses, and overturned that freedom and opposition to tyranny which for the Greeks before us was the guiding measure of what is good.[230]

[297] Indeed, it was a thoroughly disgraceful and scandalous collusion of cowards, or rather, not to mince words, Athenians, a betrayal of the freedom of Greece. My policies rendered the city blameless in the judgment of all mankind and me likewise in your judgment, and now you ask me, Aeschines, for what meritorious conduct do I deserve

---

[229] This blacklist of Greek traitors is grim because it is long and covers the Greek heartland. All those named are obscure today, and though some evidence ties a few names to Philip, all must have been notorious at the time for some connection to Philip; otherwise, Demosthenes could not have hoped to use this list to blacken Aeschines. Polybius (18.14), a Greek historian of the second century BCE and from the Peloponnese (like several on Demosthenes' list), argued against Demosthenes that some of these men branded as traitors sought Philip as an ally against Sparta or made necessary accommodations with a vastly superior power.

[230] The most vehement show of anger in the entire speech, the very ferocity of which is meant to assure sincerity.

to be honored?[231] I will tell you. Though the politicians in Greece were corrupted—all of them, starting with you— [298] no opportunity, no friendly words, no large promises, no hope, no fear, nothing at all seduced or impelled me to betray what I saw as the honorable and advantageous course for the country, nor, whenever I advised these men, did I offer that advice as you and your accomplices did, sinking towards profit like a balance. Rather, with an honest, just, and incorruptible soul I presided over the greatest issues affecting the people of my day and directed the city's affairs throughout reliably and honorably. [299] For these reasons, I think I deserve to be honored. As for my work on the city's fortifications and trenches, which you disparaged, I consider it worthy of grateful approbation (how could it not be?), but I place it far below my work as a politician. It was not with stones and bricks that I fortified the city, and among the achievements to my name it is not in those items that I take greatest pride. If you truly want to inspect the fortifications I built, you will find arms and cities and territories and harbors and ships and horses and men serving in defense of these men. [300] Those are the defenses I assembled to protect Attica, as effective as human planning could devise, and by those means I fortified the whole territory, not just the walls around Piraeus and the city center.[232] Surely I was not defeated by Philip in planning—far from it—and not in preparation either, but the allied generals and their military forces were defeated by his good fortune. What is the proof? It is plain and clear. Consider.

[301] What was a loyal citizen to do? What was a politician to do— one who worked for his country with absolute prudence, devotion, and integrity? Was he not to protect Attica from the sea by means of Euboea, from the interior by means of Boeotia, from the Peloponnesian district by means of our neighbors on that side? Was he not to ensure that the grain convoys should sail along friendly territory all the way to Piraeus? [302] Was he not only to hold on to the territories that we already possessed—Proconnesus, Chersonese, Tenedos—by dispatching forces, defending that policy in debate, and moving decrees

---

[231] Aes. 3.236, but Aeschines directed the question to Ctesiphon.

[232] Athens and the harbor at Piraeus, which formed the urban core of Attica, were protected by a system of defensive walls. The rural expanse of Attica was protected by scattered outposts.

to that effect, but also to make alliances that would acquire territories for our side—Byzantium, Abydos, Euboea?[233] Was he not to take away the enemy's most important military forces and bring over to our city the forces that we lacked? That was all achieved by my decrees and my policies. [303] Further, Athenians, a dispassionate inquirer would discover that those policies had been formulated correctly and carried out with complete integrity, and that I never overlooked or ignored or threw away the right moment for action. Nothing in the power of one man to do or plan was omitted. If the power of some god or of fortune, the ineptitude of generals, the cowardice of you who betrayed the Greek cities, or all these things together undermined our whole enterprise to the point of destroying it, what crime did Demosthenes commit? [304] If there was one man in every Greek city who was like me in the post that I took up in Athens, or rather, if Thessaly had just one man and Arcadia one who thought as I did, none of the Greeks either north or south of Thermopylae would have met with their current adversity.[234] [305] They would all be free and independent, prosperously inhabiting their own countries in safety and complete security, and, because of me, they would owe you and all other Athenians thanks for so many wonderful blessings.

Since I wish to avoid ill will, the words I've used are far less impressive than the facts,[235] but to make you aware of them, clerk, please take the list of expeditionary forces ordered by my decrees and read it out.[236]

[LIST OF EXPEDITIONARY FORCES]

[306] Those are the deeds, Aeschines, and others like them, that a worthy, upstanding citizen must carry out. Had they been successful,

---

[233] The places mentioned in this sentence all lie along the route followed by the grain convoys from the Black Sea to Attica.

[234] See 18.63–64 for Demosthenes' view of Thessaly and Arcadia, standing, respectively, for traitorous and neutral states. Thermopylae was the crucial defensive position in central Greece against invasion from the north, hence Demosthenes' emphasis on it here.

[235] I.e., Demosthenes' actions in defense of Athens described in 18.301–303.

[236] This, the last document to be read out in the trial, must have contained a long summary of all the actions organized by Demosthenes.

you citizens were assured of being indisputably the greatest power and justly so as well. But since things have turned out otherwise, at least you still have your reputation: no one reproaches the city or its choice of policy, but people rail at fortune for deciding things this way. [307] No, by Zeus, the worthy, upstanding citizen must not stand aloof from the city's interests, hire himself out to our foes, and contrive opportunities to suit the enemy rather than our country. He must not malign the person who endeavors to propose, defend, and support measures worthy of the city. And should he privately suffer some insult, he must not remember it and lie in wait, maintaining a dishonest, festering silence, as you often do, Aeschines.

[308] Now, there is such a thing as a silence that is honest and useful to the city, clearly there is. Most of you demonstrate it forthrightly. But that's not the silence this man keeps—far from it.[237] He stands aloof from politics whenever it suits him (and it suits him often), watching for a moment when you will have had your fill of someone who speaks incessantly, when some setback has occurred due to chance, or when some other problem arises (which happens often in life). At just that moment, like a wind, a politician suddenly arises from the silence, one who's been training his voice and hoarding words and phrases, which he reels off clearly and without pausing for breath. But they yield no benefit and no tangible advantage, only trouble for some citizen and disgrace for everyone.

[309] If you prepared so studiously, Aeschines, because your motives were just and you favored the country's interests, the effort ought to have borne wonderful, choice fruit, fruit that availed everyone: military alliances, streams of revenue, commercial infrastructure, useful legislation, deterrents against known enemies. [310] Achievements like these have all been reviewed on earlier occasions and worthy, upstanding men have had many occasions to demonstrate them. Yet you show up nowhere in the ranks of such men, not first, not second, not third, not fourth, not fifth, not sixth, not in any position whatsoever, not, in any event, for achievements that increased the country's power. [311] What alliance did you bring about on behalf of the city? What

---

[237] Demosthenes rejects Aeschines' attempt (3.216–220) to depict his political reticence as a plain democratic virtue in contrast with Demosthenes' oligarchic strivings.

assistance to others or what venture that won goodwill and renown? What diplomatic mission, what service abroad that enhanced the city's honor? What issue in domestic, Greek, or foreign affairs did you set right when you had the authority? What triremes are you responsible for? What arms? What dockyards? What repairs to the walls? What regiment of horse? What in the world have you been good for? What civic, communal benefit have you rendered either the affluent or the indigent? None!

[312] "But, my good man," you may retort, "if I did none of those things, at least I was loyal and devoted." Where? When? O most deceitful of all men, when every citizen who ever uttered a word from the speaker's platform donated something towards saving the state, when Aristonicus donated the money he had raised to restore his citizenship,[238] not even then did you come forward and contribute anything, though you were not without means. How could you be? From your brother-in-law Philo you had inherited more than five talents, and from the heads of the taxation-groups you were holding a "loan" of two talents, in return for which you subverted the trierarchic law.[239] [313] But I'll let that matter go since I don't wish to lose the thread by piling argument on top of argument. It's clear from this that poverty did not stop you from contributing. Rather, you were reluctant to do anything that might thwart the people whose interests you support wholeheartedly. So then, in what circumstances are you energetic? When are you illustrious? When something can be done against the interests of these men,[240] then you are the man with the most illustrious voice, the man with the keenest memory, the best actor, the Theocrines of the tragic stage.[241]

[314] Next, you bring up the great men of the past, and you are

---

[238] Because of a debt to the state, Aristonicus (mentioned also in 18.83, 223) lost his citizen status. He raised money to pay the debt and regain his citizenship, but in the state of emergency, he just donated the money to the state. The occasion of the donations must have been the aftermath of Chaeronea (see 18.171n).

[239] "Loan" (*eranos:* an interest-free loan among friends) is an innuendo for a slush fund raised by political allies. Aeschines was opposed to Demosthenes' reform of the trierarchic law (see 18.102–109; Aes. 3.222).

[240] I.e., the jurors and thus all Athenians.

[241] Theocrines, the target of speech 58 in the Demosthenic corpus, was a well-known *sykophant.*

right to do so.[242] However, Athenians, it is dishonest of him to recall your reverence for the dead and then to judge me, a man who lives among you today, in comparison to them. [315] Who on earth does not know that every living person is exposed to envy, at least to some extent, but the dead are no longer hated even by their enemies? Since that's how nature arranged things, should I be judged and scrutinized today in comparison to earlier generations? Absolutely not! That would be dishonest and unfair, Aeschines; rather, judge me in comparison to you and to anyone else you wish among your like-minded—and still living—associates. [316] Consider this further point. Which course of action brings the city greater honor and better serves its interests? To insist on the public service of earlier generations, which was extraordinary, indeed beyond what words can describe, in order to heap scorn and abuse on the public service that occurs nowadays? Or to allot the honor and goodwill of these men to all who act out of loyalty?

[317] But if I do need to address this point, then anyone who considers it will see that my policies and decisions resemble those made by the eminent citizens of the past and have the same goals as did theirs, but yours resemble those made by the *sykophants* of the past who attacked those eminent citizens. Clearly, in their days too there were persons who ridiculed contemporaries by exalting predecessors, thereby causing the same malicious trouble that you do. [318] You say I bear no resemblance to those exemplary men? Do you resemble them, Aeschines? Or does your brother?[243] Or some other current politician? No one does, in my view! No, my good man (to avoid some other term), judge the living in comparison to the living, in comparison to men of their own day, as we always do with poets, choruses, athletes. [319] Philammon did not leave Olympia without a crown because he was inferior to Glaucus of Carystus or other athletes of the past;[244] rather,

---

[242] Aes. 3.178–188 mentioned Themistocles, Miltiades, the heroes of Phyle (democratic partisans in 403), and Aristides in the course of arguing that (in 330) honors were debased by the frequency with which they were bestowed.

[243] Of Aeschines' two brothers, Philochares and Aphobetus (see 19.237), the former was a general, and the latter was a politician; hence Demosthenes refers here to the latter.

[244] Philammon and Glaucus were boxers. The latter was celebrated for multiple victories at the panhellenic games in the late sixth century. The former was a contemporary of Demosthenes and Aeschines.

he won the crown and was acclaimed for his victory because he was the best fighter out of those who faced him. So you too, scrutinize me in comparison to the politicians of this generation, in comparison to yourself, in comparison to anyone at all. I yield to no one. [320] When the city was still in a position to choose the best policy, and there was competition among all to demonstrate loyalty to the state,[245] I was recognized as offering the best advice of all politicians, and everything was handled through my decrees, laws, and diplomacy. Yet except when there was a chance to abuse those measures, neither you nor your accomplices were anywhere to be found. And after the events that I wish had never happened, and we were no longer looking for advisers but for persons who would submit to orders, who would seek wages in return for harming their country, and who would enjoy fawning on others,[246] that's when you and every one of your group took up your posts, you, powerful and eminent, an owner of horses, while I am powerless, I admit, but more loyal to these men than you are.

[321] Two traits, Athenians, mark the genuine, responsible citizen (to speak of myself in the least offensive way): he guards the city's aspirations to nobility and supremacy when the opportunity arises and his own loyalty in every situation and condition of life. That much is determined by his own character; whether and how forcefully he succeeds is determined by other things. You can see without question that my loyalty has never wavered. [322] Consider. Not when I was sought as a hostage,[247] not when they prosecuted me before the Amphictyons,[248] not when they threatened me, not when they made me offers, not when they unleashed on me those vile persons,[249] no better than animals—never did I betray my loyalty to you. Right from the beginning the path I chose for our policy was straight and honest: to foster, to enhance, to remain true to the country's honor, power, and prestige. [323] When others reap success,[250] I do not go around the Agora

---

[245] Before Chaeronea.

[246] Philip and later Alexander.

[247] See 18.41n.

[248] The occasion is unknown though Demosthenes may still be referring to Alexander's demand for hostages in 335.

[249] Those who prosecuted Demosthenes after Chaeronea (see 18.249).

[250] Referring to Alexander's victories in Asia, the most recent being the victory over Darius at Gaugamela in fall 331.

beaming with joy, nor do I shake hands and spread the good news among people who will most likely report it there.[251] I do not shudder at news that the city prospers, weeping and hanging my head like these godless men. They deride the city, as if they were not deriding themselves at the same time, but they gaze elsewhere, and when Greek misfortune means good fortune for someone else, they applaud and declare that we should endeavor to prolong that state of affairs forever.[252]

[324] No, all you gods, may none of you grant their wish! Best would be to inspire better thoughts and intentions even in them, but if they are indeed incurable, destroy every last one of them utterly and thoroughly on earth and sea. And grant the rest of us as soon as possible release from the fears that threaten and salvation that endures.[253]

---

[251] Macedonians or Macedonian sympathizers in Athens, who will report to their masters in Macedon the names of those in Athens who support their cause.

[252] "Elsewhere" = Macedon; "someone else" = Alexander; "that state of affairs" = Macedonian hegemony.

[253] The prayer with which the speech suddenly comes to an end recalls the prayer with which it began. Now Demosthenes asks the gods to intervene against Athenian supporters of Macedon, to the point of exterminating them if necessary, and implicitly ties the verdict on Demosthenes' crown to the overthrow of Macedonian hegemony. The directness with which Demosthenes assumes divine sanction for his political program, and for eliminating fellow citizens who oppose it, seems exorbitant in comparison to the secular, polite rhetoric that is the norm in modern democracy. Yet the closing prayer brings Demosthenes' view of Athens' tradition and mission to its logical conclusion. Without calling for revolt—which under the circumstances was not feasible—Demosthenes commits himself and his audience, if they vote for him, to continuing the spirit of Chaeronea.

19. ON THE DISHONEST EMBASSY

〰〰

INTRODUCTION

Background

Athens was at war with Macedon since 357, when Philip, recently acceded to the Macedonian throne, seized the northern Greek cities of Amphipolis and Pydna, which Athens considered within its sphere of influence. The Athenians made no headway, apart from repelling Philip's attempt to seize Thermopylae in 352. Meanwhile Philip extended his power into Thrace and Thessaly. In 348 Athens attempted to prop up its ally Olynthus, but Philip took the city anyway, securing his hold on Chalcidice. When Philip signaled his readiness to negotiate a settlement in 347, the Athenians were receptive, and the seeds of the conflict between Demosthenes and Aeschines were sown.

In early 346, the Athenians elected a team of ten envoys to travel to Pella, Philip's capital, and open negotiations. This delegation, known as the First Embassy, included Aeschines and Demosthenes. When they returned to Athens in the spring, the envoys presented the people with the terms of an agreement: the Athenians and their allies were to conclude peace and alliance with Philip and his allies, each side keeping those territories they possessed at the time of the agreement. On the motion of Philocrates, a leading politician and one of the ten envoys, and with the support of both Aeschines and Demosthenes, the Athenians adopted what became known as the Peace of Philocrates and swore the oaths that ratified the treaty.

Another diplomatic mission, known as the Second Embassy and consisting of the same ten citizens as the previous one, was then delegated by the people to travel to Philip and receive from him the oaths that would ratify the treaty on his part. Yet even as the Second Embassy departed, certain issues between the Athenians and Philip remained unsettled and potentially disruptive. First, Philip was then campaigning in Thrace and the Greek areas of the Thracian Chersonese. Nearly two months passed before the Second Embassy finally met Philip in Pella and received his oaths. The delay allowed the king to add several territories to his domain, including some formerly attached to Athens, that he did not possess when the Athenians had ratified. More important was the uncertainty regarding Philip's intentions towards the main parties to the Third Sacred War then being fought in central Greece: Phocis had close ties with Athens but was not an official Athenian ally under the terms of the peace agreement and thus not protected under it; Thebes, on the other hand, Athens' long-standing enemy, could pose a threat to Athens if Philip settled the war in Thebes' favor.

For Athens the Peace of Philocrates was an utter failure. The Athenians officially recognized all of Philip's gains in the north since 358, yet within weeks of ratifying the agreement, Philip moved an army into central Greece and occupied the pass at Thermopylae, thus threatening all Greek states south of that point. He also compelled the Phocians to surrender and made known his intentions to punish them severely, which duly followed later in 346. The Athenians were so alarmed that they took emergency measures behind the walls of the city and harbor. Philip withdrew back to the north, and the peace held, since none of his actions was strictly a violation of the accord, and the Athenians could do little in any case. But in addition to validating Philip's conquests of their former territories in the north, the Athenians saw their security permanently shattered as Philip stationed a garrison near Thermopylae and strengthened the Thebans at the expense of the Phocians. Far from being settled, the problem of how to respond to Macedonian expansion was exacerbated. For the next several years Demosthenes and Aeschines opposed each other bitterly as debate raged in Athens over both responsibility for the bungled diplomacy of 346 and fresh efforts to counteract further Macedonian expansion.

Demosthenes must have perceived the problems arising from the badly negotiated Peace of Philocrates before others did because he dissociated himself from it at the earliest possible moment.[1] Soon after the Second Embassy arrived back in Athens in the summer of 346, he

---

[1] 19.17–18, 33.

initiated proceedings to prosecute Aeschines for misconduct on that mission, using the procedure of an audit (*euthynai*) to achieve his goal. All citizens who served the people in any public office or were assigned any public task underwent this audit at the conclusion of their service. For those whose service required the handling of money, there were two stages to the audit. Envoys, who received money for traveling expenses and perhaps for other purchases too, necessarily underwent the two-stage audit. First, a board of accountants (*logistai*) performed a financial audit of the funds that were handled and spent. Once the financial audit was complete, the citizen went before a board of auditors (*euthynoi*) who considered any kind of malpractice that may have occurred during the citizen's service. In both stages of the audit, the regular procedures allowed opportunities for any citizen who wished to approach the presiding board and level an accusation against the citizen undergoing the audit. If such an accusation was brought and found by the presiding board to be credible, the case was referred to a popular court for adjudication with the accusing citizen as prosecutor.[2]

Aeschines successfully completed the financial audit of his activity on the Second Embassy. It was at the second stage, before the *euthynoi*, that Demosthenes leveled his charges of misconduct, which he specifies thus in the speech: "Aeschines uttered not a single word of truth in his report, prevented the Assembly from hearing the truth from me, recommended policies completely opposed to our interests, ignored everything you [the people] instructed him to do on the embassy, wasted time while the city's opportunities for great, far-reaching action were thrown away, and together with Philocrates took gifts and payments in return for all these services."[3]

In the face of this provocation, Aeschines did not respond with an attack on Demosthenes, who was in too secure a position at that moment to be vulnerable. Instead, Aeschines attacked Timarchus, a political ally of Demosthenes who had moved to prosecute Aeschines for

---

[2] On the procedures, see Hansen 1991: 222–224; Todd 1993: 112–113.

[3] 19.8. The second stage of the audit must have occurred later in 346, not long after the completion of the financial audit, even though the case was not adjudicated before a court until 343; on the chronology, see Harris 1995: 95–96. Such delays were not uncommon, since politicians were constantly maneuvering to find the most opportune moment to press such charges home.

misconduct on the embassy.[4] Charging Timarchus with prostitution, an act that disqualified a citizen from exercising his political rights, Aeschines won the case in the face of Demosthenes' support of the defendant and drove Timarchus from the political arena.[5] In the speech of prosecution, delivered in the winter of 346/345, Aeschines held out hope that the Peace of Philocrates might yet work to Athens' advantage and boasted of his role in procuring it.[6] Thus, in spite of the evident problems with the peace, Aeschines continued to stake his career on the principle behind the diplomatic efforts of 346—that rapprochement with Macedon was possible and in Athens' best interests—and he never escaped his connection with the peace.

In the following years, Athens' position with regard to Macedon did not improve. Political tension in Athens tightened in 343. Early that year Pytho of Byzantium attempted to renew diplomatic contacts between Philip and Athens. Aeschines supported that effort as an opportunity to recoup the losses suffered in 346.[7] When the renewed diplomacy proved vain, it was no longer possible for anyone in Athens to deny that the Peace of Philocrates was a disaster. At that point Philocrates fled into exile rather than face the people on a charge of treason (*eisangelia*) brought by Hyperides, a staunch anti-Macedonian politician and ally of Demosthenes. Philocrates' flight having rendered Aeschines vulnerable,[8] Demosthenes seized the moment to bring to trial his prosecution of Aeschines for misconduct on the Second Embassy.

Demosthenes had two goals: to eliminate from public opinion any remaining suspicion that he bore any responsibility for the Peace of Philocrates and, with Philocrates gone, to drive from Athens the most prominent remaining advocate of diplomatic rapprochement with Philip. That would put Demosthenes in an effective position to guide Athens' foreign policy. Though several of Athens' most prominent

---

[4] 19.2, 257, 284–286.

[5] See Aes. 1.

[6] Aes. 1.169, 174.

[7] Harris 1995: 114.

[8] A major theme of Demosthenes' speech is Aeschines' close connection with Philocrates (e.g., 19.8, 23, 279n, and frequently throughout). In defense, Aeschines tries to associate Demosthenes with Philocrates (see 19.202n), but the charge did not stick.

politicians lent their support to Aeschines,[9] Demosthenes was largely successful. In defense (Aes. 2), Aeschines could not establish that Athens was better off as a result of the peace agreement, and he could no longer recommend diplomacy, or offer any other policy, as a viable means to counter Philip and repair the damage of 346. But Aeschines secured an acquittal by a slim margin,[10] presumably because he was able to establish in the minds of the jurors enough doubt that he was actually as corrupt as Demosthenes insisted. For Demosthenes this was victory enough. Though Aeschines maintained sufficient standing to be chosen by the people for further diplomatic missions,[11] after this trial his influence on Athenian politics was limited. Demosthenes, on the other hand, went on to dominate Athenian politics and to shape policy towards Macedon, until the Athenian defeat at Chaeronea in 338 created the next occasion to reassess.

Demosthenes' Argument

The underlying strength of Demosthenes' argument is its simplicity. The main points of his argument are as follows: Both Aeschines and Philocrates were hired by Philip to turn the Peace of Philocrates into a boon for Philip and a disaster for Athens. The success of their efforts is evident in the undeniably dire straits that Athens currently faces: Philip holds Thermopylae and threatens Attica; Thebes controls Boeotia; Philip, Thebes, and Thessaly control the Delphic Amphictyony; Athens lost Phocis, which had provided Athens with a buffer and considerable military resources; Athens' status as the leader of Greece against barbarian tyranny has suffered a blow.

After a brief introduction (1–8), Demosthenes launches directly into this argument by presenting a narrative of events that extends through the first half of the speech (9–177). He recounts both Aeschines' public (hence verifiable) behavior and the disastrous course of events in such a way that they are explicable only on the premise that

---

[9] Especially Eubulus; see 19.290n, Aes. 2.184.

[10] Pseudo-Plut., *Lives of the Ten Orators* 840c.

[11] He served in 339 as one of Athens' representatives to the Delphic Amphictyony, and he served in 338 on the delegation of envoys dispatched to negotiate terms with Philip following the defeat at Chaeronea (18.149, 282).

Aeschines was bribed by Philip to act against Athens' interests. The strongest element in this narrative concerns Aeschines' report to the Assembly upon the return of the Second Embassy to Athens: Aeschines lulled the Athenians into inaction by relaying exorbitant, false promises of what Philip would do for Athens. Those vain promises loom large in contrast to what actually transpired, namely, Philip's seizure of Thermopylae and his destruction of Phocis. Demosthenes eliminates the possibility that Aeschines was duped by Philip or merely negligent by tying him closely to Philocrates, who, having recently escaped into exile rather than stand trial on a charge of treason, was universally deemed corrupt and culpable. Demosthenes established that tie at the opening of his speech: he decried Aeschines' support of Philocrates at the crucial moment following the First Embassy when the Athenians decided to accept the peace agreement (9–16). From that point on, Demosthenes portrays Aeschines and Philocrates as working in concert at every stage.

The narrative is not presented in a continuous, chronologically ordered manner. Rather, it is broken up into segments, interrupted at unpredictable intervals by indignation at Aeschines' corruption and by explicit or ironic disparagement of Aeschines' character and background, then resumed with little warning or recapitulation. Beyond vilifying Aeschines and making him (in addition to Philocrates) responsible for the disastrous turn of events, Demosthenes gives the impression of absolute control of his material, instilling in the audience confidence in his account. The original audience was aware of the basic plot, of many of the details, and of Demosthenes' agenda, and so they could pick up Demosthenes' thread at any moment with the briefest reference. Yet by compelling the audience to attend to his allusive, morally compelling narration, Demosthenes was forcing them to accept his view of events. A modern reader may well find it difficult at first to follow the narrative but will quickly come to recognize Demosthenes' way of referring to the central events and circumstances, since Demosthenes keeps repeating them.

Once the narrative is complete and Aeschines' role in events firmly established, Demosthenes restates the charges (177–181) and turns to supporting arguments (182–301): refutations of Aeschines' anticipated defense; attack on Aeschines' character and background; criticism of Aeschines' prosecution of Timarchus, which includes a masterful use

of poetic quotation at Aeschines' expense; the need to convict in order
to advance Athens' interests and to defuse the corruption spreading
throughout Greece; an attack on Eubulus, an influential politician
who was to speak in court in support of Aeschines. The speech winds
down as Demosthenes recapitulates the key moments in the primary
narrative, though each moment is retold from a different point of view
(302–336). Demosthenes concludes by asking the audience to ignore
the defendant's speech, which, because of his impressive vocal abilities,
is bound to deceive, and by reminding them that Athens' interests and
moral duty require them to convict (337–343).

Synopsis

1–8: Prooemium: focusing the jurors' attention; statement of the
charges

9–16: Aeschines' support of Philocrates following the First
Embassy

17–71: Aeschines' and Philocrates' false promises following the Second Embassy; Philip's seizure of Thermopylae and destruction
of Phocis

72–82: Anticipation of Aeschines' defense of his conduct following
the Second Embassy

83–97: Athens' position with Thermopylae in Philip's hands and
the Phocians destroyed

98–130: Aeschines bribed by Philip; failure to repudiate Philip and
Philocrates

131–149: Punishing Aeschines necessary to recoup Athens' losses
and eradicate corruption

150–177: Delay taking Philip's oaths during the Second Embassy;
Demosthenes' ransom of the Olynthian prisoners (166–173)

177–181: Review of the charges

182–191: Refutation of Aeschines' counterarguments

192–240: Invective: the Olynthian woman (196–198); Aeschines'
background (199–201); Demosthenes' integrity vs. Aeschines'
depravity (202–236); Aeschines' brothers (237–240)

241–257: Aeschines' prosecution of Timarchus; quotations of the
poets

258–287: Corruption throughout Greece; benefit of and precedent
for convicting Aeschines

288–301: Attack on Eubulus, Aeschines' main supporter
302–314 (Beginning to conclude): Aeschines' shift from loyal citizen to traitor (cf. 9–16)
315–331: Philip's scheme to hire traitors to deceive Athens; the basic narrative retold, now from Philip's point of view (cf. 150–177, 17–71)
332–336: Athens' losses caused by Aeschines (cf. 83–97)
337–340: Ignore Aeschines' speech because of his deceptive voice
341–343: Conclusion: the need to convict on pragmatic and moral grounds

ON THE DISHONEST EMBASSY

[1] How much lobbying, Athenians, this trial has occasioned and how much influence has been exerted are evident, I think, to nearly all of you, for you saw the people badgering and accosting you just now as you were being chosen by allotment.[12] But I shall make a request that should by rights be granted even to those who request nothing: that you hold no obligation nor any man to be of greater importance than justice and the oath that each of you swore before entering the court;[13] and keep in mind that justice and the oath advance your interests and those of the whole city, but partisan supporters make their entreaties and pursue their schemes for private gain. You are assembled here by law to thwart such efforts, not to assist the wrongdoers in realizing them. [2] Clearly, any citizen who undertakes public business honestly offers himself for examination indefinitely, even when he has concluded his audit (euthynai). But Aeschines here does just the opposite. Before coming into court to defend his record, he ruined one person who objected at his audit,[14] and he now goes around threatening the others. That is an absolutely terrible way to behave under our form of government, and it is extremely bad for you. For if a citizen who has held and discharged some office eliminates his accusers by spreading fear of himself rather than by behaving justly, you will lose all control over everything.

---

[12] Lots were used to assign jurors to the court.
[13] The Heliastic Oath; see 18.2n.
[14] Timarchus, prosecuted by Aeschines in 346/5 (Aes. 1), accused Aeschines of misconduct at the latter's audit following the Second Embassy.

[3] I am confident and thoroughly convinced that I shall prove that this man committed many terrible crimes and deserves the most extreme punishment. But in spite of this conviction, I am troubled—I tell you openly and shall not hide it: every case tried before you, Athenians, seems to depend as much on the circumstances of the moment as on the facts of the matter; and I fear that because the embassy took place a long time ago[15] you may have forgotten his crimes or become inured to them. [4] So let me tell you how, in spite of these obstacles, you can reach a just decision and verdict today: you must consider and think through, jurors, what are the matters for which the city should hold an envoy responsible. First, the report he delivered; second, his advice; third, the instructions you gave him; next, his use of the time at his disposal; and on top of all this, whether he was corrupt or not in discharging all these duties.

[5] Why precisely these points? First, because your deliberations about policy depend on his report: if it is true, you have the necessary information, but if not, you have just the opposite. And since you treat an envoy as an authority on the issues related to his mission, you find his recommendations especially reliable. Indeed, no envoy should ever be convicted of giving you bad or harmful advice. [6] And surely he should carry out what you instructed him to say and do and expressly voted that he should accomplish. Fine. But why his use of time? Because opportunities for great, far-reaching action often arise for a brief moment; if he deliberately surrenders or betrays this opportunity to the enemy, he will not be able to get it back, no matter what he does. [7] As for the question of integrity, all of you, I know, would say that to profit at the expense of the city is a terrible and infuriating thing; however, the lawgiver did not define the matter that way, but simply said that no gifts of any kind were to be accepted. He believed, I take it, that once a citizen has accepted a gift and been corrupted by money, he can no longer serve the city as a reliable judge of useful policy.

[8] So if I prove and demonstrate clearly that Aeschines here uttered not a single word of truth in his report, that he prevented the Assembly from hearing the truth from me, that he recommended poli-

---

[15] The Second Embassy returned to Athens more than three years before the trial.

cies completely opposed to our interests, that he ignored everything you instructed him to do on the embassy, that he wasted time while the city's opportunities for great, far-reaching action were thrown away, and that together with Philocrates[16] he took gifts and payments in return for all these services, then convict him and impose a penalty that fits the crimes. If I do not demonstrate these claims, or do not demonstrate all of them, consider me a scoundrel and acquit him.

[9] Although I have many other serious charges besides these, Athenians, that would give anyone good reason to despise him, before proceeding to my main arguments, I wish to remind you, though most of you surely need no reminder, what political position Aeschines first espoused and what public statements against Philip he thought he needed to utter. You will see that his own actions and public speeches at the beginning of his career furnish proof that he is corrupt. [10] Well, then, he is the first Athenian to have noticed—as he told the Assembly at the time[17]—that Philip had designs on Greece and was bribing some of the leading men of Arcadia. Along with Ischander, the number two actor in Neoptolemus' troupe,[18] Aeschines came before the Council and before the Assembly to discuss the matter, and he persuaded you to send envoys in every direction to gather the Greeks in Athens to plan war against Philip. [11] Upon his return from Arcadia, he recounted the long, wonderful speeches that he said he delivered before the Ten Thousand in Megalopolis, defending you against Philip's representative Hieronymus,[19] and he explained how much harm

---

[16] Philocrates was the main negotiator of the peace agreement with Philip reached in 346 (known as the Peace of Philocrates), which ended badly for Athens. Philocrates was charged by Hyperides with treason (*eisangelia*) earlier in 343 and fled into exile rather than stand trial. See further the Introduction to 19, 19.14n.

[17] Shortly after the crisis over Olynthus in 349–348. "First" is ironic: Philip's designs were by that time obvious and a concern to many, not least to Demosthenes himself.

[18] Ischander was from Arcadia but is otherwise obscure (19.303). Neoptolemus of Scyros, a well-known tragic actor, was successful in Athens, entertained at Philip's court, and advised Athens to conclude peace with Philip.

[19] Megalopolis was the chief city of Arcadia and the seat of the Ten Thousand, the Assembly of the Arcadian confederacy. The address by Aeschines took place in 347. Hieronymus is included in the blacklist of Greek traitors in 18.295.

Philip's bribed and paid agents were inflicting not just on their own states but on Greece as a whole.

[12] He adopted that policy and gave that sample of himself when Aristodemus, Neoptolemus, Ctesiphon, and others, whose information from Macedon was completely worthless, persuaded you to dispatch envoys to negotiate peace with Philip.[20] Aeschines, in fact, was one of those chosen for this embassy,[21] though not because it was thought that he would betray your interests, nor that he trusted Philip, but as one who would keep watch over the other envoys. Because of his earlier speeches and his evident hatred of Philip, you all naturally had that opinion of him. [13] After this he approached me and tried to interest me in working together on the embassy, imploring me to join him in keeping watch over that vile scoundrel Philocrates. And until we returned here from the First Embassy, Athenians, I, at any rate, had no idea that he was corrupt and had sold his services. For apart from the speeches that, as I mentioned, he had previously delivered, in the first of the Assemblies devoted to the peace treaty[22] he rose and began with a statement that I believe I can reproduce in the very words he addressed to you. [14] He said: "Athenians, if Philocrates spent much time considering how he could best hinder peace, I do not believe that he could do better than to put forward the proposal before us now.[23] But so long as a single Athenian is left, I would never advise the city to accept peace on these terms, though I do say that peace must be made." That was the kind of speech he delivered, brief and sensible. [15] That is what all of you heard him say in the earlier Assembly. Yet in the later one, when the terms of the peace treaty had

---

[20] These were the efforts of late 347 through early 346 to open negotiations between Philip and Athens. Aristodemus of Metapontus was one of the great tragic actors of his day and was instrumental in bringing the parties together. On Neoptolemus, see 19.10n. The Ctesiphon mentioned here is most likely not the one who moved the honorary decree for Demosthenes in 336.

[21] The First Embassy. Demosthenes and Philocrates were also members of this embassy, which consisted of ten citizens altogether.

[22] On 18 Elaphebolion in the spring of 346. A second Assembly devoted to the same topic took place the next day. See 19.57n.

[23] Philocrates was the chief sponsor of the agreement that had been negotiated with Philip and moved the decree that formally proposed it for adoption by the Athenians; hence it became known as the Peace of Philocrates.

to be approved, while I was supporting the decree passed by our allies[24] and working to ensure that the peace would be fair and equitable, while you also took that view and were unwilling to hear even a word from the despicable Philocrates, Aeschines rose, addressed the Assembly, and supported him with a speech that, O Zeus and all the gods, merits death many times over. [16] He said you should not recall your ancestors or put up with talk of trophies and sea battles[25] but should enact and inscribe a law forbidding you from aiding any Greeks who had not previously aided you. And this shameless wretch uttered those words while the envoys from all over Greece, whom you had summoned at his insistence before he sold himself, were standing right there and listening.

[17] Hear now, Athenians, how Aeschines frittered away the time and absolutely ruined the city's interests after you elected him again to the embassy to secure the oaths,[26] and how much he hated me for trying to stop him. We returned from that embassy—the one to secure the oaths, which is the subject of today's accounting—utterly deceived without even a shred, large or small, of what was promised and predicted when you adopted the peace treaty; for these men[27] simply went their separate way and conducted the embassy contrary to the decree. So we came before the Council. Many people are aware of what I am about to say since the Council chamber was full of regular citizens.[28] [18] I came forward and gave the Council a full and truthful report; I lodged charges against these men, and beginning from the

---

[24] Athens' allies were the members of the Second Athenian Confederacy. They wanted the Athenians to delay their decision on peace until representatives from the rest of Greece reported their positions to the Athenians (Aes. 2.60). Aes. 3.69–70 recalls further details of this decree.

[25] "Sea battles" suggests in particular Athens' greatest victory, that over the Persian fleet at Salamis in 480. See 18.203–210 for a fine example of recalling ancestors and victories.

[26] The Second Embassy, which left Athens in spring 346 to secure from Philip the oaths that would ratify the treaty which the Athenians had just voted to accept.

[27] Here and throughout the speech, Demosthenes uses the phrase "these men" to refer to Aeschines and his unnamed cronies. "This man" normally refers to Aeschines.

[28] Aside from the citizens serving as members of the Council, many citizens who were not on the Council attended that session just to listen.

first hopes that were raised when Ctesiphon and Aristodemus delivered their report[29] and later when you adopted the peace treaty, I recounted Aeschines' statements to the Assembly and the predicament into which these men brought the city. I also advised the Council not to neglect the remaining issues (namely, the Phocians and Thermopylae),[30] not to make the same mistakes as before, and not to let affairs reach a desperate state by clinging to one hope and promise after another. The Council was persuaded.

[19] When the day of the Assembly arrived and it was time to address you, Aeschines here was the first of all of us to rise to speak—and by Zeus and the other gods, try to recall along with me whether my account is accurate, for this, now, is the main thing that thoroughly sabotaged and wrecked your interests. As for reporting what happened on the embassy or if he chose, as he might have, to dispute the truth of my statement to the Council, Aeschines refrained from even broaching these points, but he delivered so impressive a speech, promising so many huge advantages, that when he finished, he had all of you in his pocket. [20] He announced that he had returned after persuading Philip to agree to everything that was in the city's interests regarding both the Delphic Amphictyony[31] and everything else; he recounted a long speech, including a summary of the high points, that he said he delivered to Philip in denunciation of Thebes;[32] and on the basis of what he had accomplished on the embassy, he calculated that within two or three days, without your stirring from home, going on campaign, or suffering any inconvenience, you would hear that the Thebans were abandoned, under siege, and cut off from the rest of Boeotia, [21] that Thespiae and Plataea were being resettled,[33] and that it

---

[29] See 19.12.

[30] I.e., defending Phocis against Thebes and maintaining control of Thermopylae as a defense against Philip.

[31] On the Delphic Amphictyony, see 18.143n.

[32] At this time Thebes was Athens' greatest rival in central Greece and viewed by the Athenians with great suspicion.

[33] These two Boeotian cities were frequently opposed to Thebes and allied with Athens. Thebes seized them in 373 during the period of Theban ascendancy. During the Third Sacred War it was in Athens' interests to see these cities resettled and independent of Thebes.

was not the Phocians but the Thebans who were being forced to restore Apollo's wealth, since they had planned to seize the temple. He
claimed that he instructed Philip that those who planned the deed
sinned against the god no less than those who carried it out with their
own hands, and as a result, the Thebans had put a price on his head![34]
[22] He added that some Euboeans,[35] upset and fearful about the
friendship that had arisen between Philip and Athens, made the following statement: "Athenian envoys, we are well aware of the terms on
which you and Philip have reached an agreement for peace, and we
know that you have given him Amphipolis and that Philip agreed to
hand Euboea over to you."[36] And then there was still another matter
Aeschines was working on, though he did not want to speak about it
yet since some of his fellow envoys already resented him. That was a
veiled reference to Oropus.[37]

[23] Basking in the glory of these achievements, as one might expect, and giving the impression that he was both an excellent speaker
and a remarkable man, he stepped down deeply satisfied. I stood up,
denied that I knew anything about these matters, and made an effort
to repeat the information that I had presented to the Council. At that
point Aeschines and Philocrates stood up to face me, one on this side,
one on the other: they screamed, they booed, finally they jeered at me.
You citizens laughed and would neither listen nor believe anything except what Aeschines reported. [24] Yet by the gods, your reaction seems
to me quite natural. For once you expected that things would improve
so drastically, who could have tolerated a citizen who either denied
that these improvements would materialize or criticized what these
men accomplished? Everything then took second place to the hopes
and expectations at hand. Those who insisted otherwise appeared to

---

[34] The deed in question is the Phocians' seizure of Apollo's temple and trea-
sury in Delphi in 355, which instigated the Third Sacred War. The notion that the
Thebans put a price on Aeschines' head as a result of his turning Philip from
Thebes to Athens is treated by Demosthenes as a joke (so too 19.35, 127).

[35] Supporters of Philip, including Cleochares of Chalcis.

[36] This statement is meant to strike the audience as wishful thinking so gran-
diose as to be absurd.

[37] Oropus, a town on the border of Attica and Boeotia and long in dispute between them, was seized in 366 by Thebes.

be no more than a spiteful nuisance, while it seemed that the city had reaped utterly wonderful and useful benefits.

[25] Why have I spoken to you about this matter first, and why have I recounted these speeches? The first and most important reason, Athenians, is this: if anyone should find my account of what these men did astounding or exaggerated, he should not wonder, "And in that case, Demosthenes, you didn't immediately mention these matters and explain them to us?" [26] Merely recall the promises that these men uttered at every opportunity, as they kept others from saying a word, and recall too those wonderful assurances Aeschines gave you, and you will realize that beyond everything else, he also harmed you by holding out hopes and making misrepresentations and promises that prevented you from hearing the truth immediately, when you needed it. [27] That is the first and, as I said, most important reason why I recounted those speeches. What is the second reason, which is no less important than the first? So that you will recall that before he was corrupt his policy was circumspect and distrustful of Philip, and will ponder the trusting friendship[38] that suddenly developed afterwards. [28] If all the information he conveyed to you turned out to be accurate, and the result was successful, then you may suppose that friendship to have been formed honestly and for the sake of the city. But if the result has been the exact opposite of what he predicted and still causes the city much shame and great danger, then you should realize that he changed his policy because of his own avarice and because he sold the truth for money.

[29] Since these speeches have come up, I would like, first of all, to explain how it happened that they[39] took control of your policy towards the Phocians. None of you, jurors, should look at the magnitude of these events and regard this man's standing as too small to account for the accusations and charges at hand; rather, consider that any citizen whom you placed in this post[40] and put in charge of whatever situation might arise could have caused as much trouble as did this man, if, like him, that person chose to hire himself out and to de-

---

[38] Uttered with irony.

[39] Aeschines and Philip.

[40] As one of the ten envoys on the Second Embassy.

ceive and cheat you. [30] Just because you often assign public business to useless citizens does not mean that the endeavors for which the city is judged in the eyes of the world are likewise of no account; no, far from it. And then it was, indeed, Philip who destroyed the Phocians, and these men helped him. Yet the point to examine and consider is whether these men intentionally subverted and ruined everything that the embassy could have done to save the Phocians, not whether Aeschines destroyed the Phocians by himself. How could he have done so?

[31] Clerk, please hand over the preliminary decree passed by the Council in response to my report, and also the testimony of the citizen who moved it, so that you citizens will know that I was not silent then and only now disclaim responsibility, but I made my accusations straightaway and foresaw what was to come. Because the Council was not prevented from hearing the truth from me, it refrained from praising these men and refused to invite them to the Prytaneum.[41] Yet, as everyone knows, that never happened to any other envoys for as long as the city has existed, not even to Timagoras, whom the people condemned to death.[42] But it happened to these men. [32] Clerk, read them the testimony first, then the preliminary decree.

[TESTIMONY, PRELIMINARY DECREE]

In the decree the Council did not praise the envoys or invite them to dine in the Prytaneum. If this man says otherwise, let him show where and provide proof, and I will step down. But he cannot. Now, if all of us conducted ourselves during the embassy in the same way, the Council was right to praise no one; everyone acted terribly. But if some of us acted rightly and others wrongly, it would seem that the good envoys share in the disgrace caused by those whose conduct was wicked. [33] How then can all of you easily figure out who is the wicked one? Recall for yourselves who denounced the affair from the first. Clearly the wrongdoer was best served by keeping quiet and, af-

---

[41] The Council often passed a decree praising envoys for service well done, and usually included the honor of being invited to dine in the Prytaneum, the central administrative building in Athens which held a public dining hall.

[42] Timagoras betrayed Athens while serving in 367 as envoy to the Persian King Artaxerxes (see 19.137).

ter evading the question for the present, by never having to answer for what happened. But the citizen with a clear conscience considered it terrible if his silence should create the impression that he had a part in the disastrous, wicked deeds. I, indeed, am the one who accused them from the first, but none of them accused me.

[34] Thus the Council passed this preliminary decree, but when the Assembly met, Philip was already at Thermopylae—that was the first of all the crimes they committed, namely, putting Philip in charge of the matter,[43] and though you should have first heard about the matter, then deliberated, and only then made a decision about what to do, in fact, you heard about the scheme at the same time that Philip reached Thermopylae, and it was no longer easy to decide what should be done. [35] Beyond that problem, no one read the preliminary decree to the people, and the people never heard it, but this man rose and made the speech that I recounted to you just now[44] about the many great advantages he claimed to be bringing back to Athens after persuading Philip to accept them, and that for that reason, the Thebans had put a price on his head.[45] As a result, although you were shocked at first by Philip's arrival at Thermopylae and enraged at these men for failing to inform you in advance, after you were led to believe you would get everything you wished for, you became as mild as can be and would not give me or anyone else a chance to speak. [36] After that, the letter from Philip was read, which this man composed[46] without our knowing it, as a direct, explicit, written defense of the crimes of these men. The letter said that he—Philip—prevented them against their will from traveling to the cities and receiving the oaths and that he detained them in order to have their help in reconciling the Halians and the Pharsalians.[47] Thus he takes everything upon himself and makes their crimes his own. [37] As for the Phocians and the Thespians and the rest of what Aeschines told you, not one little word. It

---

[43] I.e., settling the Third Sacred War, which was the occasion of Philip's entry into central Greece in 346.

[44] 19.20–22.

[45] See 19.21n.

[46] Aeschines denies he wrote the letter (2.124–127).

[47] Halus and Pharsalus were cities in Thessaly, the former allied with Athens, the latter with Philip. The cities to which the Athenian envoys wanted to travel were Philip's allies; their oaths would ratify their participation in the peace agreement.

didn't happen that way by chance. Rather, although you ought to have punished these men for failing to accomplish and carry out what you officially instructed them to do, Philip accepts the blame and says that he bears sole responsibility, and I don't think you will be able to punish him. [38] And as for matters in which Philip sought to deceive and overtake the city, this man's report insured that later you would be unable to accuse or blame Philip for any of them, since they were not contained in a letter or in any other communication from him. Clerk, read them the letter this man wrote and Philip sent, and the rest of you consider whether it is written in the manner that I explained. Read.

[LETTER]

[39] You hear, Athenians, how fine and compassionate the letter is. About the Phocians, the Thespians, or the other matters this man reported, not a word. There's not one decent thing in it, as you will at once see for yourselves. Philip says that he detained these men to have their help in reaching a settlement with the Halians[48]—the settlement they reached meant that they were driven out, and their city was destroyed! And the man[49] who wondered what he could do to earn your gratitude says that he didn't even consider releasing our prisoners of war! [40] You have often heard in the Assembly that I brought a talent with me to recover the prisoners,[50] and you will hear it again now. Yet this man tried to deprive me of this public-spirited act by persuading Philip to include that sentence in his letter.[51] This is the most important point of all. In the first letter that we brought back[52] Philip wrote, "I would have informed you explicitly and in writing how I intend to benefit you if I was sure that an alliance would be concluded as well."[53] Yet when the alliance was concluded, he says he doesn't

---

[48] See 19.36.

[49] Philip, in the letter.

[50] A talent was a significant sum. Demosthenes brought the money with him on the Second Embassy to ransom the Athenians whom Philip captured during the conquest of Olynthus in 348; see 19.166–172.

[51] To the effect that Philip did not even consider releasing the Athenian prisoners of war.

[52] From the First Embassy.

[53] In addition to a peace treaty, Philip sought, and attained, a mutual defense alliance with Athens.

know what he could do to earn your gratitude or even what he himself promised! Clearly he knew that, unless he was cheating all along. To show that he wrote these words with that intention, clerk, please take just this part of the first letter and read it from here. Read.

[EXCERPT FROM THE LETTER]

[41] So, before an agreement about peace was reached, Philip admits that so long as he secures the alliance too, he will let you know in writing how he intends to benefit the city. But when he achieved both of these, he says he doesn't know what he could do to earn your gratitude, though if you let him know, he says he will do anything so long as it brings no disgrace or dishonor. With this pretext as his cover, he has left himself a way out if, in fact, you do let him know and are moved to demand a favor.

[42] Now, these and many other claims could have been exposed right then on the spot; you could have been informed and prevented from surrendering your interests, if "Thespiae" and "Plataea" and the claim that "Thebes was about to be punished" did not suppress the truth.[54] Yet if the intent was for the city to hear these promises and be deceived, it was right to utter them. But if the intent was actually to fulfill them, then it was better to keep silent. For if events had already reached the point where the Thebans could no longer gain any advantage if they learned of the plan, why did it not succeed? But if the plan was thwarted because the Thebans learned of it, who is the blabbermouth? Is it not this man? [43] But no—these promises were not supposed to be fulfilled, and Aeschines neither wanted them nor expected them to be, so blabbermouth is one charge he needn't face. But you citizens were supposed to be tricked by these promises, to refuse to hear the truth from me, and to remain in Attica,[55] and a decree was supposed to be voted that would lead to the destruction of Phocis. That was the reason for concocting this plan, and that was the reason for announcing it in the Assembly.

[44] I heard Aeschines make these extravagant promises, and I knew for certain that he was lying—but let me tell you how I knew: first, when Philip was about to swear his oath to ratify the peace treaty, these

---

[54] The quotations are Aeschines' promises as reported in 19.20–21.
[55] So that Philip could take Thermopylae unopposed.

men blurted out that the Phocians were excluded from it, though if the Phocians were going to be saved, the sensible thing was to pass over that point in silence; second, the promises were communicated not by Philip's envoys or in his letter but by this man. [45] So, judging from this evidence, I rose to speak and tried to counter him, but when you refused to listen, I kept quiet, though I solemnly insisted on one point—and by Zeus and the gods, remember it—that I had no knowledge of the promises and no part in them, and, I added, no confidence in them either. When you reacted angrily to that lack of confidence, I said, "If any of these promises, Athenians, is realized, see that you praise these men, honor them, and bestow crowns on them, not on me. But should things turn out differently, see that you turn your wrath on them. I have done with it." [46] "Do not," Aeschines said, interrupting, "do not have done with it now. Just see that you don't take credit later." "Of course, by Zeus, otherwise I would be wrong," I said. Then Philocrates rose and, full of disdain, said, "No wonder, Athenians, if Demosthenes and I do not think alike: he drinks water, I drink wine."[56] And you all laughed.

[47] Consider the decree that Philocrates then wrote up and handed in;[57] it makes truly wonderful listening. But if one takes into account the moment at which it was composed and the promises that this man made at the time, it will be clear that they did no less than deliver up the Phocians—with their hands all but tied behind their backs—to Philip and Thebes. Clerk, read the decree.

[DECREE]

[48] You see, Athenians, that the decree contains so much praise and fine language, as when it says, "The same peace treaty that Philip enjoys shall be extended to his descendants too, and likewise the treaty of alliance," and "Philip is to be praised because he promises to do the right thing." But in fact, he promised nothing and was so far from

---

[56] This memorable statement attributed to Philocrates is probably genuine (see Dem. 6.30). Though it is meant to characterize Demosthenes as an inept, antisocial weakling, Demosthenes does not view it as particularly stinging, otherwise he would not repeat it.

[57] To be entered into the record so as to receive official consideration by the Assembly.

promising anything that he denies even knowing what he could do to earn your gratitude. [49] Rather, this man was the one who spoke and made promises on his behalf, and when Philocrates noticed that you were swept away by his words, he put the following clause in his decree: "If the Phocians do not fulfill their obligations and hand the temple over to the Amphictyons, the Athenian people will intervene against those who are preventing the transfer from taking place." [50] Since you stayed home, Athenians, and did not march out, and since the Spartans saw through the deception early on and marched home, and since none of the other Amphictyons were there[58] except Thessalians and Thebans, it was to them that Philocrates' decree, in the finest language on earth, handed over the temple, even though in the decree he said that the temple was to be handed over to the Amphictyons—to which Amphictyons? The only ones there were Thebans and Thessalians! Philocrates did not propose "to convene the Amphictyons," or "to wait until they assembled," or "that Proxenus[59] should intervene on the side of the Phocians," or "that the Athenians should march out," or anything of the sort. [51] Indeed, Philip sent two letters that summoned you forth,[60] but not with the purpose that you should take the field—far from it! For he would not summon you when he had wasted all the time when you could have gone out on campaign,[61] nor would he have detained me when I wanted to sail back home,[62] nor would he have instructed this man to say the sort of thing that made you least disposed to go out on campaign. Rather, his intent was, if you thought that he would do what you wished, that you should not vote to oppose him and that the Phocians, who placed their hopes in

---

[58] In Delphi at the sanctuary of Apollo.

[59] The most important Athenian general at the time; he was abroad with forces at his disposal.

[60] In these letters, which would have reached Athens soon after the Athenians ratified the treaty, Philip asked his new allies to contribute troops to the force that was to settle the Third Sacred War.

[61] By delaying the ratification of the treaty and keeping secret his intentions of moving into central Greece.

[62] When the Second Embassy was nearing completion of its business in Pella, Demosthenes wished to return to Athens, as he claims, to warn of Philip's plans and organize military opposition.

you, should give up their defense and resistance and, in utter despair, hand themselves over. Clerk, read them the actual letters from Philip.

[LETTERS]

[52] These are the letters that summoned you, and, by Zeus, right away! Yet if there was anything in these letters that could be trusted, should these men have done anything other than advise you to take the field and move that Proxenus, who they knew was in the area,[63] immediately give assistance? Clearly what they did was the exact opposite, naturally. For they focused not on Philip's explicit instructions but on what they knew he intended when he wrote the letters: that was the project they were aiding, that was the goal they were working towards. [53] Now, when the Phocians learned what transpired in the Assembly, when they received Philocrates' decree, when they learned what the envoys reported and what this man promised, their destruction was assured. Consider. Some of the Phocians were astute and distrusted Philip. They were induced to trust him. Why? Because they supposed that even if Philip misled them ten times over, Athenian envoys would never dare to mislead the Athenian people; therefore, what this man reported to you must be true, and it was the Thebans, not themselves, who were about to be destroyed. [54] Others in Phocis thought that they should endure anything whatsoever in the cause of defense. But even they proved pliable when it was claimed that Philip had been persuaded to back the Phocians and that unless they went along, you, whom they expected to be their allies, would move against them. Yet others in Phocis believed that you regretted having made peace with Philip. When it was pointed out to this group that you voted to extend the peace to Philip's descendants too, they despaired of you completely. That is why these men packed all these provisions into one decree.

[55] Yet the most serious wrong these men did to you seems to me to be this: by proposing immortal peace with a mortal man whose power depended on fortuitous circumstance, they mired the city in immortal shame; they deprived the city of many benefits, including those that fortune may have bestowed; and they enlarged their wicked-

---

[63] In Oreus in Euboea.

ness to the point that they wronged not only the Athenians alive to-day but all those who shall ever exist—isn't this absolutely terrible? [56] Surely you would never have agreed to tack on to the peace treaty the clause that it "shall be extended to Philip's descendants too"[64] unless you trusted the promises uttered by Aeschines, the very promises that destroyed the Phocians when they trusted them. For when the Phocians put themselves in Philip's power and voluntarily handed their cities over to him, they suffered the complete opposite of what this man reported to you.

[57] In order that you understand that their destruction occurred as I have described it and was caused by these men, I will go over the dates on which each event took place. Should any of these men dispute the dates, let him rise and speak during the time allotted to me.[65] The peace treaty was approved on the nineteenth of Elaphebolion, and the embassy to secure the oaths was abroad for three whole months.[66] During that entire time, the Phocians were unharmed. [58] The embassy to secure the oaths returned to Athens on the thirteenth of Skirophorion.[67] Philip was at Thermopylae by then, making overtures to the Phocians, all of which they rejected. The evidence is that otherwise they would not have approached you here in Athens. The next Assembly, the one in which the lies and deceit of these men ruined everything, took place on the sixteenth of Skirophorion.[68] [59] I estimate that news of your decision reached the Phocians four days later, for the Phocian envoys present in Athens were greatly concerned to know what these men reported and what you decided. So we can assume that the Phocians learned of your policy on the twentieth, since that is the fourth day after the sixteenth. Then there fol-

---

[64] See 19.48 for this clause.

[65] A purely rhetorical gesture. The time was measured by a water-clock.

[66] This is the Second Embassy. The oaths were to be sworn by Philip and his allies to ratify the treaty on their part. The Athenians swore their oaths of ratification on the twenty-fifth of Elaphebolion, and the envoys departed Athens shortly thereafter. Elaphebolion is the ninth month of the Athenian calendar, falling in March/April.

[67] Skirophorion is the twelfth month of the Athenian calendar, falling in June/July.

[68] This is the Assembly described in 19.19–50.

lowed the twenty-first, the twenty-second, the twenty-third; on that day the truce was made,[69] whereby everything in Phocis was lost and done for. [60] How is this date established? On the twenty-seventh the Assembly met in Piraeus to discuss the dockyards when Dercylus[70] returned from Chalcis with the news that Philip had handed everything over to the Thebans, and he reckoned that the truce had been made four days earlier. From the twenty-third, there follows the twenty-fourth, twenty-fifth, twenty-sixth, twenty-seventh—this is obviously the fourth day later. So, the dates, the reports to the Assembly, the proposals, everything proves that these men aided Philip and collaborated in the destruction of Phocis. [61] None of the Phocian cities was taken by siege or captured by force, but all were utterly lost because they accepted the truce. This is the best evidence that they met this fate because these men persuaded them that Philip would keep them safe. For the Phocians certainly had no illusions about Philip! Clerk, please bring forward both our treaty of alliance with the Phocians and the Amphictyonic decrees that authorized the dismantling of the Phocians' fortifications. From these you will understand what the Phocians expected from you and what they suffered because of these godless men. Read.

[ALLIANCE BETWEEN PHOCIANS AND ATHENIANS]

[62] What the Phocians expected from you is this: friendship, alliance, military support. What they suffered because this man prevented you from aiding them—hear. Clerk, read.

[AGREEMENT BETWEEN PHILIP AND PHOCIANS]

You hear it, Athenians. It says, "Agreement between Philip and Phocians," not Thebans and Phocians, or Thessalians and Phocians, or Locrians or anyone else who was there. In another place it says, "To hand the Phocian cities over to Philip," not to the Thebans, not to the Thessalians, and not to anyone else. [63] Why? Because Philip assured you, through this man, that he entered central Greece to ensure the

---

[69] Between Philip and the Phocians.

[70] An Athenian citizen and a member of both the Second and the Third Embassy; on the latter, see 19.121n. Dercylus left the Third Embassy to bring this news to Athens.

security of the Phocians. They trusted this man completely, looked to him for everything, made peace because of him. Clerk, read the rest of the documents. Consider where the Phocians put their trust and what they suffered. Did it turn out to be what this man promised or anything close to it? Read.

[AMPHICTYONIC DECREES]

[64] Nothing worse, Athenians, nothing greater than this has ever happened in Greece during my lifetime, or, I believe, at any previous time. Yet these men are responsible for one man having the power to bring about so huge a disaster, despite the presence of the city of Athens, which by ancestral tradition is the leader of Greece and does not allow such things to happen. The manner in which the wretched Phocians perished is evident not only from these decrees [65] but also from the deeds that were committed, a terrible and piteous sight, Athenians. When we recently made our way to Delphi, we could not help but see everything—houses razed, fortifications demolished, countryside empty of adult men, a handful of women and children, miserable old people. No one could find words to describe the troubles they now have. And still I hear all of you talk about the vote they once cast against the Thebans, when the question of enslaving us was put to the question.[71] [66] How would your forebears vote, Athenians, if they could see again, how would they judge those who are responsible for destroying this city? Even if they stoned these men with their own hands, they would not, I expect, consider themselves defiled.[72] How is it not disgraceful—or worse than disgraceful, if that's possible—that those who saved us then and cast the saving vote in our favor should, because of these men, meet the opposite fate and be allowed

---

[71] In the negotiations on Athens' terms of surrender in the Peloponnesian War (403), the Thebans and Corinthians sought to impose the harsh punishment mentioned here, which the Athenians averted. Demosthenes does not mention that beyond the Phocians, who had their own reasons to be wary of Thebes unchecked by Athens, it was the Spartan opposition to Thebes and Corinth that was decisive (see Xen., *Hellenica* 2.2.19–20).

[72] I.e., the victims of the stoning imagined here, those who destroyed the Phocians, are so sinful that they are incapable of bringing blood-guilt, which would require expiation, on those who did the stoning.

to suffer what no other Greeks have done? Who is responsible? Who used trickery to bring this about? Is it not this man?

[67] There are many good reasons, Athenians, to consider Philip a fortunate man, but there is one reason above all, and by the gods and goddesses, I can name no one else in my lifetime who has been fortunate in the same way. To conquer great cities, to acquire vast territory and all such things are, I suppose, enviable and glorious achievements—how could they not be?—but one could name many others who have done the same. [68] But this bit of luck belongs just to him and to absolutely no one else. What is it? When his affairs compelled him to seek out corrupt men, he found men more corrupt than he wanted. Is not that the right way to view these men? When Philip had so much at stake and nevertheless hesitated to lie on his own behalf, either in the letters he wrote or when any of his envoys spoke for him, it was these men who hired themselves out and deceived you. [69] Even Antipater and Parmenion, though they were serving a master and would not have to face you afterwards,[73] found a way to avoid being the agents of your deception. But these men were Athenians, from the freest city of all, and official envoys; yet they undertook to deceive you, though they had to look upon you in daily encounters, had to live among you for the rest of their lives, and had to undergo an audit of their deeds in office before you. How could there be more cowardly or shameless men than these?

[70] So that you realize that Aeschines has actually fallen under your curse and that sanctity and piety forbid you to acquit him once he has uttered such lies, let the clerk take up the curse that is prescribed by law and recite it.

[CURSE]

This is the prayer, ordained by law, which the herald utters on your behalf at every Assembly and in the Council too whenever it meets.[74] Now, this man cannot say that he did not know about it: when he was

---

[73] Antipater and Parmenion were Philip's two most important generals. They would not, of course, have to submit to an audit in a court in Athens.

[74] The curse aimed to protect the Athenians from traitors in their midst; it is known from various sources. See Rhodes 1972: 36–37.

a petty clerk and served the Council in that capacity, he himself dictated it to the herald.[75] [71] How then would it not be a bizarre, monstrous act on your part if what you command, or rather, expect the gods to do on your behalf, you yourselves fail to do today when it lies within your power, and if you yourselves set free the very man whom you entreat the gods to obliterate along with his family and household? Do not do it! Should anyone escape your notice, leave it to the gods to punish him. But should someone fall into your hands, do not give the gods any more commands in regard to him.

[72] I hear that Aeschines will be so brazen and shameless that he will disown everything he did, the reports he gave, the promises he made, the tricks he used against the city, as if the trial were being conducted before anybody but you who know all the facts, and that he will then shift the blame to the Spartans, to the Phocians, and to Hegesippus.[76] But that's laughable, or rather utterly shameless. [73] For whatever Aeschines is going to say about the Phocians, the Spartans, or Hegesippus—that the Phocians spurned Proxenus, that they are an impious people,[77] that—whatever in the world he may accuse them of, it all happened before these envoys returned to Athens, and it did not stand in the way of safeguarding Phocis. Who says this? [74] Aeschines, this man right here. For it was not "if only for the Spartans," or "if only Proxenus hadn't been spurned," or "if only for Hegesippus," or "if only for this or that" the Phocians would have been saved—that is not what Aeschines reported at the time. Rather, he omitted all these matters and explicitly said that he returned to Athens after persuading Philip to safeguard the Phocians, to resettle Boeotia,[78] and to arrange

---

[75] See 19.249 on Aeschines' service as secretary.

[76] One of the leading anti-Macedonian politicians and probable author of speech 7 in the Demosthenic corpus, Hegesippus is not mentioned in Aes. 2.

[77] Aes. 2.133–134 pleads that the Phocians refused to hand over certain strongholds to the Athenian general Proxenus (see 19.50n) as promised in negotiations in 347, that the Phocians refused to recognize the customary truce allowing free passage to the Eleusinian Mysteries, and that the Spartans too refused to take over positions near Thermopylae.

[78] Demosthenes discussed these deceptive promises earlier (19.19–22). On resettling Boeotia, see 19.21n.

affairs in your interests, that these things would take place in two or three days, and that on account of these achievements, the Thebans put a price on his head.

[75] But do not let him go on about what the Spartans or the Phocians did before he gave his report. Do not listen to it, and do not let him denounce the Phocians for being wicked. When you saved the Spartans that time, it was not because they were virtuous, and likewise those damned Euboeans and many others too, but because it was in the city's interests for them to remain safe, as is indeed the case with the Phocians now.[79] After this man delivered his report, did the Phocians, the Spartans, you, or anyone else commit some offense that prevented his promises from being realized? Ask him that, because he'll have nothing to say. [76] Only five days passed during which Aeschines reported false information; you trusted him; the Phocians heard about it, surrendered, perished. This makes it crystal clear that every kind of deceit and cunning was utilized to destroy the Phocians. So long as Philip could not move into central Greece because the negotiations for peace were going on but was making preparations, he would take the Spartans aside and promise to arrange matters in their interests. In this way he sought to prevent them from going over to the Phocians with your assistance. [77] But when he reached Thermopylae and the Spartans, having discovered the plot, withdrew, he then commissioned this man to deceive you: he hoped that if you failed to perceive that he was supporting Thebes, he could avoid the further delays, combat, and waste of time that would arise from a Phocian defense mounted with your assistance. He could then put everything under his control without a struggle, which is what happened. So just because Philip deceived both Spartans and Phocians, do not on that account fail to punish this man for the deceptions he worked on you. That would not be right.

[78] If Aeschines asserts that in return for the loss of Phocis, Ther-

---

[79] Following their victory over Sparta at Leuctra in 371, Thebes invaded Laconia in 370, and the Athenians sent a force to aid the Spartans. In 357 the Athenians mounted an expedition to save Euboea from Theban domination. Elsewhere Demosthenes presents these expeditions as examples not of defending Athenian interests but of noble generosity (18.98–100).

mopylae, and the rest, the city retained the Chersonese,[80] by Zeus and the gods, do not accept it, jurors, and do not, on top of the wrongs you suffered from the embassy, allow him to bring disgrace on the city in his defense speech too, claiming that you sacrificed your allies' safety to retrieve one of your private possessions. That is not what you did, but the peace was already in effect, and the Chersonese had been secured for four whole months while the Phocians were unharmed. It was afterwards that this man told the lies that deceived you and destroyed them. [79] Besides, you will find that the Chersonese is more precarious now than it was then. Would it have been easier to punish Philip for attacking the Chersonese before he seized these places,[81] or now? In my view, much easier before. So what does retaining the Chersonese amount to if the man who would like to capture it is now spared the fears and dangers that he faced earlier?

[80] I also hear that Aeschines will profess astonishment that it is Demosthenes and not some Phocian who is accusing him.[82] Better to hear the true story from me first. Of the Phocians who were driven from their country, I think the best and most respectable ones now live as exiles, and they have suffered so much that they keep a low profile. None of them would wish to arouse enmity against himself personally because of the disaster that struck them all. And though other Phocians would do anything for money, there is no one to give it to them. [81] For I would certainly never give anyone anything to stand beside me here and shout out what they suffered: the truth and the facts themselves shout loud enough. Nonetheless, the Phocian people are so wretched and despondent that rather than worry about accusing individual citizens at their audits in Athens, they are busy being enslaved and dying in terror at the hands of the Thebans and Philip's soldiers, whom they are forced to feed, though they themselves have been dispersed into villages and had their arms confiscated. [82] So don't let him take up this line of argument, but make him show that the Phocians were not destroyed or that he did not promise that Philip would protect them. For the point of auditing an envoy is this: what was ac-

---

[80] The Chersonese, modern Gallipoli, was crucial for Athenian interests because of the grain supply from the Black Sea and fell within Athens' sphere of influence since the fifth century.

[81] Phocis and Thermopylae.

[82] Aes. 2.142–143 introduces Phocian testimony to support his case.

complished? what did you report? If your report was true, you are safe; if it was false, pay the penalty. If the Phocians are not in court, what does that matter? As I see it, you did your utmost to render them incapable of helping their friends or repulsing their enemies.

[83] Beyond the shame and disgrace attached to these actions, it is a simple matter to show that the same actions have plunged the city into the midst of great danger. Are any of you unaware that the Phocians' war and their control of Thermopylae gave us protection against Thebes and made it impossible for Philip to invade the Peloponnese, Euboea, or Attica?[83] [84] However, although the city enjoyed this security because of its geographical position and the prevailing state of affairs, you gave it up, influenced by the lies and deceptions of these men; and though that security was fortified by armed forces, an unremitting war, large cities containing allied troops,[84] and considerable territory, you allowed it to disappear. So the earlier expedition to Thermopylae[85] was in vain, though it cost you more than two hundred talents if you include the participants' personal expenses, and your hopes with regard to the Thebans[86] have proved vain too. [85] But although Aeschines did many appalling things for Philip, hear what is truly his most egregious act of insolence towards the city and all of you: Philip decided at the outset to make Thebes the beneficiary of everything he did; however, by reporting the opposite and exposing your unwillingness to accept it, this man sharpened both your hatred of the Thebans and Philip's friendship with them. How could anyone have used you with greater insolence?[87]

[86] Clerk, take the decree of Diophantus and the decree of Callis-

---

[83] During the Third Sacred War (355–346) Thebes fought at the head of the Delphic Amphictyony against Phocis and was thus unable to direct resources against Athens. By controlling Thermopylae, the main route from the north into central and southern Greece, Phocis made it difficult for Philip to move beyond that point.

[84] The cities containing allied troops were in Phocis. "Unremitting war" is the Third Sacred War.

[85] In 352, the Athenians mobilized quickly in aid of the Phocians to prevent Philip from seizing Thermopylae. Philip backed down.

[86] I.e., to punish them.

[87] In Demosthenes' view, Thebes was Athens' natural ally against Philip. Hence Aeschines' act of deception worsened what was already a bad situation for

thenes and read them,[88] so that you will realize that when you did what was necessary, you won sacrifices and praise in Athens and elsewhere, but when these men deceived you, you brought your wives and children in from the countryside and voted to celebrate the festival of Heracles within the city walls, even though there was peace. I wonder whether you will release unpunished the man who deprived even the gods of their traditional honor.[89] Clerk, read the decree.

[DECREE]

These are the measures, Athenians, that you decreed at that time as a fitting response to your achievements.[90] Clerk, now read the second decree.

[DECREE]

[87] These are the measures that, because of these men, you decreed at this time.[91] Yet this was hardly the result expected either when you first made the peace and alliance or later when you consented to add the words "to Philip's descendants too."[92] Rather, because of these men, you hoped to enjoy utterly wonderful benefits. Furthermore, even after that crisis, if news ever arrived that Philip's troops and mercenaries

---

Athens: it increased the antagonism between Athens and Thebes and drove Thebes closer to Philip.

[88] The decree of Diophantus authorized a festival of thanks to the gods for the success of the Athenian mission to Thermopylae in 352 (see 19.84n). Following Philip's seizure of Thermopylae in 346, the decree of Callisthenes authorized emergency defensive measures, including moving the women and children of Attica within the walls of the city and harbor.

[89] Because under the emergency the Athenians could not celebrate the festival in the traditional manner, which entailed observances in the countryside, Aeschines, deemed responsible for the emergency, is said to have deprived the gods of their traditional honor.

[90] The festival of thanks to the gods in response to the success at Thermopylae in 352.

[91] The emergency defensive measures in response to Philip's seizure of Thermopylae in 346.

[92] See 19.48, 56.

reached Porthmus or Megara,[93] you were stunned, as you all know. So if Philip is not yet treading on Athenian soil, you mustn't contemplate it at your ease. No, if these men have put Philip in a position to do this whenever he wishes, you must recognize the fact and keep that terrible prospect in view, and as for the man who is responsible for putting Philip in this position, you must despise him and punish him.

[88] I know that Aeschines will avoid speaking about the charges lodged against him, and to lead you as far away from the facts as possible, he will recount how much good all men derive from peace and likewise how much evil from war, and this encomium of peace will be characteristic of his entire defense.[94] Yet even this tactic incriminates him. For if others derive benefit from the very thing that causes us so much trouble and turmoil,[95] how could this state of affairs be explained unless these men accepted bribes and mismanaged something that is naturally good? [89] "How so?" he may say. "Is it not because of the peace that you possess and will continue to possess three hundred triremes and the requisite equipment and money?" To that you should respond that peace has significantly increased Philip's resources too, especially in the status of his arms, territory, and revenues, which have become significant. [90] "But we too are not without resources." On the contrary, since it is the condition of one's assets, especially with regard to allies, that determines whether men use their possessions for themselves or cede them to a stronger party, because our assets have been sold by these men, they are ruined and depleted, while Philip's are formidable and have grown significantly. Surely it is not right that because of these men, he should become more powerful in both respects, allies and money, yet we should count the gain that peace would have brought us anyway as compensation for what these men bartered away.[96] The gain does not compensate for the goods bartered

---

[93] Porthmus, the harbor of Eretria in Euboea, and Megara were two places near Attica where, earlier in 343, Philip intervened militarily in an attempt to set up regimes friendly to him.

[94] Aes. 2.172–177 is an encomium of the advantages that Athens has derived from peace in the past.

[95] Viz., peace.

[96] What they "bartered away" is Phocis, a crucial ally whose loss, as Demosthenes argued in 19.83–85, severely weakened Athens' situation.

away—far from it, since we would have the gain in any event, and if not for these men, the goods bartered away would be ours in addition to the gain.

[91] Surely you would consider it grossly unfair, Athenians, if Aeschines should become the target of your ire because the city encountered many troubles for which he bore no responsibility, and likewise were he to be acquitted because of something important that someone else accomplished. So examine the deeds for which he is responsible, and show gratitude if he deserves it and be angry when that seems warranted. [92] How can you decide this fairly? By not allowing him to confuse matters—the mistakes the generals made,[97] the war against Philip, the benefits of peace—but by looking at each item by itself. For example: were we at war with Philip? We were. Does anyone blame Aeschines for that? Does anyone wish to charge him in regard to the conduct of the war? No one does. So on this subject, at least, he is acquitted and need say nothing about it. For the defendant ought to provide witnesses and offer arguments on the points in dispute, not mislead the audience by defending himself on matters already agreed upon. So make sure, Aeschines, that you say nothing about the war, for no one charges you with any crime on that score. [93] After that, certain citizens tried to persuade us to make peace. We were persuaded. We sent envoys.[98] They brought back Macedonian envoys to negotiate for peace. Here again, does anyone fault Aeschines for this? Does anyone claim that he was the first to propose peace or that he was wrong to bring back envoys to negotiate? No one does. So he shouldn't say a word about the mere fact that the city made peace, since he is not responsible for it. [94] If someone asks me, "What, then, do you mean, sir, and from what point do you begin your accusations against Aeschines?"—from the point at which, Athenians, as you were deliberating not whether or not to make peace (for that, at least, had already been decided) but on what terms you would do so, he opposed the speakers defending what was right, took money, spoke in support of the man who was bribed to move the proposal,[99] and

---

[97] Aes. 2.71–73 blames the Athenian generals.

[98] The First Embassy.

[99] Philocrates. The proposal is the one that the Athenians should make peace with Philip on the terms defended by Philocrates in the Assembly mentioned in 19.15–16.

afterwards, having been elected to the embassy to secure the oaths,[100] failed to carry out any of your instructions, destroyed the very allies who survived the war intact, and uttered lies of a magnitude and consequence that no one else has ever matched before or since. From the beginning of the affair until Philip first began to talk of peace, Ctesiphon and Aristodemus managed the first stages of the deception.[101] But when the project was ripe for action, they handed it over to Philocrates and this man, and they took up the task and ruined everything.

[95] Now that he must justify his conduct in court—this man who, I take it, is a scoundrel, a blasphemous villain, and a clerk!—he will conduct his defense as if he were on trial for peace. It's not that he wishes to account for more crimes than anyone accuses him of—for that would be madness—but he sees that since there is nothing good in his record but, in fact, it is all crimes, a defense based on peace has, if nothing else, at least a benevolent sound. [96] And I fear, Athenians, I fear that, without realizing it, by maintaining the peace we act like people who borrow at high interest; for these men surrendered the object that furnished safety and security—the Phocians and Thermopylae. It was not because of this man that we made peace in the first place—and what I am about to say is strange but absolutely true. Anyone who is truly pleased with the peace should give credit to the generals, since everybody blames them. For if they fought as you wished them to, you would not have even listened to talk about peace. [97] So peace is the work of the generals, but the precarious, fragile, unreliable peace is the work of these men who took bribes. So stop him from talking about peace; stop him, and make him talk about his record. For Aeschines is not being tried for the peace, no, but peace has a bad name because of Aeschines. Here's the proof. If a peace agreement had been reached but you were not misled in any way and no one was destroyed, is there anyone whom the peace would have harmed, apart from its being bad for our reputation? Although even this is this man's fault, because he threw his support to Philocrates, nothing irreparable, in any event, would have taken place. But as

---

[100] The Second Embassy.

[101] See 19.12n on Ctesiphon, Aristodemus, and the opening of negotiations between Philip and Athens.

things are, much that is irreparable has taken place, and this man is responsible.

[98] All of you know, I take it, that this whole affair led to doom and disaster because of the disgraceful cowardice of these men. Yet I have no intention, jurors, of using these troubles to attack them with fabricated charges or inviting your cooperation in such a scheme: if what happened was the result of folly or stupidity or any other form of ignorance, I myself acquit Aeschines and urge you to do the same. [99] However, no such excuse could be fairly admitted for a politician. For you do not order or force anyone into public life, but people enter politics when they are convinced they are up to it. You behave with honesty and decency and welcome such people, and far from being resentful, you elect them to some post and put your affairs in their hands.[102] [100] A politician who gets the job done will be acclaimed and profit beyond the norm on account of it; but if he fails, shall he make excuses and prevaricate? That would hardly be right. It would not appease the allies who perished or their children or their wives or anyone else if my stupidity, to say nothing of this man's, was the cause of such misery. Far from it. [101] Nevertheless, forgive Aeschines these horrible, unprecedented crimes, if the harm he did seems the result of stupidity or some other form of ignorance. But if it seems the result of corruption, of taking money and bribes, and if the facts themselves clearly make the case, by all means put him to death if you possibly can, but failing that, make him a living example for the future. Now consider for yourselves whether the proof of this matter is not entirely just.

[102] When Aeschines here made those speeches—the ones concerning Phocis, Thespiae, and Euboea[103]—if he had not been bribed and was not consciously deceiving you, then there are only two possible explanations: either he heard Philip actually promise that he would act in that way and do those things, or else, having been mesmerized and duped by Philip's overall generosity, he expected it to carry over to these other matters too. Apart from these alternatives,

---

[102] Demosthenes is flattering his audience with this generous account of the people's attitude towards their politicians.

[103] See 19.21–22.

nothing else is possible. [103] In either case, Aeschines of all men had reason to hate Philip. Why? Because Philip's part in the affair caused him the most terrible disgrace: he has deceived you; he is viewed with contempt; he is on trial. He would have been tried for treason [104] long ago if matters had run their proper course. It is only because you citizens are naive and complacent that he is undergoing an audit (*euthynai*), and doing so at the time of his choosing. [104] Has any of you heard Aeschines raise his voice and accuse Philip? Well? Has anyone seen him criticize Philip or say anything? No one has. All Athenians are quicker to accuse Philip, even ordinary citizens who have not been harmed by Philip, at least not personally. I was waiting to hear him make the statement—if indeed he was not bribed—"Athenians, do with me as you wish. I trusted Philip, I was deceived, I made a mistake, I confess it. But beware of that man, Athenians. He is a cheat, a trickster, a villain. Do you not see what he did to me, how he deceived me?" I hear nothing of the kind, and neither do you. [110] [105] Why? Because he was not deceived and not misled, but he hired himself out and took money to make the speech and betray us to Philip. As Philip's hireling he was worthy, upstanding, and just; for you, however, as envoy and fellow-citizen he turned traitor and deserves to die not once, but three times over.

[111] These are not the only proofs that he was paid to make that speech. Not long ago some Thessalians arrived here with envoys from Philip, seeking your vote in favor of Philip's membership in the Amphictyonic Council. [106] Who of all men had the most reason to challenge these envoys? Aeschines here. Why? Because Philip did the opposite of what this man assured you he would do. [112] He said that Philip would fortify Thespiae and Plataea, that he would not destroy the Phocians, and that he would put an end to Theban insolence. But Philip made the Thebans greater than they should have been, he de-

---

[104] By the process of *eisangelia*.

[105] The traditional enumeration accidentally left a gap here. Nothing is missing from the text.

[106] This embassy must have reached Athens in late 346. When the Third Sacred War was settled, Philip had the Phocians removed from the Amphictyonic Council and took for himself the two seats on the Council that had belonged to them.

stroyed the Phocians utterly, and he refrained from fortifying Thespiae and Plataea, and he also enslaved Orchomenus and Coronea.[107] How could two outcomes be more opposed to each other than these? And yet Aeschines did not challenge the envoys and uttered not a word in protest. [113] But that's not even the worst of it: he was the only man in the entire city actually to support the envoys. Not even Philocrates—loathsome creature—dared to do that, but Aeschines here did. When you raised a clamor and refused to listen to him, he stepped down from the platform and revealed his true feelings in front of Philip's envoys, declaring that many citizens make noise, but few fight when they need to—you remember it, I'm sure—though he himself, I take it, is a marvelous soldier, O Zeus![108]

[114] Next, if we could not demonstrate that any of the envoys had received anything, and if it were not possible for all of you to see it, torture or similar methods would be the only way to investigate the matter.[109] But if Philocrates not only acknowledged the fact in your presence many times in the Assembly but also made the situation clear to you—by selling wheat, building a house, threatening to go off to Macedon even if you did not dispatch him, importing timber, openly exchanging gold in the marketplace[110]—surely he cannot deny taking money, since he acknowledged it himself and made a show of it. [115] Now, while Philocrates takes his money, ruins his reputation, and puts himself in danger, is there anyone so foolish or hapless as to renounce the honest citizens whom he might have joined and to choose instead to go on trial as an associate of Philocrates? I don't think there is. If you consider the matter closely, you will find, Athenians, that all this is clear and substantial proof that Aeschines has taken money.

---

[107] Like Thespiae and Plataea (see 19.21n), Orchomenus and Coronea were Boeotian cities that Athens would have liked to see strengthened in opposition to Thebes.

[108] Aes. 2.167–170 responds to the charge of shirking implied by this ironic comment.

[109] Slaves could give testimony in court only under torture, to which both prosecution and defense had to agree. The practice was more often talked about than used.

[110] Macedonian gold for Athenian coins. Wheat and timber, valuable commodities in Athens, were Macedonian staples and exported from there.

[116] Now, look at the latest episode, which is no less a proof that this man was paid off by Philip. You are surely aware that recently, when Hyperides indicted Philocrates for treason,[111] I stepped forward and said I was troubled by one aspect of the indictment, namely, that Philocrates should have committed so many serious crimes by himself while the nine other envoys did nothing.[112] I said that that couldn't be, for Philocrates would have amounted to nothing unless he had some of the envoys as accomplices. [117] "Now, I should not be the one to absolve or incriminate anyone," I said, "but let the facts themselves reveal the guilty and absolve the innocent. Let each of them volunteer to rise, come before you, and declare that he had no part and took no comfort in Philocrates' scheme. Whoever does that," I said, "is exonerated in my eyes." I think you remember that speech. [118] Yet no one came forward or availed himself of the opportunity. All the others had some excuse. One said he was not subject to an audit; another thought he was probably somewhere else at the time; a third claimed Philocrates as an in-law.[113] But this man had no excuse; he simply sold his services once and for all, not limiting his employment to what's happened so far: if he is acquitted now, clearly his next step will be to rejoin Philip and work against you. Even if you let him go, he will not let up, but to avoid uttering a single word against Philip, he would rather be reviled, put on trial, exposed to anything at your hands than do anything to defy Philip's pleasure. [119] What is this connection with Philocrates, what is this great regard for him? Even if Philocrates had conducted the embassy in the most exemplary fashion and achieved the most advantageous outcome but yet admitted to taking money while on the embassy, as he did indeed admit, this connection

---

[111] Earlier in 343 by the process of *eisangelia*. Having fled into exile rather than stand trial, Philocrates was condemned to death *in absentia*.

[112] Both the First and Second Embassies consisted of ten Athenians representing Athens (among whom were Philocrates, Aeschines, and Demosthenes) and Aglaocreon of Tenedos representing Athens' allies. Aglaocreon was a close associate of Aeschines and testified for Aeschines at the trial (2.126). Hence the "nine other envoys" who Demosthenes claims were Philocrates' accomplices were the eight other Athenian envoys (i.e., all apart from Demosthenes and Philocrates) and Aglaocreon.

[113] One would be reluctant to speak against a relative.

is the very thing that an honest member of the embassy ought to shun, guard against, and solemnly repudiate in his own behavior. Aeschines has not done that. Is the situation not clear, Athenians? Does it not shout out loud and declare that Aeschines took money and is always wicked for the sake of money, not because he is stupid or ignorant or made a simple mistake?

[120] "Yet who testifies that I took bribes?" he will ask. A splendid question! The facts, Aeschines, which are the most trustworthy of all witnesses, for the facts cannot be impugned or blamed for being what they are because they've been seduced or are doing a favor for someone; rather, what you have done through betrayal and corruption determines what the facts turn out to be when examined. But in addition to the facts, you will testify against yourself right now. Stand up, please, and answer.[114] Surely you won't claim you are inexperienced and thus have nothing to say, you who spoke to the limit of the clock while successfully prosecuting cases that lacked witnesses and were as outlandish as a drama.[115] It's clear you're a very clever fellow.

[121] However, though Aeschines here has done many repugnant things and displayed enormous cowardice, a view, I take it, which you all share, nothing, in my judgment, is worse than the act I am about to describe, and nothing will prove more decisively that he has been caught taking bribes and is thoroughly corrupt. When, thanks to the wonderful, great hopes fostered by this man, you organized yet another diplomatic mission to Philip, the third one, you elected this man and me and most of the same citizens as before.[116] [122] Straightaway

---

[114] While Aeschines, of course, does not move or say anything, Demosthenes pauses to set up the following gibe.

[115] A mocking allusion to the occasion in 345 when Aeschines successfully prosecuted Timarchus for sexual misconduct and thereby ended the latter's political career (Aes. 1; Demosthenes helped to defend Timarchus). The "clock" refers to the time allotted to the prosecutor to speak. "Drama" is a gibe at Aeschines' former career as a tragic actor.

[116] The Third Embassy to Philip left Athens shortly after the Assembly meeting in which Aeschines conveyed hopes that Philip would settle the Third Sacred War in Athens' interests (19.19–50); this embassy was designed to further that likelihood. While en route, the envoys learned of Philip's seizure of Phocis and dispatched Dercylus, one of the envoys, back to Athens with the grim news (see 19.60).

I rose, took an oath of exemption,[117] and though some people caused a commotion and urged me to go, I said that I would not. This man remained in his elected post. When the Assembly later broke up, the envoys got together and discussed which of them would stay behind in Athens. For with things still up in the air and the future unclear, all kinds of views were being expressed by people gathering in the Agora. [123] The envoys feared that a special meeting[118] of the Assembly might suddenly be called, and then, if you heard the truth from me, you might make the right decision about the Phocians, and Philip might lose his grip on the situation. If you had just voted something and had given the Phocians some ray of hope, you would have saved them. For if you were no longer misled, Philip could not last; he could not, since he had no grain in the countryside, which had not been planted because of the war, and he could not import grain, since your triremes were there and controlled the sea. Moreover, the Phocian cities were numerous and hard to take except by a long siege. If Philip took one city a day, there were twenty-two of them.

[124] For all these reasons, then, they left this man in Athens to prevent you from changing any of the decisions that you were deceived into making. Now, for him to withdraw without an excuse was risky and would arouse considerable suspicion—"what do you mean? You're not leaving and won't be an envoy after you assured us of so many wonderful benefits?" But he had to stay. What to do? He pretended to be sick, and his brother, having come before the Council with the physician Execestus, took an oath to exempt this man here on the grounds that he was sick, and he was elected in Aeschines' place. [125] But five or six days later, when the Phocians had been destroyed, and this man had completed the task for which he was paid (as he would any other), Dercylus turned back after reaching Chalcis and reported to you at a meeting of the Assembly in Piraeus that Phocis was destroyed.[119] This news, Athenians, naturally filled you with

---

[117] A citizen whom the people elected to an office could remove himself by taking an oath that he could not perform the duties because of a legitimate excuse. It is not known what excuse Demosthenes alleged in this case.

[118] See 19.154n.

[119] See 19.60n on Dercylus.

grief for the Phocians and trepidation for yourselves, and you voted to move the women and children in from the countryside, to prepare the outlying guard posts, to fortify Piraeus, and to celebrate the festival of Heracles inside the city. [126] When, in the wake of these events, clamor and confusion beset the city, that was the moment when this skilled, clever, smooth-talking man went off as an envoy to the person who had done all this. He was not elected by the Council or the Assembly, he paid no attention to the illness for which he was just exempted, or to the envoy who had been chosen in his place, or to the law that ordains death as the penalty for such transgressions, [127] or to the truly terrible fact[120] that he was going into the heart of Thebes and the Theban army, even though he had announced that a price was put on his head in Thebes and that the Thebans were then in control of Phocian territory as well as holding all Boeotia. But he was so deranged, so preoccupied with profit and taking bribes, that all this meant nothing. He simply ignored it and went on his way.

[128] That was the course of events, yet far more terrible is what he did when he got there. All of you here and all other Athenian citizens were so horrified and outraged at what was happening to the poor Phocians that you kept both the Council's representatives (theōroi) and the Thesmothetae from traveling to the Pythian festival, and you dropped the traditional delegation (theōria) entirely.[121] Yet this man traveled to the Thebans and Philip, who were sacrificing in celebration

---

[120] Ironic (see 19.21n).

[121] Theōroi (lit. "observers") were sent by Greek cities to represent them at the major panhellenic festivals. The theōria was the entire procession of theōroi to a festival. In Athens the six Thesmothetae ran the lawcourts and were among the nine chief magistrates (see 18.112n). The Pythian festival, one of the chief panhellenic festivals, was celebrated quadrennially in Delphi in honor of Pythian Apollo. This festival was managed by the Delphic Amphictyony, in whose name Philip had just punished the Phocians and overseen the transfer of Delphi from the Phocians to the Thebans (see 19.50). By refusing to send a procession to the Pythian festival, the Athenians showed their displeasure at this turn of events and the current policy of the Delphic Amphictyony. Demosthenes implies that under the circumstances, it was an act of piety for the Athenians to refuse to attend the Pythian festival.

of their political and military victories. He feasted and shared in the libations and prayers Philip offered to mark the destruction of your allies' walls, territory, and forces; and he joined Philip in wearing a crown and singing paeans; and he drank to Philip's health.[122]

[129] These facts cannot be described one way by me and another way by him. Those concerning his exemption from the embassy are set out in the public documents stored in the Metroon, under the control of the public slave, and a decree expressly records Aeschines' name.[123] As for his behavior in Philip's camp, the other envoys who were there and informed me will testify. For I was not a member of that mission, since I was officially exempted. [130] Clerk, please read the decree and call the witnesses.

[DECREE, WITNESSES]

What prayers do you suppose Philip and the Thebans offered when they poured their libations? Was it not that they and their allies be given a mighty victory in war and just the opposite for the Phocians' allies?[124] Did not this man offer this prayer and lay this curse on his country? It is now your duty to turn that curse upon his head.

[131] So by going there he broke a law that prescribes death as the punishment; his behavior when he got there clearly merits death several times over; and what he did on the previous embassies would justly lead to his execution. Consider, then, what penalty is sufficiently harsh and clearly appropriate for such crimes. [132] Wouldn't it be disgraceful, Athenians, if all of you, indeed the entire citizen body, should first publicly condemn everything connected with the peace, distancing yourselves from the Amphictyony and treating Philip with hostility and suspicion, because what happened was ungodly, outrageous, unjust, and harmful to your interests, but then, when you've come into

---

[122] The crown and paeans (songs of praise addressed to the gods) celebrate victory. Aeschines responds to these accusations at 2.162–163. See also 18.287.

[123] The public archive was kept in the Metroon, the shrine to the Mother of the gods in the Agora near the Council-house.

[124] The Phocians' allies are the Athenians. The prayer attributed to Philip and the Thebans is a traditional one for combatants; hence, Demosthenes' audience will readily believe the attribution.

court to conduct an audit of these events and sworn the oath on behalf of the city,[125] you should acquit this man, who is responsible for
all the misery and whom you caught red-handed committing these
crimes? [133] What other Athenian, indeed, what other Greek would
not rightly criticize you if he saw that while you were angry at Philip
for extracting peace from war by buying it from those who sold it to
him—a deed that could be excused—you nevertheless acquitted this
man here, who so disgracefully sold you out, though your laws prescribe the most severe punishment for anyone who does that?

[134] Perhaps my opponents will argue that you will move Philip to
hostility if you convict the envoys who negotiated peace. If that's true,
then, try as I might, I cannot see that I could charge this man with
anything worse. For if Philip paid money to get peace but now has become so great and terrible that, heedless of your oaths and duty, you
are considering what you could do to earn his gratitude,[126] what punishment would be appropriate for those who are responsible for this
situation? [135] But I think I can show that you are more likely to
move Philip to a friendship that is in your interests. For you must realize, Athenians, that Philip does not despise your city, nor did he prefer the Thebans to you[127] because he considered you less important
than them. Rather, these men spoke to Philip and gave him some advice, which I, in fact, once told you about in the Assembly without a
protest from any of them. [136] Democracy, they told him, is the most
erratic and capricious thing there is, like a wind that swirls on the sea,
moving wherever chance takes it. One man comes, another leaves. No
one takes responsibility for common interests or even gives them any
thought. But Philip ought to have a few friends in Athens to do business and manage affairs among you, for instance, the very man who
was offering the advice. And if Philip made this arrangement, he would
easily get from you whatever he wished.

[137] I suppose if Philip had heard that the men who gave him this

---

[125] See 18.2n on the Heliastic Oath.

[126] The notion that Athenians would try to earn Philip's gratitude recalls the
charge raised against Philip and Aeschines earlier (19.39–41).

[127] I.e., in settling the Third Sacred War in favor of Thebes rather than Athens.

advice were put to death [128] immediately upon their return, he would have done just what the Persian King did. And what did he do? Under false pretenses the King had given Timagoras,[129] according to reports, forty talents. But when the King learned that you executed Timagoras and that he did not have the authority even to preserve his own life, let alone to do any of the things he had promised, the King realized that the recipient of his largess was not the person in charge. So, first he sent word that he was giving you back Amphipolis, which at the time was recorded on his register of friends and allies.[130] Then he never offered anyone another bribe. [138] Philip would have done the same had he seen that any of these men was punished, and if he sees it now, he will do it. But what should he do if he hears that these men address the Assembly, enjoy your esteem, prosecute others? Should he look to spend more money when he can spend less? Should he cultivate all of us when he can cultivate two or three? He would be crazy. Philip did not simply choose to confer public benefits on Thebes, far from it, but he was persuaded to do so by their envoys. [139] Let me tell you how it transpired.

Envoys from Thebes reached Philip just when we too were there. He wanted to give them money, and quite a bit too, so they said. But the Theban envoys refused and took nothing. Later, in a genial mood at drinks during a festive meal he offered them various items of war booty, and in particular silver and gold drinking vessels. The Thebans turned down everything and did not compromise themselves at all. [140] Finally, Philo, one of their envoys, made a speech, Athenians,

---

[128] The method of execution that is specified (*apotympanismos*) entailed binding the victim to a plank and leaving him to die by exposure.

[129] On Timagoras, see 19.31 and note. The episode described here took place in 367.

[130] Amphipolis, a strategically placed town on the Thracian coast, was in Athens' control from 437 to 424. Though Athens sought to reestablish control, Amphipolis remained independent until Philip captured it in 357. The diplomatic transaction described in this paragraph is a mere gesture: when the Persian King took Amphipolis off his rolls, he did not actually control it; and when he restored it to Athens, that changed nothing on the ground and did not enable Athens to assert control over the city.

that ought to have been made on your behalf rather than the Thebans'. He said he was pleased and delighted to see Philip acting with such cordial generosity towards them. They themselves were bound by ties of friendship and hospitality even without these gifts, but they asked him to direct this generosity toward their city's affairs, which were their concern at the moment, and to act in a manner that was worthy of both himself and the Thebans. They agreed that in this way the city as a whole and they themselves would be on his side.

[141] Consider what happened to the Thebans as a result of that speech and what the consequences were for us, and examine truthfully how important it is not to put your city's interests up for sale. First, the Thebans obtained peace just when the war was taxing and exhausting them, and they were losing. Next, their enemies, the Phocians, were utterly ruined, and entire cities and fortifications were destroyed. Is that all? No, by Zeus, but in addition to that, they took over Orchomenus, Coronea, Corsiae, Tilphosaeum,[131] and as much Phocian territory as they liked. [142] That is what the Thebans got from peace, which is more than they could have prayed for. And what did the Theban envoys get? Nothing, apart from the credit for bringing about their country's gain. That, Athenians, is a fine and momentous mark of their integrity and reputation, which these men sold for money. Now, let me compare what the city of Athens got from peace and what the envoys of Athens got, then you consider whether the city and these men fared alike. [143] The result for the city was to surrender all its assets and allies and conclude a treaty with Philip that committed you to stopping anyone who might attempt to protect your assets and allies, and to regarding anyone who might wish to restore them to you as a foe and an enemy, but the one who stole them as a friend and ally. [144] These are the positions that Aeschines here supported when his accomplice Philocrates proposed them. Though I succeeded on the previous day in persuading you to ratify your allies' decree[132] and to summon envoys from Philip, this man's tricks forced a postponement to the next day, whereupon he persuaded you to adopt the motion of

---

[131] Boeotian places that Thebes sought to control. Tilphosaeum was a fortified high place near Lake Copais. On Orchomenus and Coronea, see 19.112n.

[132] See 19.15n on this decree.

Philocrates that contained these provisions and many others that were even worse.

[145] So that was what the city got from peace, and it's not easy to think of anything more disgraceful. And what did the envoys get, who brought this about? I pass over everything you have seen with your eyes—houses, timber, wheat[133]—but there is also the property and farms in the territory of our defeated allies, from which Philocrates derives an income of one talent and Aeschines here, thirty minas.[134] [146] Is it not a terrible disgrace, Athenians, that your envoys derive an income from your allies' disasters and that the same peace has meant, for the city that dispatched the envoys, the defeat of its allies, the surrender of its assets, and humiliation instead of glory, but for the envoys who brought this harm to the city it has produced income, prosperity, possessions, and wealth instead of the most desperate poverty? To prove that these are the facts, clerk, please call the witnesses from Olynthus.[135]

[WITNESSES]

[147] I would not be surprised if Aeschines should dare to claim that an honorable peace, one that met my requirements, was not achievable since the generals bungled the war. But if he does say this, by the gods remember to ask him whether it was this city or some other that he was representing as an envoy. If it was another city, one that he says prevailed in war and had capable generals, he has taken Philip's money with good reason.[136] But if it was this city, why does Aeschines still clearly accept gifts even after the city that he represented lost its assets?[137] Indeed, if there was anything aboveboard in

---

[133] See 19.114n.

[134] See 18.41n on Aeschines' property.

[135] It is uncertain why Demosthenes calls Olynthians as witnesses: the points at issue concern Phocis. Perhaps these witnesses recently traveled through Phocis, or the passage may be corrupt.

[136] Ironic: if the envoy's city was defeating Philip, Philip could secure peace on favorable terms only by bribing the envoy to concede such terms.

[137] Thus Aeschines' acceptance of money from Philip is compensation not merely for arranging peace on terms favorable to Philip but also for service to

what happened, the outcome should have been the same for both the city and the envoys who were sent to represent it.

[148] Consider this question too, jurors: do you think that the Phocians enjoyed a greater military advantage over the Thebans than did Philip over you? There's no doubt the Phocians had the greater advantage: they held Orchomenus, Coronea, and Tilphosaeum; they drove the Thebans from Neon; they killed two hundred and seventy Thebans at Hedylion and erected a trophy;[138] their cavalry was superior; and the Thebans were beset by an Iliad of woes.[139] [149] You had no troubles of that kind—and may you never have any—but the worst part of the war with Philip was your inability to inflict as much damage on him as you wished; you had absolutely no fear that you yourselves might suffer from him. How then did it happen that, by the same peace treaty, the Thebans, whose military power was so inferior, not only saved their own possessions but added those of their enemies as well, while you, the Athenians, lost in peace that which you preserved through war? It happened because the Theban envoys did not sell their country, but these men sold yours.[140] My next point will convince you even further that events took place in this way.

[150] When the peace that Philocrates proposed and this man supported was concluded, and Philip's envoys received your oaths and left—and up to this point, at least, nothing irreparable had taken place, for the peace was disgraceful and dishonored the city, but it was balanced by the wonderful benefits that were to accrue to us[141]—I

Philip that has continued well after the peace was concluded. "Gifts," which are exchanged between equals, are (as often) an ironic euphemism for outright bribes.

[138] Hedylion was a mountain in Boeotia. Neon was a Phocian town that was saved from a Theban assault. On Orchomenus, Coronea, and Tilphosaeum, see 19.141n.

[139] This remarkable metaphor, based on the enormous suffering of war contained in Homer's *Iliad,* became proverbial later in antiquity.

[140] The transmitted text is uncertain here. It contains a clause that does not make sense in the context: "But, by Zeus, he will say that our allies have been exhausted by the war." Something has been lost to connect this clause with what follows, or it represents something that Demosthenes himself never completed, or it is a later interpolation.

[141] Ironic: see 19.24. Nothing was irreparable before the peace was ratified because the Athenians were still in a position to safeguard their interests.

urged you and told these men that we should sail to the Hellespont as quickly as possible and make sure that in the intervening period we held onto our territories in that region and did not allow Philip to take possession of any of them.[142] [151] I knew full well that those who are not careful lose for good any territory they might give up while peace is being made at the end of a war. For no one who has once decided for peace on the basis of his chief interests has ever wished to go back to war over places that were previously ignored, but whichever party seizes those places first keeps them. Further, it was my belief that, if we sailed there, the city would be assured of one of the following benefits. Either, having given his oaths in our presence as required in the decree, Philip would return the city's possessions that he took and keep his hands off the rest, [152] or else, if he did not do this, we would inform you here straightaway, and after seeing his greed and treachery in those distant and small places you would not abandon the ones that are nearby and more important, namely, Phocis and Thermopylae. But if Philip refrained from seizing your territories and did not deceive you, your objectives would be entirely secure, and you would receive fair treatment from him voluntarily.

[153] I had good reason for these expectations. If the Phocians were secure and in control of Thermopylae, as they were then, Philip would have no threat to hold over your heads that might cause you to relinquish your rights. Lacking both a land route and naval power, Philip was in no position to reach Attica, whereas if he wronged you, you could immediately close off his markets, deprive him of money, and blockade him from everything else. Then he would be enslaved to the gains to be derived from peace, not you. [154] This is not a plan that I am making up as a pretense now after the fact. I conceived it right at that moment, made provisions for your interests, and informed these men, as I will prove to you. There were no more scheduled meetings of the Assembly since they had all taken

---

[142] This is the time between the oaths given by the Athenians and those that would be given by Philip, who was then campaigning near the Hellespont. Only when both parties had given their oaths would the treaty be fully ratified and officially in force. One clause of the treaty held that both parties were to keep all the territory they held at the time the peace went into effect. Demosthenes feared that Philip would use the intervening period to add to his territory at Athens' expense.

place by that time,[143] but the envoys were dawdling and had not departed. So as a member of the Council, which the people had put in charge, I moved a decree to the effect that the envoys should depart as soon as possible and the general Proxenus should find out where Philip was and convey the envoys there. The words I utter now are the exact same as those used in my proposal. Clerk, please take the decree and read it.

[DECREE]

[155] Now at that point I got the embassy underway, but the envoys resisted, as you will plainly see from what they did next. When we reached Oreus and met up with Proxenus,[144] these men forgot about sailing and completing their mission and took a circuitous land route instead. We wasted twenty-three days getting to Macedon and then sat in Pella the rest of the time waiting for Philip to arrive, the whole journey amounting to about fifty days![145] [156] During that time the peace treaty was in effect, but Philip took Doriscus, Thrace, the area by the walls, Hieron Oros,[146] and arranged everything to suit himself. Meanwhile I was constantly speaking up and reiterating my arguments, at first like someone contributing to open debate, then like someone trying to instruct the uninformed, finally like someone who puts aside all restraint in the face of the most wicked and corrupt men. [157] The man who was conspicuous in opposing my pleas, who contested everything that I recommended and you voted for, was this man. You will find out presently whether all the other envoys shared his views. I have nothing to say about any of them at the moment, and I do not accuse them: none of them should have to be compelled to demon-

---

[143] In each of the ten administrative periods of the year (roughly thirty-six days), there were four regular meetings of the Assembly. Special meetings could be called but required notice and preparation (see 19.123).

[144] On the northern tip of Euboea where Proxenus was anchored with the fleet, Oreus was the staging point for the journey farther north.

[145] To sail from Oreus directly to a port near Pella, Philip's capital, would have taken two or three days.

[146] The "area by the walls" probably refers to Heraeum on the northern coast of the Propontis. Hieron Oros ("Sacred Mountain") is in the same district. Doriscus is inland near the Thracian Chersonese.

strate his integrity today, but that matter depends on each man himself and whether he had any part in the crimes. You have all seen that what was done was disgraceful and vile and paid for. Who was involved in it will be evident from the affair itself.

[158] "But during that time, by Zeus, the envoys were receiving the oaths from Philip's allies, or else they were taking care of other business." Far from it! Rather, although they were abroad for three whole months and spent a thousand drachmas of your money on expenses, they did not receive the oaths from a single city, either on their way to Macedon or on their way back, but the oaths were administered at the inn by the temple of the Dioscuri (anyone who has been to Pherae knows the place I'm speaking of), when Philip was already on his way here at the head of his army.[147] It was a disgrace, Athenians, and you deserve better. [159] But for Philip, it was the highest priority to have the oaths administered that way. These men first tried to add a clause, "excluding Halus and Phocis," to the peace treaty,[148] but they were unable, since you forced Philocrates to expunge that clause and explicitly to write in "the Athenians and their allies" instead. Yet Philip did not want any of his allies to give their oaths to such a treaty—for they had no intention of joining the expedition against those territories of yours that he now controls, and the treaty would give them an excuse for abstaining. [160] Philip also wanted no witnesses to the promises he made for the sake of peace and no public disclosure of the fact that Athens was not losing the war, but he was seeking peace and promising the Athenians much to get it. So to prevent these facts from becoming known, he deemed it crucial for these men to stay put. They indulged him in everything, making a display of excessive flattery. [161] Now, when all these points are established—that these men wasted the available time, surrendered territory in Thrace, did nothing to carry out your official instructions or to further the city's interests, delivered a false report back in Athens—how is it possible for right-minded jurors intent on fulfilling their oaths to allow Aeschines to go free? To establish the truth of my statements, clerk, first read the decree that di-

---

[147] Pherae was in Thessaly, about halfway between Pella and Athens.

[148] Halus was a city of southern Thessaly that was besieged by Philip and that the Athenians vainly tried to include, along with Phocis, in the peace treaty.

rected how we were to administer the oaths,[149] then read Philip's letter, then the decree proposed by Philocrates and the one passed by the Assembly.[150]

[DECREE, LETTER, DECREES]

[162] To show that we would have reached Philip at the Hellespont had any of the envoys followed the advice I gave and the orders you set out in the decree, clerk, call the witnesses who were there.[151]

[WITNESSES]

Clerk, now read the other testimony too, which contains Philip's response to Euclides, present in court, who reached Philip later.[152]

[TESTIMONY]

[163] Listen as I explain that these men are in no position to deny that they were acting on Philip's behalf. When we were setting out on the First Embassy to negotiate peace, you sent a herald on ahead to secure pledges of safe conduct.[153] On that occasion, as soon as the envoys reached Oreus, they did not wait on the herald or waste any time, but they sailed straight for Halus even though it was under siege. From there they went to Parmenion,[154] who was directing the siege, and traveling through the enemy's army to Pagasae, they went on ahead and met the herald in Larissa. Such was the extraordinary zeal they displayed on that trip. [164] But when peace was in effect and travel

---

[149] This decree, one clause of which is quoted in 19.278, instructed the envoys to receive the oaths individually from Philip's allies.

[150] The decree proposed by Philocrates contained the clause explicitly excluding the Halians and Phocians from the treaty; the one passed by the Assembly contained the clause that explicitly included in the treaty only the Athenians and their allies (19.159). Philip's letter is one of those referred to in 19.40.

[151] In Oreus, the staging point for the journey to Philip (19.155).

[152] According to an ancient scholar, Euclides, otherwise unknown, was sent to Philip to protest his activities in Thrace, in particular his defeat of the Thracian king Cersebleptes, an Athenian ally against Philip. See 19.174n.

[153] The state of war between Macedon and Athens at the time of the First Embassy necessitated the use of a herald for this purpose.

[154] Philip's chief general.

was completely safe, and you gave the order for haste, it did not occur to them at that time either to hurry if they were going by land or else to sail. Why? Because it served Philip's interest in the first instance to conclude peace as quickly as possible, but in the second instance to extend the time as much as possible before his oaths were administered. [165] To show that these statements too are accurate, clerk, please read the following testimony.

[TESTIMONY]

Is there any way that men could demonstrate more conclusively their utter devotion to Philip's cause than that on the same route they stood still when your interests would have them hasten, yet they rushed onwards when they should not even have moved until the herald arrived?

[166] Consider now what each of us chose to do while we were sitting there idly in Pella. I chose to find and rescue the prisoners of war,[155] spending my own money and asking Philip to purchase their freedom with the gifts of hospitality that he was giving us. You will hear in a moment what Aeschines was doing during that time. But first, what did it mean that Philip was giving us money in common? [167] Let there be no misunderstanding—Philip was sounding us out. How? By contacting each of us privately and offering, Athenians, quite a large sum of money. If anyone rebuffed him (I shouldn't comment on my own response, since the deeds and events themselves will make that clear), he supposed that we would all naively accept what he gave us in common, and so long as we had all taken something, however small, out of the common largess, those who had sold their services privately would be safe. That was the reason the gifts were offered, on the pretext, of course, of being gifts of hospitality. [168] When I thwarted this scheme, these men just divided up the additional portion among themselves. But when I asked Philip to spend the money on the prisoners of war, he could hardly denounce the envoys or say, "But this man or that man has the money," or shun the expenditure.[156] So he

---

[155] See 19.40n on these prisoners.

[156] The first two alternatives were not feasible because either would be tantamount to admitting that the envoys had taken bribes. That forced both Philip and

agreed to do it, but he deferred the matter, claiming that he would send the prisoners back during the Panathenaea. Clerk, read the testimony of Apollophanes [157] and then that of the others who were there.

[TESTIMONIES]

[169] Let me tell you how many prisoners of war I personally freed. During the time that we were in Pella but before Philip's arrival, some of the prisoners, indeed precisely those who were free on bond, [158] suspecting, I guess, that I would be unable to convince Philip to free them, said that they wanted to secure their own freedom and to avoid being under any obligation to Philip. So they borrowed the money, three minas or five or whatever sum happened to be the ransom of each. [170] Now, when Philip agreed to free the rest of the prisoners, I called together those to whom I personally had advanced money [159] and explained what happened. I wanted to avoid the impression that their initial haste had left them at a disadvantage and to prevent the poor among them from ransoming themselves out of their own resources; so I gave them the ransom money as a gift. To prove that these statements are true, clerk, read these testimonies.

[TESTIMONIES]

[171] That is the sum of money that I gave as a gift to those unfortunate citizens. When you presently hear this man say, "Well, Demosthenes, since you claim to have realized from my support of Philocrates that our mission was corrupt, why then did you join the ensuing embassy, the one sent to receive the oaths, and not take an oath of exemption?" remember that I had promised the citizens whom I liberated that I would bring the ransom money and do what I could to protect them. [172] To break my word to fellow-citizens and abandon them in their adversity would have been terrible. And if I took an oath

---

the envoys to agree to Demosthenes' demand to ransom the prisoners with the money that Philip gave them.

[157] Nothing is known of this man.

[158] Apparently the bond gave these prisoners some freedom of movement just within Pella.

[159] The verb used here implies a loan without interest.

of exemption, it would not have been honorable or even safe for me to travel there on my own. So if not for my desire to save those citizens, may I perish utterly and thoroughly if I would have joined the embassy with these men, even for a very large sum of money. And the proof is that twice you elected me to serve on the Third Embassy, and twice I took the oath of exemption; and while I was abroad on the Second Embassy, everything I did was in opposition to them. [173] So in this way, whatever was under my control during the embassy turned out for your benefit, but whatever these men, being the majority, controlled, ended in utter disaster. And if anyone had listened to me, everything else would have turned out in the same way. For I was not such a wretched fool that, although to gain your favor I was giving money even as I saw others taking, I did not also desire whatever could be done without expense to bring about much greater advantages for the whole city. That is exactly what I did, Athenians. But these men, I'm afraid, were too much for me.

[174] Now, compare what this man and Philocrates did with my actions; the comparison will make matters clear. First, in violation of the decree and what they told you, they declared the Phocians, the Halians, and Cersebleptes[160] excluded from the peace. Second, they tried to alter and annul the decree that governed our diplomatic mission. Next, they officially listed the Cardians as Philip's allies,[161] and while voting not to send you the letter I wrote, they sent one written by themselves, which was completely dishonest. [175] Next, when I criticized these policies, not only because I thought them despicable but also because I feared that these men would involve me in their destruction, this fine gentleman here said that I had proposed to Philip that I would overthrow your democratic government, even though all

---

[160] Cersebleptes, king of the Odrysians in Thrace, had been Athens' rival for influence in the Chersonese. In the mid 340s, under pressure from Philip, Cersebleptes looked to Athens for support but never became officially an Athenian ally. Aes. 2.81–93 defends his record with regard to Cersebleptes.

[161] Cardia, a city in the Chersonese, was formerly within the Athenian sphere of influence. It was apparently independent of either side in the peace treaty, but Demosthenes accuses his opponent of trying to bring Cardia officially within Philip's sphere of influence.

the while he never stopped for a moment talking to Philip in private. I'll say nothing about the rest, but when Dercylus,[162] not I, was watching Aeschines during the night in Pherae with the assistance of this slave of mine, present in court today, he caught him leaving Philip's tent, so he told the slave to inform me and to remember it himself. Finally, after the rest of us departed, this loathsome, shameless man stayed behind with Philip for one day and night. [176] To prove these assertions, I will first present the testimony that I drafted myself and for which I undertake responsibility under the law.[163] Then I will summon each of the other envoys, and I will require them either to testify or to swear an oath denying any knowledge of this matter. If they swear the oath, I will demonstrate to you beyond doubt that they are perjurers.[164]

[TESTIMONY]

[177] You have seen the troubles and difficulties that plagued me during the entire trip. Since these men commit such crimes under your very eyes, when you are in a position to confer rewards or mete out punishment, what do you think they did while they were there and close to the man who was handing out money?

Now, I wish to review my accusations from the beginning to show that I have fulfilled every promise I made at the beginning of my speech.[165] I have demonstrated that Aeschines' report to the Assembly was entirely false and that he deceived you, and I relied on the facts themselves as witnesses, not on mere assertions. [178] I have demonstrated that he was responsible for your refusal to hear the truth from

---

[162] See 19.60n on Dercylus.

[163] Demosthenes refers to his liability under the procedure *dikē pseudomartyriōn* (false testimony), which made witnesses legally liable for their sworn written testimony in court. Normally litigants could not be witnesses in their own case (cf. Dem. 46.9), but the apparent exception here may be due to Demosthenes' introduction of his testimony as the basis for the summons that follows immediately.

[164] Aes. 2.126–127 provides contrary testimony on these points. A litigant could summon witnesses and compel them either to confirm official testimony or to swear an oath disclaiming the testimony. Failure to respond to the summons made witnesses liable to legal action.

[165] The accusations listed here follow those listed in 19.8.

me because you were captivated by his promises and assurances; that every policy he recommended was contrary to your interests; that he repudiated the peace advocated by our allies and supported the one advocated by Philocrates; that he frittered away the time so that even if you wished you were unable to mount an expedition to Phocis; and that he committed many other terrible deeds while abroad, betrayed everything, sold his services, took bribes, missed no opportunity for mischief. That is what I promised in the beginning; that is what I have demonstrated.

[179] Now consider the next point; the argument you are about to hear is straightforward. You swore to cast your votes in accord with the laws and decrees of the Assembly and the Council of Five Hundred.[166] It is clear that everything this man did on the embassy was contrary to the laws, to the decrees, to justice. Thus, every sensible juror ought to convict him. Even if he committed no other crime, two things he did are sufficient grounds for putting him to death: he betrayed to Philip not only the Phocians but Thrace too. [180] Yet no one could identify two places in the entire world more important to the city than Thermopylae on land and the Hellespont at sea.[167] These men disgracefully sold both places and against your interests handed them over to Philip. It would be endless to describe how great a crime it was, apart from everything else, to betray Thrace and its fortifications,[168] and it is not difficult to show how many people you either put to death or punished with stiff fines for that reason: Ergophilus, Cephisodotus, Timomachus, Ergocles long ago, Dionysius, others.[169] Practically all of them together did less harm to the city than this man. [181] In the past, Athenians, you were still methodical in looking ahead and guarding

---

[166] On the Heliastic Oath, see 18.2n. "The Council of Five Hundred" is the full name for what is elsewhere simply "the Council."

[167] Phocis bordered on Thermopylae, the gateway to central and southern Greece. Thrace was on the northern shore of the Hellespont, through which grain was shipped from the Black Sea region to Athens.

[168] See 19.156n.

[169] Ergophilus, Cephisodotus, and Timomachus were generals who were convicted in the late 360s, early 350s. Ergocles, an associate of Thrasybulus (the leader of the democratic resurgence in 403), was sentenced to death in 390/89. Dionysius was a common name, and the man referred to here is unknown.

against trouble. Nowadays you neglect problems that are not imminent and troubles that are not right in front of you, and then you cast
futile votes here, for instance, "that Philip is to swear oaths to Cersebleptes," "that he is not to take part in the Amphictyony," "that he is
to revise the peace treaty." [170] None of these decrees would have been
necessary if this man had been willing to sail to Macedon and do his
duty. But in fact, by telling us to go by land, he destroyed what could
have been saved by sailing, and by lying, he destroyed what could have
been saved by speaking the truth.

[182] I am informed that he will soon express his irritation that he
is the only public speaker to be held accountable for his speeches.[171] I
leave aside that people who deliver speeches for the sake of money
are naturally held accountable for what they say; but let me say this. If
Aeschines jabbered a bit and made mistakes while acting in a private
capacity, do not examine it too closely, let it go, overlook it. But if he
purposely deceived you for the sake of money while he was your envoy, do not acquit him, and do not allow him to claim immunity for
what he said. [183] For what else should envoys be held accountable if
not their speeches? Envoys are not in charge of triremes, territory, soldiers, or citadels (for no one entrusts these things to envoys) but of
words and time. Now, if Aeschines did not waste the time available
to the city,[172] he is not guilty; if he did waste it, he has committed a
crime. If the words in the report he gave were true or in the city's interests, he should be acquitted; if they were false, paid for, and against
the city's interests, he should be convicted. [184] There is no greater
crime someone could commit against you than to speak false words.
For how could people whose government is based on speeches govern
themselves securely unless the speeches are true? And if someone is
bribed to speak in support of policies that favor the enemy, how does
that not also put you at risk? [185] When someone wastes time in an
oligarchy or a tyranny, it is not the same crime as in your city. Far from
it. In those forms of government, I believe, everything is done immediately by dictate. But with you first the Council must consider every

---

[170] These quotations illustrate decrees of the Assembly that turned out to be
no more than useless attempts to respond to difficult situations ad hoc.

[171] Aes. 2.178.

[172] This refers to the time squandered by the envoys before they received
Philip's oaths ratifying the peace treaty (see 19.150–165).

matter and issue a preliminary decision, and that cannot happen any day but only when heralds and envoys have been notified in advance. Next, the Assembly must meet, and that takes place when the laws specify. Then the politicians who offer the best policy must defeat and overcome those who oppose them out of ignorance or corruption. [186] On top of all this, when a decision has been reached and a course of action seems advantageous, time is needed for resources the people lack, to allow them to acquire what they need to execute the policy they decided. So the man who wastes time in the kind of government we have does not just waste time; no, he has completely ruined the city's policy.

[187] Now, there is a phrase anyone interested in deceiving you can easily use: "the troublemakers in the city, those who prevent Philip from doing good things for the city." To that I will make no response, but I will read you letters from Philip, and I will remind you of every occasion on which you were deceived. You will thereby realize that when Philip tricked you, he surpassed "the saturation point," as that trite expression has it.[173]

[PHILIP'S LETTERS]

[188] Though Aeschines' record as envoy includes many shameful acts, all working against your interests, he now goes around asking people, "What would you say about Demosthenes, who accuses his fellow envoys?" By Zeus, of course I do: whether I like it or not, since I was subject to your plots during the entire journey, I now have the choice of either giving the impression that I joined you in those deeds or accusing you. [189] But I deny that I even was your fellow-envoy: as envoy you committed many despicable crimes while I served the best interests of these people. Philocrates was your fellow-envoy, and you were his, and Phryno too.[174] All of you worked together and had the same goals. "But what of the salt? What of the table? What of the libations?" That is his tragic lament, as if those who betrayed these things were not the guilty ones, but the ones who did what was

---

[173] The expression that spoke of "the saturation point" has not survived. Presumably Demosthenes means that Philip's letter contains deceit after deceit. If he commented on specific points after the letter was read, these comments did not survive in the written text of the speech.

[174] Phryno was a member of the First and Second Embassies (see also Aes. 2.12).

right.[175] [190] Now, I know that all the Presiding Officers share in the sacrifice conducted before every meeting, and they dine together and make libations in common.[176] Yet the good ones among them do not for that reason imitate the bad ones, but if they catch any of their colleagues committing a crime, they notify the Council and the Assembly. Likewise for the Council: they offer sacrifices at the beginning of the year; they feast together. The generals share libations and other rituals, as do virtually all those who hold office.[177] Does that give them reason to grant immunity to colleagues who commit crimes? Far from it! [191] Leon prosecuted Timagoras, his fellow-envoy for four years. Eubulus prosecuted Tharrhex and Smicythus, his colleagues at the common mess. In the old days the famous Conon prosecuted Adimantus, his colleague as general.[178] So who violated the salt and the libations, Aeschines? The traitors, dishonest envoys, and bribe-takers, or those who indicted them? Clearly the guilty have, like you, violated the libations of the entire country, not only their own.

[192] Listen for a moment to a few words that have little to do with the embassy, so that you may realize that these envoys are the most vile and reprehensible of all those who have ever journeyed to Philip, whether for public or private purposes. When Philip took Olynthus and was organizing his Olympic festival,[179] he invited actors from all over to participate in the communal festivities. [193] While he was en-

---

[175] The salt, table, and libations shared by the envoys suggest a common purpose fortified by common rites (cf. Aes. 3.52). Demosthenes mocks Aeschines' pathetic attempt to portray Demosthenes as a traitor to that association; Aeschines answers at 2.22. "Tragic lament" mocks Aeschines for his career on stage.

[176] On the Presiding Officers (*prytaneis*), see 18.169n and the Series Introduction.

[177] Most civic offices, including the generalship, were held by several individuals who functioned as collegial members of a board.

[178] On Timagoras, see 19.31n. On Eubulus, see 18.21n. Tharrhex and Smicythus are otherwise unknown. Conon and Adimantus were generals in the last year of the Peloponnesian War. The latter was accused of treason because he alone of the Athenian prisoners from Aegospotami was not put to death by Lysander, the Spartan commander (Xen., *Hellenica* 2.1.32).

[179] Not the quadrennial panhellenic festival celebrated in the Peloponnese, but a festival celebrated near Mt. Olympus in northern Greece. Olynthus fell to Philip in 348.

tertaining them and awarding crowns to the victors, he asked Satyrus, our well-known comic actor, why he alone made no request. Had Satyrus detected some pettiness in Philip or some aversion towards him? Satyrus is said to have replied that he had no need of any of the things that the others wanted, and although what he would really like to ask for would be the easiest favor in the world for Philip to bestow, he nevertheless feared he would not get it. [194] When Philip urged him to speak and rather impetuously boasted that there was nothing he would not do for him, Satyrus, it is said, brought up Apollophanes of Pydna, his host (*xenos*) and friend. Now, Apollophanes had been treacherously murdered, whereupon his relations, fearful for his young daughters, removed them and brought them to Olynthus. "These girls," Satyrus continued, "who are now of marriageable age, became prisoners when Olynthus was taken and are now in your hands. I beg and beseech you, give them to me. [195] Please listen and understand what kind of gift you would be giving me, if you do give it. I would not gain any profit from it but would add a dowry at my cost and marry them off. I will not allow them to endure anything unworthy of me or their father." When the guests at Philip's banquet heard this request, the shouts of approval were so loud and boisterous that Philip was actually touched and granted the request, even though the Apollophanes in question was among those who killed Alexander, Philip's brother.[180]

[196] In comparison with this banquet attended by Satyrus, let's consider another banquet these men attended in Macedon. Observe whether the two cases resemble each other closely. The envoys were invited to the house of Xenophron, the son of Phaedimus who was one of the Thirty Tyrants, and so they went. I did not go.[181] When it came time to commence the drinking, an Olynthian woman was brought in; she was quite attractive but of free birth and modest, as the event proved. [197] At first, it seems, according to what Iatrocles

---

[180] In 368. Aes. 2.156 disparages Demosthenes' version of Satyrus' story.

[181] Demosthenes implies that while he would not even enter the house of a descendant of one of the Thirty Tyrants, the oligarchs who terrorized Athens in the aftermath of the Peloponnesian War, the other envoys had no such scruples. Phaedimus is a faulty reminiscence of Phaedrias (Xen., *Hellenica* 2.3.2). Aeschines rejects Demosthenes' version of the following story, calls the party's host Xenodocus, and claims that he was a Macedonian (2.4, 153–158).

told me the next day, the envoys pressured her rather gently to drink and eat a bit of dessert. But as the affair wore on and their spirits grew heated, they kept prodding her to lie on the couch and sing something as well. The woman became distressed, for she didn't want to sing and wasn't able to, whereupon this man and Phryno, declaring her behavior an outrage, said they would not allow her, a loathsome, accursed Olynthian prisoner of war, to put on airs. "Summon a slave," they said, and "bring a whip." A servant produced a strap, and, since the men, I believe, were drunk and easily provoked, when she said something and began crying, the servant ripped off her tunic and flogged her back repeatedly. [198] Beside herself at this dreadful turn of events, the woman jumped up and fell at the knees of Iatrocles, upsetting the table. If he hadn't rescued her, she would have been killed by their drunken rage; for this piece of trash [182] is fierce when he drinks. The story of this woman was told even in Arcadia among the Ten Thousand. [183] Diophantus gave you a report about it, which he will be compelled to furnish under oath right now. And there was also much talk of it in Thessaly and elsewhere.

[199] This foul specimen knows full well what he's done, yet he will dare to look you in the face, and in a moment he'll be using his glorious voice to talk of the life he's led. It makes me gag. Do these jurors not know that you started off reading books in your mother's initiation rites, and as a child you hung around with the holy bands of drunken revelers? [184] [200] And that you later served as a petty clerk to civic magistrates and could be bribed for two or three drachmas? And that you just recently found happiness as a freeloader, playing the bit parts in productions financed by other citizens? [185] So, what kind of life will you talk about? The one you did not live, since it's clear what your life was like. The arrogance of it! This man put someone else on

---

[182] Aeschines.

[183] The Ten Thousand was the name of the Arcadian Assembly.

[184] In this invective Demosthenes uses many of the same barbs that he later used with even greater success in speech 18; see 18.258–265 and the notes in that passage.

[185] Demosthenes contrasts Aeschines, the bad, impoverished actor, with citizens who concretely promote the public welfare by taking up the *chorēgia,* the obligation to pay for choral productions in the city's festivals. See 18.257, 262, 267.

trial for prostitution![186] But I'll take that up later. Clerk, please read the testimonies first.

[TESTIMONIES]

[201] Jurors, since Aeschines has been convicted of so many heinous crimes against you—what misdeed has he not exhibited? He's a corrupt, bootlicking, accursed, lying traitor to his colleagues,[187] everything that is utterly reprehensible—he will not mount a defense against even a single one of them, and he will not be able to put forward any legitimate or straightforward argument in his own defense. What he is going to say, as I have ascertained, borders on madness, but someone who has nothing honest to say is compelled, I suppose, to try anything.

[202] I have heard that he will say that I was an accomplice in every deed that I am now denouncing, that I supported those actions and worked with him to accomplish them, but then I underwent a sudden change and accused him.[188] With regard to the facts, a defense of this kind is neither honest nor relevant, though it is one way to accuse me. For if I did what he charges, I am indeed a despicable creature, but that doesn't make his actions any better; far from it. [203] Nevertheless, I believe that it is incumbent on me both to establish that Aeschines will be lying if he levels such charges and to demonstrate what an honest defense would consist in. Now, a defense that is honest and straightforward would show either that the alleged acts never took place or that they served the city well. But neither alternative is open to Aeschines. [204] Surely he cannot argue that the city is better off because the Phocians are destroyed, Philip controls Thermopylae, the Thebans hold sway, Euboea is occupied, Megara is threatened, and the peace is unratified; when he delivered his report to the Assembly,[189] he promised that the outcome would be precisely the opposite and would be to your advantage. And since you are well aware of events, having

---

[186] Timarchus, the defendant in Aes. 1.

[187] See 19.70 on accursed, 19.191 on traitor to colleagues.

[188] Demosthenes needed no prior knowledge of Aeschines' case to anticipate this argument. Aes. 2.14–20, 54–56 argues that Demosthenes was Philocrates' accomplice.

[189] See 19.20–22.

seen them for yourselves, he will also be unable to persuade you that they never took place. [205] Therefore, it remains for me to show that I did not collaborate in any of these actions. Do you want me, jurors, to put aside all the evidence that I resisted these men in the Assembly, quarreled with them while abroad, and opposed them throughout? Shall I instead present these men as witnesses that they and I worked towards opposite goals in every instance and that they accepted money to do you harm, while I refused to take any? Consider.

[206] Who would you say is the most loathsome man in Athens, the one absolutely brimming with impudence and contempt? No one would name, even by mistake, anyone but Philocrates. And who would you say talks loudest of all and uses that voice of his to say most clearly what he wants? Aeschines, of course, the man before us now. And who would these men say is timid and cowardly before the mob or rather, as I say, judicious? I am, for never once have I hectored you or bullied you against your wishes. [207] Consequently, whenever the discussion in the Assembly has been about these men, you always hear me accusing them, criticizing them, and stating unequivocally that they are corrupt and have sold the city's interests completely. And when they heard these charges, none of them has ever yet rejected them, opened his mouth, or even shown his face. [208] So why is it that the most loathsome, loudest men in the city are so badly defeated by me, though I am both the most timid and the most soft-spoken of all? Because the truth is strong and the opposite is weak, namely, the awareness that they sold the city's interests. This saps their boldness, this stops their tongue, plugs their mouth, chokes them, silences them.

[209] Surely you remember the most recent occasion, just the other day in Piraeus, when you denied Aeschines a place on the embassy: [190] he screamed that he would charge me with treason [191] and indict me and alas and alack. To do that would mean long trials and numerous speeches, instead of two or maybe three simple words that even a slave

---

[190] The embassy in question is unknown. Some have suspected the embassy mentioned in 18.134, but it is probably not that one because on that occasion, the Areopagus Council forced Aeschines off an embassy to which the people had initially appointed him.

[191] By the process of *eisangelia*.

bought yesterday could recite:[192] "Athenians, the situation is outrageous. This man accuses me of crimes that he himself helped to perpetrate; and he says that I took money, though he took his share." [210] Now, Aeschines did not utter those words, he did not pronounce them, and none of you heard them. Instead, he just started making threats. Why? Because he knew what his record was, and those words held him in thrall. He could not bring himself to face up to them but shrank before them, his will held fast by his guilty conscience. But nothing prevented him from hurling insults and abuse of every kind.

[211] Yet the most important point of all is a matter of deeds, not words. After I served as envoy for the second time,[193] I was seeking to do my duty and submit my accounts for the second time. But Aeschines went to the auditors with a number of witnesses and tried to prevent them from admitting me into court; he alleged that I had already undergone the audit (*euthynai*) and was now exempt. This was utterly ridiculous. What was the point? When Aeschines submitted his accounts from the First Embassy, no one brought any accusations; so he sought to avoid a second court appearance for the embassy for which he is on trial now, the one on which all the crimes occurred. [212] Because I faced the auditors a second time, he had to face them again too. That's why he tried to prevent them from admitting me. This deed, Athenians, clearly proves two points: Aeschines has convicted himself, so that it would be impious for any of you to acquit him,[194] and he will have nothing to say about me that is true. For if he had any true complaints against me, he would have spoken up and accused me then and, by Zeus, he would not have tried to keep me out of court.

[213] To show that these statements are true, clerk, please call the witnesses who will testify to them.

Yet if Aeschines attacks me for something over and above the embassy, you should ignore him for many reasons. I am not the one on trial today, and when my speech is over, no one will add water to my clock. So if Aeschines tries that tactic, it can mean only that he has no

---

[192] A slave bought yesterday could scarcely speak Greek.

[193] On the Second Embassy.

[194] The jurors' oath (18.2n) obliges them to condemn the guilty; see also 19.71.

legitimate arguments. For what defendant would prefer to level accusations if he were able to mount a defense? [214] Consider another point too, jurors. If I were on trial with Aeschines prosecuting and Philip judging, and if I were unable to argue my innocence and instead slandered Aeschines and tried to drag him into the mud, do you not think that Philip would be angered at having his supporters slandered in his own presence? Do not sink below Philip's level, but compel Aeschines to defend himself on the charges for which he is being tried. Clerk, read the testimony.

[TESTIMONY]

[215] Since my conscience was clear, I recognized my obligation to submit my accounts and to comply with all the requirements of the law, but Aeschines did just the opposite. How, then, could he and I have done the same thing? And how can it be right for him to bring up charges today that he never saw fit to mention before? It cannot, of course. But he will bring them up nevertheless, and by Zeus, with good reason. You know, of course, that since mankind has existed and trials have taken place, no one has ever yet been convicted of a crime by his own confession, but criminals defy, deny, lie, make excuses, do anything to avoid punishment. [216] You must not be misled by any of these tactics today but must decide the matter based on your own knowledge. You must pay no attention to my words or his, or to the witnesses that he, with Philip's financial backing,[195] will prepare so that they give any testimony whatsoever (and you will see how eagerly they will testify on his behalf), or indeed to the splendor and power of his voice or to the feebleness of mine. [217] If you are sensible, your task today is not to judge politicians or speeches but to examine the facts as all of you know them and then to thrust the disgrace resulting from the outrageous, appalling destruction of the city's affairs upon those who are responsible. What is it then that you citizens already know without having to hear it from us?

---

[195] Playing on both Philip's corruption of the witnesses and Aeschines' career in the theater, Demosthenes ironically describes Philip as *chorēgos* (lit. "chorus producer"), the name given to citizens who financed plays and other choral performances in Athens for public benefit (see 19.200n).

[218] If peace brought you everything that these men promised, if you agree that you are so full of dishonor and cowardice that—when no enemy occupied your land, no one blockaded you at sea, and no other imminent danger faced the city, when you could import cheap grain and your circumstances were no worse in other respects than they are now, [219] when you knew beforehand because these men assured you that your allies would be destroyed, that the Thebans would gain power, that Philip would seize the region near Thrace, that forces would threaten you from Euboea, and that everything that has happened would happen—if in that situation you gladly made peace, then acquit Aeschines, and do not commit perjury too[196] in addition to so much humiliation already—for he has done you no wrong, but I am thoroughly out of my mind to accuse him now. [220] However, if it's exactly the opposite, and these men made many pleasant promises—that Philip was well disposed towards the city, that he would safeguard the Phocians, that he would put an end to the Theban insolence, and in addition that, if peace were reached, he would more than make up for the loss of Amphipolis and would return Euboea and Oropus—if by making these promises, these men utterly deceived you, tricked you, and all but stripped you of Attica, convict them, and do not bring the curse down upon yourselves and commit perjury[197] on top of the other outrages (I don't know what else they should be called) you suffered and for which these men took payment.

[221] Now, consider the next point, jurors. Is there any reason I would have chosen to prosecute these men had they done nothing wrong? You won't find one. Is it pleasant to have many enemies? It's not even safe! Did I harbor any hatred of this man before? None. Then why? "You were afraid, and cowardice prompted you to seek safety in prosecution"; this is the line he takes, as I've been told. But if, as you say, Aeschines, there was no mischief or crime,[198] why would I be

---

[196] By violating the Heliastic Oath to acquit the innocent and convict the guilty.

[197] By allowing the traitors' crimes to go unpunished, the jurors would involve themselves in the curse that hangs over the traitors because of their treachery (see 19.70). On the perjury, see previous note.

[198] On the embassy.

afraid? Yet if he concedes that crimes did occur, consider, jurors, what those who are actually guilty deserve to suffer, when I, though not guilty at all, feared they would bring me down with them. So that's not the reason. [222] So why do I bring charges against you? By Zeus, I'm just a *sykophant,* looking for you to buy me off.[199] Now, which scenario better served my interests? Should I have taken the money offered by Philip, which was considerable and as much as any of these men received, and thereby made both Philip and these men my friends? For they would indeed be my friends, they would, if I shared their goals; it is not some inherited quarrel that turns them against me, but my refusal to join their schemes. Or should I have extorted a share of what they took and thereby made Philip and these men my enemies, ransomed the prisoners of war at considerable personal expense, and incurred disgrace and loathing while wresting from these men a small profit? [223] That is not what I did; rather, for the sake of justice and truth and the rest of my life, I reported the facts and refused to profit, supposing, as do many of you, that I would earn your esteem for being honest and that I should not trade my standing in your eyes for any gain. I despise these men because I saw on the embassy that they are detestable scoundrels, and now that their corruption has made you angry about the entire embassy, I have also lost the public honors that were coming to me.[200] But I am bringing charges now and prosecuting at Aeschines' audit with a view to the future: by means of a trial in court, I wish to establish in your presence that my course of action and that taken by these men are mutually opposed.

[224] Yet I fear, yes, fear—and I shall tell you exactly what I think—that later on, you citizens will drag me down with the rest of them though I've done nothing wrong at all, since right now you are discouraged. For you seem to me, Athenians, to be exhausted, merely waiting on the terrible fate in store. You see struggles elsewhere but take no precautions yourselves, and you neglect the city even though it has long been seriously declining. [225] Do you not think it appalling and outrageous? Even if I had decided to be silent, I am com-

---

[199] I.e., in return for dropping the prosecution, which was the *modus operandi* of *sykophants.* Of course, Demosthenes is speaking ironically.

[200] See 19.31n on honors for successful envoys.

pelled to speak now. I suppose you know Pythocles, son of Pytho-dorus,[201] who is here in court today. He and I used to get on quite well, and up to this very day no unpleasantness has occurred between us. Yet since he's been to visit Philip, he turns away when he sees me, and if for some reason he cannot escape an encounter, he leaves immediately so as not to be seen in my company. Yet he walks around the Agora with Aeschines and seeks his advice.

[226] Haven't things reached a thoroughly wretched state, Athenians, when those who have chosen to serve Philip have their conduct towards each side watched so closely by him that each of them supposes that nothing he does in Athens will escape Philip's notice, as if he were standing by in person and personally decides in each case who is his friend and who not? Yet you are so deaf and blind to those who devote their lives to you, who strive for your esteem and never betray it, that these accursed men and I now compete on an equal basis even though you know full well what's going on. [227] Would you like to know the cause of this state of affairs? I shall explain, but please do not be angry at me for speaking the truth. Since Philip, of course, has but one body and one soul, he both loves his benefactors and hates his opponents with undivided enthusiasm. Yet each of you, in the first place, fails to view the city's benefactors and enemies as likewise his own, [228] and, secondly, assigns greater importance to other matters that frequently lead you astray—pity, envy, anger, indulging those who ask for favors, thousands of other things. And anyone who could escape all this will nevertheless not elude those who would prefer to see such men as he eliminated. Mistakes in each of these cases, creeping in little by little, together damage the city.

[229] Do not, Athenians, do this today, and do not acquit this man who has committed such crimes against you. Really, what will people say about you if you acquit him? That some men set out from Athens as envoys to Philip—Philocrates, Aeschines, Phryno,[202] Demosthenes. Well? One reaped no profit from the embassy and used his own resources to ransom the prisoners of war; another, having sold the

---

[201] Apart from his connection with Aeschines and enmity with Demosthenes (18.285, 19.314), Pythocles is little known.

[202] See 19.189n on Phryno.

city's interests, used the money for whores and delicacies in the market.²⁰³ [230] One, that scoundrel Phryno, sent his own son to Philip before enrolling him as a citizen;²⁰⁴ another did nothing unworthy of the city or himself. One had already financed a chorus and a trireme but still considered it his duty to take on additional expenses voluntarily, to ransom the prisoners, and to allow no citizen to remain in that distressing state through poverty; another, so far from saving anyone who was still a prisoner, worked with Philip to take an entire region that belonged to our allies and to turn its more than ten thousand soldiers and nearly one thousand cavalry into prisoners.²⁰⁵

[231] What happened then? The Athenians, who had known about this for some time, seized the men. And? Those who had taken money and gifts, who had disgraced themselves, the city, and their own children, were acquitted, since the Athenians believed that they were the sensible ones and that the city was thriving. And what about the prosecutor? They thought he was an imbecile, that he failed to understand the city, that he had no idea where he was throwing his money away!²⁰⁶ [232] Who, Athenians, will look on this example and strive for justice in his public conduct? What envoy will serve honestly if it means both not taking money and at the same time being regarded as no more trustworthy in your eyes than those who did take it? You are not merely judging these men today, no, you are also enacting a law for all time hereafter about whether it's proper for all envoys to be mercenary and disgracefully aid the enemy or honest and work on your behalf honorably and without corruption. [233] You do not need to hear testimony on any other points, but, clerk, please call the witnesses to testify that Phryno sent his son to Philip.²⁰⁷

---

²⁰³ Philocrates.

²⁰⁴ Young men were officially enrolled as citizens at age eighteen. Demosthenes suggests an obscene purpose in Phryno's gift of his son to Philip, which is soon elaborated (19.233).

²⁰⁵ Aeschines. The region is Phocis.

²⁰⁶ In this paragraph, Demosthenes imagines a parody of justice that he would dearly like to avert. In this nightmarish scenario, ransoming the prisoners was throwing money away.

²⁰⁷ The testimony is delayed until 19.236.

Yet Aeschines did not put Phryno on trial for sending his own son to Philip for a shameful purpose. Rather, if someone in his youth was rather more handsome than others, if this someone had no idea that his appearance might excite suspicion, and if he later lived a bit recklessly, Aeschines put him on trial for prostitution.[208]

[234] Let me say a few words about the public banquet and my decree; I nearly omitted what I most need to speak about.[209] When I drafted the motion concerning the First Embassy and again in the Assembly that was convened to discuss peace, it was not yet evident that these men had said or done anything wrong. So I followed custom by commending them and inviting them to banquet in the Prytaneum. [235] By Zeus, I also hosted Philip's envoys, and quite splendidly too, Athenians. For when I saw them crowing about how the Macedonians are so sumptuous and splendid in bestowing hospitality, I knew immediately that I had to surpass them in this matter myself and come off as more generous. This is what Aeschines will be referring to when he says that "Demosthenes himself commended us," and "Demosthenes himself invited the envoys to the banquet." But he will not explain when this happened. [236] It happened before the city was the victim of any crimes and before it became clear that these men had sold their services: the envoys were just back from their first trip, the Assembly was about to hear their report, and neither had this man yet made clear his support of Philocrates nor Philocrates the terms he would propose. So if Aeschines mentions those events, remember that they occurred

---

[208] The "someone" in question is Timarchus, whom Aeschines prosecuted for prostitution in 346/5 (Aes. 1). Demosthenes implies that Aeschines' failure to prosecute Phryno for a truly grievous moral crime shows that the prosecution of Timarchus, which Aeschines drenched in morality, was just a matter of political expediency.

[209] While a member of the Council in 347/6, Demosthenes moved a decree praising the envoys of the First Embassy and inviting them to dine in the Prytaneum (see 19.31n on this standard practice). He also moved a decree affording hospitality to Philip's envoys, Antipater and Parmenion. See 18.28 for Demosthenes' later attempt to defend this part of his record. Aeschines attacks Demosthenes for praising the Athenian envoys of the First Embassy (2.45–46, 53, 121) and for Demosthenes' reception of the Macedonian envoys (2.111).

before the crimes took place. After that, there was no familiarity and no common ground between them and me. Clerk, read the testimony.[210]

[TESTIMONY]

[237] Now, perhaps Aeschines' brother will speak on his behalf, either Philochares or Aphobetus. There is a great deal that you could fairly say to both of them, and one must, Athenians, speak freely without reservations. Even though you, Philochares, paint perfume jars and tambourines (*tympana*) and you, Aphobetus, are, like Aeschines, a petty clerk and run-of-the-mill—nothing contemptible there, but hardly the proper background for a general—we Athenians chose you for diplomatic posts, military commands, the highest offices.[211] [238] If none of you did anything wrong, we are not the ones who ought to thank you, but you would rightly thank us. For we dignified you while passing over many who deserved the offices more. So if one of you did commit a crime in the offices that you occupied, a crime of that sort, how much more just would it be for all of you to be hated rather than spared? Quite a bit, I would think. Perhaps Aeschines' brothers will press hard with their booming voices and insolent manner, urging that "it is understandable to aid a brother." [239] Do not give in. Keep in mind that if his brothers are obliged to think of him, you are obliged to think of the laws, of the city as a whole, and above all, of the oath that you yourselves swore before taking your seats in court. If they implore any of you to save this man, consider whether it has been shown that he committed no crime against the city or that in fact he did. If their appeal is to save him if he is innocent, then I agree that you should, but if they implore you in any case no matter what, then they are asking you to perjure yourselves. For if the ballot is secret, it will not escape the gods, a fact the lawgiver understood quite well: while none of these men will know who among you showed them favor, the gods and the divine realm will know who voted against justice. [240] Each of you is better off deciding for justice and right and thus protecting your hopes of divine favor for your children[212] and yourselves rather

---

[210] That concerning Phryno, his son, and Philip (19.233).

[211] Philochares was a general, and Aphobetus was a politician. The tambourines recall Glaucothea's rites (see 18.284n). Decorating perfume jars was menial.

[212] Divine punishment could extend to the next generation.

than conferring a hidden, invisible favor on these men and acquitting the man whose own testimony convicts him. To prove that you did great harm as envoy, Aeschines, is there anyone I could find to testify against you more powerfully than you? Since you thought it necessary to inflict so much trouble on the man who sought to publicize your record as envoy,[213] clearly you expected a bad outcome if these citizens discovered what you did.

[241] If you are sensible, this man's earlier prosecution[214] will come back to haunt him not only because it is a massive sign of his conduct on the embassy but also because the arguments he used in that prosecution are now valid against him. Surely it is fitting that others should exploit against you, Aeschines, the very standards of justice that you employed in prosecuting Timarchus. [242] On that occasion Aeschines said the following to the jurors: "Demosthenes will defend Timarchus and censure my conduct on the embassy. Then, if his speech distracts you, he'll gloat and go around asking 'how did I manage to distract the jurors from the matter at hand and get away with stealing the case right from under them?'"[215] Don't you try that, Aeschines, but defend yourself on the charges for which you are being tried. You had your chance to accuse and say anything you wanted when you were prosecuting Timarchus.

[243] Furthermore, since you had no witnesses to prove your case against Timarchus, you even quoted epic verses to the jurors:

No rumor ever dies completely if it is spread
abroad by many people. It too is a god.[216]

Since all these people, Aeschines, say that you did indeed take bribes while you were on the embassy, so in your case too, I suppose, "no rumor ever dies completely if it is spread abroad by many people." [244] Why, look how many more people blame you than blamed Ti-

---

[213] Timarchus.

[214] Aes. 1, *Against Timarchus*.

[215] Aeschines exacerbated the charge by portraying Demosthenes as a sophistic teacher, gloating with his students over a deceitful triumph (1.175).

[216] Hesiod, *Works and Days* 763–764, quoted by Aeschines against Timarchus at 1.129. At 2.144–145, Aeschines responds to this attempt by Demosthenes to turn his own words against him.

marchus. Not even all of his neighbors knew Timarchus, but absolutely no one, Greek or barbarian, denies that you envoys accepted bribes on the embassy. So, if rumor is indeed true, you envoys are incriminated by the rumor spread by the masses, since you yourself insisted that rumor must be reliable, for "it too is a god," and that the poet who wrote those verses was wise.

[245] There were also iambic verses that Aeschines found and recited, including these:

> If any man enjoys the company of bad men,
> I've never examined him: I know he is
> like those he likes to be around.[217]

Then, having described his opponent as "frequenting the cock fights and hanging around with Pittalacus"[218] and the like, he asked: "Don't you know what to think of such a person?" I will now show that these iambic verses apply to you too, Aeschines, and when I address the audience, my words will be right on the mark: "If any man enjoys the company"—especially while on an embassy—of Philocrates, "I've never examined him: I know he" has accepted bribes, like Philocrates, who has admitted as much.

[246] Though Aeschines labels others speechwriters and sophists in an attempt to abuse them, I will show that these names apply to him.[219] The iambic verses just quoted come from Euripides' *Phoenix*. Yet neither Theodorus nor Aristodemus, both of whom often employed Aeschines as their third actor, ever acted in that play; it was performed, rather, by Molon and perhaps some other actor from long

---

[217] These are the last three of nine verses from Euripides' *Phoenix* (now lost) that Aeschines quoted against Timarchus (1.152).

[218] Aeschines excoriated Timarchus for attending cockfights and prostituting himself to Pittalacus, a public slave (1.53–54).

[219] These labels branded the opponent as an expert but dishonest and untrustworthy manipulator of public discourse (see 18.276n). Strictly speaking, a speechwriter (*logographos*) was one who, in return for compensation, composed speeches for others to deliver in court on their own behalf. Demosthenes had previously been a speechwriter, but he ceased that activity once he entered politics, with which it was not compatible. Aeschines called Demosthenes these names at 1.94, 125, 175, and in the later speeches at 2.180, 3.16, 173, 202.

ago.[220] But Sophocles' *Antigone* was often performed by Theodorus, and it was often performed by Aristodemus too. That play contains some splendid iambic verses that you would find edifying, and though Aeschines performed those verses often and knows them by heart, he omitted them from his speech. [247] Of course, you are well aware that in every tragic drama the third actors enjoy the particular privilege of playing tyrants and those who bear the scepter. Consider the verses that the poet puts into the mouth of Creon-Aeschines in this play, verses that Aeschines neither uttered to himself in regard to the embassy nor recited to the jurors. Clerk, read.

IAMBIC VERSES FROM SOPHOCLES' *ANTIGONE*

It is impossible to understand the mind
or thought or conviction of any man until
rule and law have plainly put him to the test.
If a man governs the whole city
but fails to abide by the best counsels
and holds his tongue out of fear,
now as before I consider him most evil.
And a man who holds a friend above
his own country, I call him worthless.
Let all-seeing Zeus take notice—
neither would I be silent if in place of safety
I saw ruin advancing on the citizens,
nor would I ever count my country's enemy
as my friend: I know our country
saves us, and we preserve our friends
by sailing steadily upon the ship of state.[221]

[248] Aeschines recited none of these verses to himself during the embassy, but, bidding a fond farewell to sage Sophocles, he held Phil-

---

[220] Theodorus and Aristodemus were two of the best-known actors of their day; Aristodemus was mentioned above (19.12) in connection with negotiations between Philip and Athens. Molon was acting during the late fifth century (Aristoph., *Frogs* 55). On Aeschines as a third actor, see 18.129n.

[221] Lines 175–190 of the play. In the following passage, Demosthenes weaves verbatim quotations of these verses seamlessly into his attack on Aeschines.

ip's hospitality and friendship far "above his" city and more profitable to himself, and as he "saw ruin advancing" close by—Philip's expedition against the Phocians—he uttered no warning and gave no alert, but, on the contrary, he kept it hidden, colluded, and obstructed those who wished to speak. [249] He did not recall that "our country saves us" and that "sailing upon the ship of state," his mother performed initiations and purifications and drained her clientele of their property, whereby she raised her sons to be such great men, while his father taught school, as the older citizens tell me, by the house of "the hero," the doctor, making what living he could but nevertheless doing so on that ship of state.[222] And the sons took bribes while working as petty clerks in all the civic offices until, finally, elected by you citizens to the rank of secretary, they were maintained for two years in the Tholos,[223] and now Aeschines has been dispatched as an envoy by that ship of state. [250] He thought nothing of these facts and took no steps to keep the ship of state sailing steadily; in fact, he capsized and sank it and so far as lay in his power maneuvered the ship into the hands of the enemy. And you are not then a sophist? And a wicked one to boot! You are not a speechwriter? And a fiend to boot! You ignored the verses that you performed many times and knew by heart, but you found verses that you never acted at any point in your life and brought them on the public stage in order to harm a citizen.

[251] Consider the story that Aeschines told about Solon. He claimed that a statue of Solon portraying him with his hand inside his hanging cloak was erected as an example of the modesty of the public speakers of Solon's day, whereupon Aeschines rebuked and abused Timarchus for his brazenness.[224] But according to the Salaminians, the statue is less than fifty years old, and since Solon lived about two hundred and forty years ago, not only was the craftsman who put Solon

---

[222] On the occupations that Demosthenes assigns Aeschines' parents and their vituperative import, see 18.258–265 with notes. An ancient scholar explains that this doctor, Aristomachus, was known as the hero because of his size.

[223] As secretary, Aeschines served the *prytaneis* (the Presiding Officers of the Council; see 18.169n), who worked and dined in the Tholos, a building in the Agora. The Council's secretaries also had dining privileges in the Tholos.

[224] Aes. 1.25–26, which includes an attack on Timarchus for appearing naked in the Assembly while drunk. The statue in question was on Salamis.

in that stance not Solon's contemporary but neither was his grand-father! [252] That is what Aeschines told the jurors, and he imitated the stance, but what is far more useful to the city than the stance— observing Solon's mind and purpose—that Aeschines did not imitate; in fact, he did quite the opposite. When Salamis revolted from Athens, and the Athenians imposed the death penalty on anyone who might propose its recovery, Solon personally assumed the risk by composing and reciting an elegiac poem, which enabled him to recover Salamis for Athens and remove the attendant humiliation.[225] [253] But when this man supported the terms proposed by Philocrates, he abandoned Amphipolis and peddled it away, even though the Persian King and all Greeks recognized it as yours. That was the time to think of Solon, was it not? Yet not only did he abandon Amphipolis while in Athens but when he went to Macedon he never even mentioned the name of the place that was the reason for his presence there as envoy.[226] Indeed, he told you as much himself in his report. Surely you citizens recall him saying: "Though I too was prepared to speak about Amphipolis, I skipped it to give Demosthenes the opportunity to discuss it." [254] But when I addressed the Assembly, I said that this man had left me none of the points he wished to make to Philip, for he would sooner lend a man his blood than his words. Rather, having accepted Philip's money, he could not, I take it, offer any protest, because Philip gave him the money precisely to retain Amphipolis.[227] Clerk, please take Solon's elegiac verses and read them, so that you citizens understand that Solon too despised men like this.

[255] It's not that you must speak with your hand inside your cloak. No, Aeschines, you must negotiate with your hand inside your cloak. But in Macedon you stretched your hand out and held it there, bringing disgrace on these people, though in Athens you offer righteous talk.

---

[225] In the early sixth century, Athens defeated Megara and occupied Salamis (Plut., *Life of Solon* 8). Several verses of Solon's ode on Salamis survive.

[226] On Amphipolis and the Persian King, see 19.137n. In the negotiations of 346, Amphipolis must have figured among Athens' claims, but it was hardly the embassy's main goal. In the Peace of Philocrates, Athens' claim to Amphipolis was officially abandoned.

[227] See Aes. 2.43, 48, 52 for his account of who was responsible for addressing Philip regarding Amphipolis.

And though you practiced and rehearsed your wretched little speech, do you expect to get away with so many serious crimes, even if you put a cap on your head and go about abusing me? [228] Clerk, read.

ELEGIAC VERSES [229]

It is Zeus' plan and the will of the blessed immortal gods
    that our city will never be destroyed:
such is the great-hearted sentinel, scion of a mighty father,
    Pallas Athena, who holds her hands above.
But in their folly the citizens themselves, obedient
    to money, wish to destroy their great city,
and the people's leaders are intent on evil; much suffering
    lies in store for them because of great transgressions.
They know not how to check their greed or harmonize
    present delight in the peace of the banquet.
. . . .
    they grow rich, embracing unjust deeds.
. . . .
    sparing neither sacred possessions nor public ones,
they steal and plunder, one from the other,
    and do not guard the reverend foundations of Justice—
the silent one who knows what goes on and what went on before
    and in time comes to exact full revenge.
That comes now, an inescapable wound upon the whole city,
    and the city swiftly falls into evil servitude,
or it rouses civil strife and sleeping war,
    which destroys the lovely youth of many.
For hostile men soon consume the lovely city
    through alliances dear to the wicked.
These evils stir among the people; many of the poor
    arrive in a foreign land,

---

[228] The cap mocks Aeschines for trying to imitate Solon, who is said to have worn a cap when reciting his poem on Salamis (see Plutarch, cited in 19.252n; the purpose of the cap is unclear, though it may have been a herald's cap).

[229] This poem (Solon 4 West), preserved only here, is not the Salamis ode. It is impossible to know how many verses Demosthenes actually had the clerk read, but it could have been the entire passage.

sold and bound with outrageous bonds.

. . . .

Thus the common evil enters the home of every man,
and the courtyard gates no longer bar the way:
it leaps over the high fence and assuredly finds its man,
even should one flee to the corner of the inward room.
My heart commands me to teach the Athenians this lesson:
lawlessness secures the city abundant evils,
but lawfulness makes all things orderly and sound
and often encloses the unjust in chains;
it smoothes the rough, puts an end to greed, expunges violence,
and withers the growing blossoms of ruin;
it straightens crooked judgments, tames
haughty deeds, ends dissension,
and stops the anger of grievous quarrel. Through it
all things among men are sound and wise.

[256] Athenians, you hear what Solon has to say about men like
Aeschines, and about the gods, who in his view preserve the city. I
have always believed that Solon's view is true, and it is my wish that the
gods do preserve our city. I also believe that the very fact that this audit has taken place today somehow reveals the gods' concern for the
city. [257] Consider. A man does a thoroughly disastrous job as envoy,
gives up territory where you and your allies were responsible for wor-
shiping the gods,[230] and then disenfranchises a citizen who, though
once his accuser, duly appeared in court.[231] Why should it happen this
way? So that he may meet with neither sympathy nor clemency for the
crimes he committed. When he prosecuted Timarchus, he chose to
denounce me, and later he kept threatening in the Assembly to bring
charges and the like. Why should it happen this way? So that I might
prosecute him with the utmost compassion on your part, with the
fullest understanding of his evil tricks, and with experience of all his
actions.

---

[230] The Phocian cities destroyed by Philip were no longer able to maintain
their ancestral rites.

[231] Timarchus' penalty in the prosecution brought by Aeschines was the loss
of his civic rights.

[258] Though he managed to avoid a trial to this point, he is now brought to court at a time when unfolding circumstances, if nothing else, make it impossible as well as dangerous for you to allow this corrupt man to go free. It is always your duty, Athenians, to despise and punish corrupt traitors, yet to do so now would be particularly timely and beneficial to all Greeks everywhere. [259] Athenians, Greece has fallen victim to a terrible disease, one that is relentless and will require considerable good fortune and attention on your part. The most prominent citizens and respected leaders in the cities are haplessly betraying their own freedom and voluntarily enslaving themselves, all the while talking euphemistically of Philip's friendship and goodwill and so on. Although the other citizens and whoever else has any authority in each of the cities should be chastising their leaders and putting them to death forthwith, far from taking any action, they actually admire and emulate those leaders and to a man seek to be like them.

[260] This condition with its attendant rivalries had, until yesterday or the day before, robbed the Thessalians of their regional power and their general reputation among the Greeks, but now it is stripping them of their freedom: Macedonian forces occupy the citadels in some of their towns.[232] The condition has spread to the Peloponnese, where it has caused massacres in Elis, driving those wretched people so furiously insane that in pursuit of civic supremacy and Philip's patronage, they pollute themselves with the blood of kin and fellow-citizens.[233]

[261] Nor has it stopped there, but it has spread to Arcadia, where the entire region is turned upside down. Like you, the Arcadians are duty bound to cherish freedom, for apart from you, they are the only Greeks native to their soil.[234] But now they revere Philip and erect a bronze statue and award him a crown. Recently they voted to admit him to their cities, should he pay the Peloponnese a visit.[235] Things are the

---

[232] Philip began to intervene in Thessaly in the late 350s, and he began to exercise authority there directly in the mid 340s.

[233] Earlier in 343 an oligarchic coup, supported by Philip, replaced democracy in Elis.

[234] Popular Athenian mythology held that through their ancestor Erichthonius, born from the earth of Attica, the Athenians were native to their soil (autochthonous). Other Greek cities made similar claims for themselves.

[235] Ironic: Philip did not pay visits without the company of his army.

same in Argos. [262] To speak plainly, by Demeter, the situation requires no small amount of caution, since the disease is moving in from all sides and has now reached us, Athenians. While you are still safe, be wary and disenfranchise the citizens who first spread the disease among us. Otherwise, take care that you don't realize how aptly I speak only when you can do nothing about it. [263] Do you not see, Athenians, the clear, vivid example that the Olynthians have become? The poor souls, they perished on account of nothing other than the kind of behavior I just described. From what happened to them, you should be able to understand it well.

At a time when the Olynthian cavalry numbered a mere four hundred, and the Olynthians put no more than five thousand men in the field altogether, when Chalcidice was not yet unified into a single federation, [264] the Spartans attacked Olynthus with a massive force on both land and sea.[236] As you citizens surely know, Sparta was then sovereign, so to speak, over land and sea. Well, even though the Spartans attacked with such overwhelming force, the Olynthians lost neither the city itself nor a single stronghold, but they prevailed in several battles and killed three Spartan commanders, ultimately settling the war on their terms. [265] But when corruption made inroads among certain Olynthian politicians and through foolishness, if not bad luck, the Olynthians trusted them in preference to those who genuinely spoke on the people's behalf, when Lasthenes roofed his house with timber donated from Macedonia, when Euthycrates raised abundant cattle without paying anyone a fee,[237] when one politician suddenly owned sheep, another horses, when the citizenry, who were the victims of this business, far from taking umbrage or demanding redress from the guilty, ignored them, emulated them, honored them, and regarded them as real men— [266] when, I say, things progressed to this point and corruption prevailed, the Olynthians possessed one thousand cavalry, more than ten thousand infantry, and had allies among all the surrounding cities, and you Athenians supported them with ten thousand mercenaries, fifty triremes, and a citizen contingent of four thousand men. But none of these forces could save them. In less than

---

[236] In 382–379. See Xen., *Hellenica* 5.2–3.

[237] Demosthenes treats Lasthenes and Euthycrates as paradigmatic Greek traitors (see 18.48, 19.342).

a year of fighting, the Olynthians lost all the cities of Chalcidice, and Philip no longer had reason to attend to the traitors; he didn't know what to take first. [267] Five hundred cavalry along with their arms were surrendered by their own commanders and seized by Philip, which is more than any single man has ever taken. The light of the sun engendered no shame in the men who did these deeds, nor did the native soil on which they stood, nor the temples, nor the graves, nor the humiliation that such actions were bound to bring forth afterwards. Such madness and insanity, Athenians, comes of corruption. You, therefore, you the people must come to your senses, and instead of permitting such behavior, you must punish it publicly. It would be truly absurd if you voted a harsh condemnation for the Olynthian traitors but failed to punish the criminals in your midst. Clerk, please read the decree concerning the Olynthians.[238]

[DECREE]

[268] All Greeks and barbarians believe you did the right and noble thing, jurors, when you voted to condemn traitorous, villainous men. Given that bribery precedes treachery and causes people to become traitors, consider anyone you see taking bribes, Athenians, to be a traitor too. Whether he betrays strategic advantages or policies or an army, in my view he destroys whatever lies within his control, and all such men deserve your loathing equally.

[269] Of all men, Athenians, you alone can look to your own past as a guide in these circumstances and imitate the example of the ancestors whom you rightly praise. Even if you are currently at peace, and so this is not the moment to imitate them in combat, on campaign, or by facing the dangers that won them glory, you can at least imitate their prudence, [270] for that always serves a purpose. To be prudent requires no more trouble or exertion than it does to be imprudent. It will take the same amount of time for each of you, sitting here now, either to decide the right policy and vote for it, thereby benefiting the city as a whole and living up to the standards of your ancestors, or to decide the wrong policy and vote for that, thereby harming the city and falling short of your ancestors' standards. And what did your ancestors think about traitors? Clerk, take this document and read it. You citi-

---

[238] The Athenians outlawed Lasthenes and Euthycrates (see previous note).

zens must understand that you are lax about matters that your ancestors considered a capital crime. Clerk, read.

[INSCRIPTION]

[271] As you hear, Athenians, the inscription says that Arthmius, son of Pythonax, from the city of Zelea, was declared a villain and public enemy of the Athenian people and their allies, and his entire family along with him.[239] Why? Because he brought Persian gold to the Greeks. So this means, I take it, that your ancestors endeavored to prevent any person at all from doing Greece any harm for the sake of money, but you do not even try to prevent a fellow-citizen from harming your own city. [272] "Yes, by Zeus, but the inscription stands in any old place."[240] On the contrary, though the entire space of the Acropolis is sacred and covers a considerable expanse, the inscription stands just to the right of the great bronze statue of Athena that was paid for with donations from the Greeks and dedicated by the city as a memorial of the Persian War.[241] At that time, therefore, justice was so hallowed and punishing such wrongdoers so admirable that the memorial statue of the goddess and the penalty inflicted on criminals of this sort were deemed worthy of placement in the same spot. But now there is laughter, fearlessness, disgrace, unless you presently put a stop to this excessive laxity.

[273] Yet as I see it, Athenians, you would do well to imitate your ancestors not just in one respect but in everything they did. All of you, I'm sure, are familiar with the following story. Callias, son of Hipponicus, negotiated the peace treaty that everyone still talks about, whereby the Persian King was not to journey by land any closer to the coast than a day's ride for a horse or to sail by warship beyond either the Chelidonian islands or the Cyanian islands.[242] Yet because Callias

---

[239] Arthmius' mission to bribe Greeks on behalf of the Persian King occurred in the early to mid fifth century. Zelea is a town in the Troad. Arthmius is a favorite villain of fourth-century orators (see Dem. 9.41–46; Aes. 3.258–259).

[240] An imagined objection, to the effect that the inscription is not prominently displayed and thus of no importance.

[241] The statue of Athena Promachos ("fighting in the front") by Phidias, dedicated in 449.

[242] Callias fought at Marathon (490) and was one of the most prominent and wealthy Athenians of his generation. The Peace of Callias (mid fifth century)

supposedly accepted gifts while on the embassy, your ancestors nearly executed him and at his audit (*euthynai*) forced him to pay fifty talents. [274] Now, no one could claim that the city concluded any peace treaty, before or since, more honorable than that one. But that didn't matter to your ancestors. In their view, their own valor and the city's renown were responsible for the treaty, whereas the envoy's honesty or lack thereof stemmed from his character, and they insisted that citizens engaged in public business demonstrate honest and impeccable character. [275] Your ancestors considered corruption so repugnant and harmful to the city that they did not allow it for the sake of any enterprise or any individual. But you, Athenians, have seen one and the same peace demolish your allies' fortifications while it erects houses for the envoys and strip the city of its possessions while it brought these men riches they never dreamed of. Yet far from taking their lives, you require a prosecutor, and you use words to try men whose criminal deeds are evident to all.

[276] One need not speak only of the old days and use just those examples to urge you towards retribution. Many people have been punished during the lifetime of you who are here today. I'll pass over most of them but will mention one or two who were sentenced to death for diplomatic missions that did the city far less damage than this one. Clerk, please take this decree and read it.

[DECREE]

[277] With this decree, Athenians, you condemned those envoys to death, one of whom was Epicrates. From the older citizens I hear that he was a good man, often active on behalf of the city, and clearly a democrat, since he served with the partisans in Piraeus who restored democracy.[243] Yet none of these facts availed him, rightly. One who

---

marked a cessation in hostilities between Athens and Persia, but for lack of evidence, most details are disputed. The Chelidonian islands lay off the coast of Lycia. The Cyanian islands, or Symplegades, lay at the mouth of the Black Sea just past the Thracian Bosporus.

[243] In 404–403, when the Spartans imposed a narrow oligarchic regime (the Thirty Tyrants), the democratic resistance was concentrated in Piraeus. Those who served in this band were considered heroes in the restored democracy. Epicrates served as envoy to the Persian King in 391 and after fleeing into exile was convicted *in absentia*.

ventures to administer such important business must not be halfway honest, nor after he gains your confidence ought he then to abuse it for the sake of doing greater mischief. Rather, he must simply undertake not to wrong you. [278] Now, if these men here failed to commit any of the crimes for which Epicrates and his colleagues were sentenced to death, put me to death forthwith. Consider. The decree against Epicrates says: "Since they conducted the embassy contrary to written instructions," which is the first charge against them. And didn't these men act contrary to written instructions? Doesn't their decree direct them to include "the Athenians and the Athenians' allies" in the peace, whereas they declared that the Phocians were excluded from it? Doesn't their decree direct them to "receive the oaths from the magistrates in the cities," whereas they received the oaths from the representatives sent by Philip? Doesn't their decree forbid them "from meeting alone with Philip," whereas they never ceased doing business with him in private? [279] Epicrates' decree says: "Some were convicted of making false reports to the Council," yet these men are shown to have done this in the Assembly too. Shown by whom? That is what's splendid! By the facts themselves, for, of course, everything turned out to be the opposite of what they reported. Epicrates' decree continues: "And of issuing false dispatches." These men did the same. "And of defaming the allies and accepting bribes." Well, instead of defaming the allies, they completely destroyed them, and that's much more serious, I suppose, than defamation. As for taking bribes, if they denied it, the case would have to be proved, but since they admitted it,[244] surely they should have been arrested.

[280] So what will you do, Athenians? You are the offspring of that illustrious generation, and some of you still with us actually belong to it. The facts are before you. Will you permit Epicrates, the democratic benefactor and partisan of Piraeus, to be cast out and punished; will you permit Thrasybulus, son of Thrasybulus the democrat who restored democracy from Phyle,[245] to incur a fine of ten talents as hap-

---

[244] Aeschines may not admit it, but Philocrates, whom Demosthenes has closely tied to Aeschines, "admitted" it by escaping into exile rather than facing the charges in court.

[245] Thrasybulus was the leader of the democrats who defeated the Thirty Tyrants (see 19.277n). Phyle, an Attic deme northwest of the city towards Boeotia, was the staging point for the final victory.

pened the other day; will you permit like treatment for the citizen descended from Harmodius and your greatest benefactors, those whom, to mark their deeds on your behalf, you include by law in the festive libations at all your sanctuaries and sacrifices, whom you exalt in song and venerate on a par with the heroes and gods;²⁴⁶—[281] will you permit all these citizens to face the penalties ordained by law and gain no benefit from clemency, from compassion, from the sobbing children who bear your benefactors' names,²⁴⁷ from anything at all, and yet the man whose father, Atrometus, teaches school, whose mother, Glaucothea, heads a wild cult for which her predecessor was put to death,²⁴⁸ whose family are people of that sort, whose father and every forebear, like himself, have never availed the city in any way, when you have this man in your power, you will set him free? [282] What command has he held in the cavalry, in the navy, in the field? Which chorus, which public expenditure, which fiscal obligation (*eisphora*) has he provided? What loyalty has he demonstrated, what danger has he braved? Which of these has this man or his relatives ever done for the city? Even if he could lay claim to all these distinctions but not to those other ones—namely, serving honestly as envoy and remaining free of corruption—surely he still deserves to die. But if he can lay claim neither to these distinctions nor to those, will you not punish him? [283] Will you not recall what he said when he prosecuted Timarchus?—that a city that does not use muscle against criminals is of no use, nor is a state where clemency and influence outstrip the laws, and that you must not take pity on Timarchus' mother, who is an old woman, on his children, or on anyone else, but must understand that

---

²⁴⁶An ancient scholar records the general Proxenus (19.50n, 155) as the unnamed descendant of Harmodius whom the Athenians fined. In 514 Harmodius and his lover Aristogeiton plotted to kill the tyrant Hippias. They were able to kill only the tyrant's brother Hipparchus and were themselves executed, but they were soon revered in Athens as tyrannicides and received cult status as heroes of democracy. Proxenus is descended only from Harmodius, but Aristogeiton is included among Athens' "greatest benefactors."

²⁴⁷It was not uncommon for Athenian litigants to make emotional displays and bring forward relations to elicit pity on their behalf (see 19.310).

²⁴⁸On the activities of Aeschines' mother and father, see 19.199, 249, 18.258–265 with notes. Glaucothea's ill-fated predecessor was Nino.

if you abandon the laws and the state, you will find no one to take pity on you.[249]

[284] So because Timarchus took notice of this man's crimes, the poor man will remain deprived of his rights, but you will grant this man his freedom? Why? If Aeschines thinks it right to inflict such heavy punishment on a man who wrongs himself,[250] how heavy a punishment should you, in your capacity as sworn judges, inflict on those who have grievously wronged the city, of whom he is one, as has been shown? [285] "By Zeus, that trial will improve our young people."[251] Then this one will improve our politicians, who put the city's most important interests at risk. Even they deserve consideration.

To show you that Aeschines ruined Timarchus not, by Zeus, out of concern for improving your children's character—for they already possess good character, Athenians, and may the city never fare so badly that our young men need Aphobetus[252] and Aeschines to improve their character—[286] but because Timarchus, while on the Council, moved a decree that ordered the death penalty for anyone caught shipping arms or naval equipment to Philip, here is the proof. How long has it been since Timarchus began speaking before the Assembly? A long time.[253] Well, even though Aeschines was in the city during that entire time, it was not until he went to Macedon and sold his services that he took offense and considered it outrageous for someone like Timarchus to address the Assembly.[254] Clerk, please take Timarchus' decree and read it.

---

[249] Nothing in Aes. 1 fits with what Demosthenes says here.

[250] Timarchus was prosecuted for prostituting himself and then speaking in the Assembly.

[251] An imagined objection, to the effect that Aeschines' prosecution was necessary because young Athenian men must be warned of the dangers of illicit sex, a point made by Aes. 1.187, 2.180.

[252] Aeschines' brother (see 19.237).

[253] Timarchus was a member of the Council for the first time in 361/360 (Aes. 1.109). Aeschines' prosecution of Timarchus took place in 346/5.

[254] By law, a citizen who had engaged in male prostitution was forbidden from addressing the Assembly. The alleged prostitution of Timarchus took place during his youth, so that Aeschines presumably could have prosecuted him on the same charge the first time he spoke in the Assembly.

[DECREE]

[287] So the one who advanced your interests by moving a decree that forbade the shipment of arms to Philip during wartime under penalty of death was insolently destroyed. The other, this man, who actually handed over your allies' arms to Philip, mounted a prosecution and spoke about prostitution, O earth and gods, while his two brothers-in-law were at his side. You would shriek if you saw them: the degenerate "Nicias" who hired himself out to Chabrias on the way to Egypt, and the villain "Cyrebio" who parties at processions without a mask.[255] But that's nothing, for he was looking at his brother Aphobetus. So you see, on that day all the talk about prostitution flowed back to its source.

[288] To make clear how badly Aeschines' wicked lies humiliated our city, I will leave aside all other matters and discuss one that all of you are aware of. Formerly, Athenians, all other Greeks would try to discover what your decisions would be, but now we are the ones who go around trying to find out what others intend to do, trying to hear what the Arcadians think, what the Amphictyons think, where Philip will be next, is he alive or dead. [289] Is that not what we do? Yet what worries me is not whether Philip is alive, but whether the city's desire to despise and punish criminals is dead. Philip doesn't scare me so long as you do your part, but if those who seek employment in his service fear no retribution from us, if they find support among certain politicians who enjoy your trust, and if individuals who have always denied aiding Philip shall now rise to speak for Aeschines—that's what scares me. [290] Tell me, then, Eubulus, when your cousin Hegesilaus was on trial and just the other day when Thrasybulus, Niceratus' uncle, was on trial, why did you reject their requests to testify for them dur-

---

[255] Chabrias, a well-known mercenary general of the first half of the fourth century, fought alongside the Spartan Agesilaus in Egypt in 360. Demosthenes uses derogatory nicknames to refer to Aeschines' brothers-in-law, Philo and Epicrates (his wife's brothers; Aes. 2.150). Cyrebio, a well-known parasite, stands for Epicrates. Individuals often wore masks while getting drunk at celebrations of the god Dionysus, and Epicrates, Demosthenes implies, lacked the shame to hide his identity. Demosthenes demeans Philo's military career (beyond the slur on his relations with Chabrias) by implicitly contrasting him with Nicias, the great Athenian general of the fifth century (see Harris 1986).

ing the first part of the trial, and then on the question of punishment, you rose and said not a word on behalf of the defendants but begged the jurors to excuse you?[256] So you refuse to testify on behalf of relations and close friends, but you will testify on behalf of Aeschines, [291] even though he joined Aristophon in his attack on you when he prosecuted Philonicus as a means of criticizing your conduct, and thus proved himself to be one of your enemies?[257] You terrified the citizens by declaring that, unless they voted for the motion that this man supported and the reprobate Philocrates proposed—the motion that turned a just peace agreement into a disgraceful one—they would have to go straight to Piraeus, pay taxes, and divert the festival fund to military purposes.[258] [292] And then, when the crimes of these men destroyed everything, you reconciled with them? Though you uttered curses in the Assembly and swore on your children's lives that you truly wished to see Philip destroyed, you will now come to the aid of this man? How will Philip be destroyed when you yourself preserve those who are on his payroll? [293] And why in the world did you put Moerocles on trial for extorting twenty drachmas from each of the mining concessionaires? Why did you prosecute Cephisophon for stealing sacred property because he took three days to deposit seven minas in the bank, when you do not indict those who actually took bribes for

---

[256] Given Eubulus' influence at the time of this trial (18.21n) and his intention to support Aeschines (see Aes. 2.184), Demosthenes needed to do what he could to discredit his testimony. Hegesilaus was accused of collaborating with Plutarch, tyrant of Eretria, to thwart an Athenian expedition in Euboea in 349/8. Thrasybulus' trial was mentioned above (19.280). Eubulus' connection with Thrasybulus and Niceratus, an Athenian politician, is unknown. The first part of the trial was devoted to deciding the defendant's guilt or innocence. If the verdict was guilty, a second part of the trial was devoted to deciding the punishment.

[257] On Aristophon, who opposed Eubulus over financial policy, see 18.162n. Nothing is known of Philonicus or this prosecution.

[258] I.e., Eubulus supported the Peace of Philocrates by threatening the citizens with drastic measures (military service, war taxes, reduced civic spending) unless they approved the proposal. Piraeus is where the Athenians docked their warships. The comment on the festival fund (theōrika) is ironic because Eubulus was formerly the magistrate in charge of this large and important civic fund and was associated with a law, then in force, that forbade even consideration of using the festival fund for military purposes on pain of death.

the destruction of our allies and have confessed and were caught in the very act, but instead you call for their protection?[259] [294] These crimes are appalling and required considerable planning and vigilance, whereas your grounds for prosecuting those others, Eubulus, are a joke, as you citizens will see from the following.

In Elis did anyone ever steal public money? Most likely. But were any of those thieves involved in the recent oligarchic coup in Elis?[260] Not one. Well? When Olynthus existed, were there also similar thieves there? I believe so. Did Olynthus fall because of them? No. Well? Don't you think Megara too had its share of people who stole and embezzled public money? Of course. Have any of them been found culpable for what recently happened there?[261] Not one. [295] But what kind of men do commit crimes of this magnitude? Men who think they deserve to be known as Philip's friends or guests, men who seek generalships and other positions of leadership, who believe they should be above the many. When Perilas was recently tried in Megara before the Three Hundred for meeting with Philip, did not Ptoeodorus, the wealthiest, noblest, most influential Megarian, come forward and demand his release, and did not Ptoeodorus then send Perilas back to Philip, whence Perilas returned with a band of soldiers while Ptoeodorus was cooking something up?[262] [296] Quite so. There is nothing, absolutely nothing, that warrants greater vigilance than letting some individual rise above the many. As far as I'm concerned, let no one be spared or put to death just because a particular person wishes it, but depending on whether a man's deeds warrant sparing him or not, you should cast the vote that he deserves. That's how it should be in a democracy. [297] Moreover, many citizens have certainly wielded influence over

---

[259] On "those who actually took bribes . . . and have confessed," see 19.279. The Athenians leased mines in Attica in return for stipulated fees. Moerocles, one of the hostages demanded by Alexander in 335 (18.41n), was accused of surcharging. Cephisophon, whose crime is obscure, is mentioned along with Eubulus in 18.21.

[260] See 19.260n. The implication is that stealing public money poses a relatively small threat to the city.

[261] See 19.87n.

[262] Perilas and Ptoeodorus are included in the blacklist of Greek traitors in 18.295. The Three Hundred was a civic body in Megara that adjudicated the case.

you at one time or another: Callistratus, later Aristophon, Diophantus, others before them.[263] But in what forum did each of them attain prominence? In the Assembly. In court, however, no one has ever, up to this very day, been above you, above the laws, or above your oaths. So do not allow Eubulus to be so today. To demonstrate that you are better off being vigilant than trusting, I will read you an oracle of the gods, who always protect the city far more than do its leading citizens. Clerk, read the oracles.

[ORACLES]

[298] You hear the gods' warning, Athenians. If this oracle came during wartime, it is the generals whom the gods are telling you to watch, since generals are the leaders in war, but if during peacetime, it is the citizens in charge of policy; for they lead, they have your trust, they are the ones you should fear may deceive you. The oracle says: "And preserve the city's unity, so that all citizens are of one mind and give the enemy no comfort." [299] Now, do you think, Athenians, that it would give Philip comfort to see the man who did so much damage spared or punished? Spared, I take it. But the oracle says that we must do whatever does not please the enemy. So, Zeus, Dione,[264] and all the gods are urging all citizens to be of one mind in punishing anyone who serves the enemy: from outside those who plot against us; from inside, their collaborators. It is the job of those who plot to tender bribes, of collaborators either to take them or to safeguard those who have already taken them.[265]

[300] But human reflection also makes clear that the most dangerous and frightening threat of all is when the leading politician[266] is allowed to become friendly with those who do not share the people's interests. Consider by what means Philip gained complete control of

---

[263] On Callistratus and Aristophon, see 18.219n. On Diophantus, see 19.86, 198.

[264] Dione was Zeus' consort at Dodona, which reveals that these oracles came from the oracle of Zeus at Dodona. After Philip took control of Delphi in the settlement of the Third Sacred War, Athens turned away from Delphi and to Dodona in northern Greece (see also 18.253).

[265] Aeschines is the collaborator who takes bribes; Eubulus is the one who would safeguard the bribe-taker Aeschines.

[266] Eubulus.

circumstances and attained his greatest triumphs. He bought action from those who were selling it, and he corrupted the leading politicians in the cities and spurred them on. [301] Now, it is in your power today, if you wish, to render both these factors useless: you need only to refuse to listen to the citizens who testify on behalf of such men, showing that they are not your masters (for now they say they are), and to punish the hireling while letting everyone know about it.

[302] Anyone who acted this way, betraying allies, friends, and the vital opportunities that decide a people's fate for good or ill, would rightly rouse your anger, Athenians, but no one more so or with greater justification than Aeschines. Since he initially took up his post among those who distrusted Philip, was the first and only one to see that Philip was the common enemy of all Greece,[267] yet then deserted, betrayed, and suddenly belonged to Philip's cause, how does this man not deserve to die many times over? [303] These are facts that even he will not be able to deny. Who first brought Ischander before you on the grounds that he was sent to Athens from friends in Arcadia? Who shouted that Philip was organizing Greece and the Peloponnese for his purposes while you were sleeping? Who delivered those long, wonderful speeches in the Assembly that featured renditions of the decrees of Miltiades and Themistocles and the oath that the ephebes take in the shrine of Aglaurus?[268] Was it not this man? [304] Who persuaded

---

[267] See 19.9–14 for Demosthenes' account of this first stage of Aeschines' political career.

[268] It is uncertain whether either the decree of Miltiades or that of Themistocles is historically genuine, but in fourth-century Athens, Miltiades was held to have moved the decree of 490 urging the Athenians to fight at Marathon without waiting for allies, and Themistocles was held to have moved the decree in 480 urging the Athenians to abandon Attica and fight the Persians on the sea (see also 18.204). A text of the Themistocles decree inscribed in the early third century BCE survives, though its authenticity has been doubted (see Fornara 1977: 53–55). As part of their induction into military service, the ephebes (Athenian youths in military training) swore an oath affirming their adherence to military discipline and their readiness to sacrifice their lives on behalf of Greek freedom (see Lyc. 1.76–80 and, for a text of the oath, Harding 1985: 133–135). The shrine of Aglaurus, daughter of Cecrops, who was said to have sacrificed herself to save Athens, was on the north side of the Acropolis (Herod. 8.53).

you to send envoys practically to the Red Sea[269] on the grounds that Philip's plotting against Greece obliged you to anticipate events and keep abreast of Greek affairs? Was not Eubulus the one who moved the proposal and Aeschines the one who was dispatched to the Peloponnese? Though only Aeschines would know what he actually said in his discussions and speeches, what he told you in his report upon his return is something that all of you, I'm sure, recall.

[305] In the Assembly he repeatedly labeled Philip a damned barbarian,[270] and he reported that the Arcadians were pleased to learn that Athens was finally considering what to do and waking up. Yet there was one thing he said troubled him most of all. When leaving Arcadia, he ran into Arestidas who was on his way back from Philip and had about thirty women and children traveling with him. Puzzled, he asked one of the travelers who the man was and who were the crowd of people with him. [306] Being told that Arestidas was returning from Philip with these Olynthian prisoners of war as a gift, Aeschines found it, he said, outrageous, and he began to weep and wail for Greece, which was in a terrible plight if it allowed such miseries to occur. At that point he recommended that you dispatch a delegation to Arcadia to bring charges against Philip's partisans. For, he said, friends there told him that if Athens should take notice and send envoys, those partisans would pay.

[307] What Aeschines said to the Assembly on that occasion, Athenians, was truly noble and worthy of the city. But after he had been to Macedon and saw the man who was his enemy and the enemy of Greece, did he say anything in the Assembly that matched or resembled his previous words? Far from it. Rather, he advised you not to remember ancestors, not to talk of trophies, not to give anyone any aid,[271] but to be surprised that people should insist on including the

---

[269] Ironic exaggeration (see 19.10). The "Red Sea" included the modern Red Sea, the Persian Gulf, and the general area of the Indian Ocean, of which the Athenians had little firm knowledge.

[270] Making known one's view of Philip as either a Greek or a barbarian indicated the speaker's attitude towards Philip (see 19.308). Demosthenes was vehement in branding Philip a barbarian (e.g., Dem. 9.31).

[271] See 19.16.

Greeks in your deliberations about peace with Philip, as if it were necessary to satisfy others regarding your private affairs. [308] He said that Philip was, by Heracles, the purest Greek, the most skillful speaker, Athens' greatest friend, that certain people in the city were so bizarre and ill-tempered as to feel no shame in abusing Philip and labeling him a barbarian. Is there any way that one and the same man could speak as he did formerly, then dare to utter these words, if he had not been corrupted? [309] Well? Is there anyone who could formerly have despised Arestidas because of the Olynthian women and children, and then support doing the same deeds as Philocrates, who brought free Olynthian women to Athens and is so notorious for his repulsive lifestyle that there is no reason for me to say anything sordid or disagreeable about him here? But if I merely mention that Philocrates brought back women, all of you, and the spectators as well,[272] know what happened next. You feel pity, I'm sure, for the poor unlucky women, though Aeschines felt no pity for them, and they did not move him to weep for Greece because they were violated by our envoys while among allies.[273]

[310] But although he behaved that badly while serving as envoy, he will shed tears for himself, and he will probably produce his children and bring them up.[274] But when you see his children, jurors, consider that because of this man the children of many of your allies and friends roam and wander as beggars in terrible circumstances. They deserve your pity far more than do the children of this unlawful, traitorous father. Moreover, these men robbed your children of their hopes too when they extended the treaty "to Philip's descendants too."[275] So when you see his tears, reflect that you now have in your power the man who demanded that a delegation be sent to Arcadia to bring charges against Philip's partisans. [311] You have no reason now to send a delegation to the Peloponnese, or to embark on a long journey, or to spend

---

[272] A ring of spectators outside the court proper observed the proceedings and are addressed here.

[273] Olynthus had been allied to Athens. See 19.196–198 for this allusion to Aeschines' supposed participation in the maltreatment of one Olynthian woman.

[274] See 19.281n; Aes. 2.179.

[275] See 19.48 for this clause, which, as Demosthenes would have it, robs future Athenians of their hopes of regaining what was lost by the Peace of Philocrates.

money for this. Instead, you can each approach the platform and cast your vote in the name of sanctity and justice on behalf of your country and against a man who, O earth and gods, first talked, as I just described, about Marathon, Salamis, battles, and trophies, but then, as soon as he had set foot on Macedonian soil, advocated just the opposite[276]—that you should not remember ancestors, not talk of trophies, not give anyone any aid, not take counsel with the Greeks, and do everything but tear down the walls.

[312] Never in your presence have more shameful words ever been spoken than those. For is any Greek or barbarian so stupid or uninformed or thoroughly hostile to our city that, if someone said to him, "Tell me, is there any part of Greece as it is presently constituted and inhabited that would still be called Greece or inhabited by the Greeks of today had not the men of Marathon and Salamis—our ancestors—accomplished those acts of valor for the sake of Greece?"—no one, I'm convinced, would say such a thing, but they'd say that the barbarians would have taken over Greece completely. [313] So no one, not even any of our enemies, would deprive those men of their praises and acclamations, but Aeschines forbids you, their descendants, to remember them, just so that he can make some money? Indeed, though the dead are excluded from every other good thing, the glory that stems from noble deeds belongs particularly to those who have died in this way. For they no longer meet with envy. If this man deprives those ancestors of their glory, it would be right for him now to be deprived of his rights as a citizen and for you to inflict that punishment on him on behalf of your ancestors. With that speech of yours, you evil creature, you stripped our ancestors of their deeds and mocked them; with your words you destroyed all their achievements.

[314] These deeds have given you a farm,[277] and you've become an important man. Yes, there's that too. Before he caused the city every kind of harm, he would admit that he was a public clerk and owed you thanks for being elected to the post, and he conducted himself modestly. But since he committed untold evils, he raises his brows, and if

---

[276] Aes. 2.152 rejects this charge of a sudden about-face.

[277] See 19.145–146, 18.41 for Demosthenes' account of Aeschines' property. Since Aeschines did not come from a family with land holdings, his ownership of land, however acquired, was grist for Demosthenes' mill.

anyone mentions "Aeschines the clerk," he is straightaway the man's enemy and declares that he's been affronted. He walks through the Agora with his cloak down to his ankles, keeping pace with Pythocles, puffing out his cheeks,[278] now at your service as one of Philip's intimate friends, one who wants to be rid of democracy and considers the present state of things a torrent of folly, this man who used to prostrate himself before the Tholos.[279]

[315] I would like to recall for you the main points that enabled Philip to enlist these detestable men and outsmart you. It is worth examining the entire intrigue closely. At first Philip wanted peace because his land was being plundered by pirates and his markets were closed, which prevented him from profiting from his resources. So he dispatched those sweet-talking gentlemen to represent him, Neoptolemus, Aristodemus, Ctesiphon.[280] [316] When we envoys reached Philip, he immediately hired this man to support the accursed Philocrates with words and actions and to outdo those of us who were trying to do what was right, and he composed a letter[281] to you in which he expressed his firm belief that a peace agreement would be reached.

[317] Yet even this was not enough to give Philip an advantage over you unless he could destroy the Phocians, and that was not an easy matter. His affairs had, as if by chance, reached a critical point in which, unless he abandoned all his aims, he would be forced to lie, break his oaths, and make all Greeks and barbarians witnesses of his wickedness. [318] For if he accepted the Phocians as your allies and swore an oath to them along with you,[282] he would necessarily be violating sworn pacts with the Thessalians and Thebans. He had sworn to help the latter take over Boeotia, the former to control the Amphictyony.[283] But if Philip did not accept the Phocians, as in fact he did

---

[278] On Pythocles, see 19.225. As the puffed cheeks make clear, Demosthenes is ridiculing Aeschines, but it is not clear what is ridiculous about his style of dress.

[279] A snub at Aeschines' former service as a secretary; see 19.249n on the Tholos.

[280] See 19.10, 12 on these persons.

[281] See 19.40.

[282] I.e., if Philip allowed the Phocians to be included in the peace treaty among the Athenian allies.

[283] These were among the Theban and Thessalian objectives against Phocis in the Third Sacred War, since Thebes had lost control over much of Boeotia, and Thessaly had been deprived of its control of the Pylaeo-Delphic Amphictyony (on

not, he supposed that you would not allow him to invade Greece but would send an expedition to Thermopylae, and if you had not been deceived, that is precisely what you would have done. If you did that, he figured that it would be impossible for him to invade. [319] There was no need for him to learn this from others, but he had his own evidence on the matter. For when he defeated the Phocians the first time, wiping out their mercenary forces along with their leader and general Onomarchus,[284] not a single living person, Greek or barbarian, assisted the Phocians apart from you, and yet he not only did not invade or achieve anything he hoped to attain by invasion but he was unable even to approach.[285]

[320] Philip understood quite well, I take it, the circumstances that confronted him. In Thessaly he was faced with internal squabbles, the Pheraeans in particular being recalcitrant. The Thebans were faltering, and their defeat in battle led to the erection of a trophy over them.[286] Philip realized that if you were to send an expedition, invasion was not possible, and if he even attempted it, he would be sorry, unless some trick could be used. "How," he wondered, "can I accomplish all my goals without obviously lying or appearing to violate my oaths? How? I know—if I find some Athenians to trick the Athenians! In that case, the stigma[287] will not extend to me." [321] Thereupon, Philip's envoys warned you that he would not accept the Phocians as your allies, and your envoys took up the point and told the people that because of the Thebans and Thessalians it would obviously be dishonorable for Philip to accept the Phocians as allies, but if he gets control of the situation and secures a peace agreement, at that point he will bring about whatever arrangements we may demand of him now. [322] So with these hopes and inducements, they secured from you the peace treaty that omitted the Phocians. Next it was necessary to prevent the expedition to Thermopylae, for which, in spite of the treaty, you had fifty triremes in wait to thwart Philip if he should

---

the latter, see Dem. 18.143n, 5.23, 6.22). Philip was indeed helping Thebes and Thessaly attain these objectives, but "sworn pacts" seems to be Demosthenes' rhetorical exaggeration.

[284] In 352 at the battle of the Crocus Plain in southern Thessaly.

[285] See 19.84n on the Athenian expedition to Thermopylae in 352.

[286] See 19.148.

[287] Of being caught in a lie.

move. [323] But how? What trick could be used in regard to this matter? If your envoys gave you no opportunity to act, pressed circumstances forward, and imposed them on you suddenly, you would not be in a position to launch an expedition even if you wanted to. Wherefore, these men plainly did just that, while I, as you've heard many times by now, could not return ahead of them and, even after I had rented a boat, was prevented from setting sail.[288]

[324] But it was also necessary that the Phocians should trust Philip and surrender to him on their own to avoid any loss of time and prevent you from passing any hostile measure. "The message that the Phocians will be safe should come from the Athenian envoys so that, even if I am distrusted, the Phocians will surrender based on their confidence in Athens. As for the Athenian people, I will summon them forth[289] so that they will think that everything they desire is arranged and will pass no hostile measure. Finally, in their report to the Assembly these men[290] will convey promises from me that will keep the Athenians from making any move whatever happens."[291] [325] In that way and using those tricks, these men, who will themselves suffer a most miserable destruction, destroyed everything. All at once, instead of seeing Thespiae and Plataea resettled, you heard that Orchomenus and Coronea were enslaved;[292] instead of Thebes being humbled and stripped of its arrogance and pride, the walls of your Phocian allies were torn down. The Thebans did the tearing down, though Aeschines had dispersed them in his speech.[293] [326] Instead of returning Euboea to you in exchange for Amphipolis, Philip is erecting more bases against you in Euboea and persists in his designs on Geraestus and Megara.[294] Instead of getting Oropus back, we are sending armed sorties to Drymus and the territory around Panactum, which is some-

---

[288] Back to Athens from the Second Embassy (see 19.51).

[289] I.e., under arms, to join him in settling the Third Sacred War.

[290] Aeschines and his cronies.

[291] As in 19.320, this passage represents Philip's thinking. The situation is described in 19.51–52.

[292] See 19.20–22, 112.

[293] Ironic: Philip punished the Phocians by dispersing them into unfortified villages, which, according to Demosthenes, was the fate that Aeschines had predicted for the Thebans (see 19.81).

[294] Geraestus is on the southern tip of Euboea. On Megara, see 19.295.

thing we never did so long as Phocis was secure.²⁹⁵ [327] Instead of reestablishing the traditional rites in Apollo's sanctuary and exacting payment to restore the god's property, genuine Amphictyons are driven into exile, and their land is laid waste, while Macedonian barbarians, who never were Amphictyons before, now rely on force to enjoy that status.²⁹⁶ If anyone says a word about the sacred money, he is thrown from the precipice, and his city loses the right of consulting the oracle first.²⁹⁷

[328] The entire set of circumstances is like a puzzle for the city. Philip avoided lying and accomplished everything he wanted, but while you expected to have just what you wanted, you have seen just the opposite of this happen. Ostensibly you are at peace, but your plight is worse than if you were at war. And from their role in these developments, these men have money and until this very day have not been punished.

[329] For many reasons I think you have long known that the whole affair is simply a matter of corruption and that these men have their payment in return for everything they did. I fear that my attempt to demonstrate the point in detail may produce a result I don't intend, and I'll annoy you because you have long understood these matters on your own. Nevertheless, listen to this point too. [330] Would you erect in the Agora, jurors, a bronze statue of any of Philip's envoys? Well? Would you bestow on them dining privileges in the Prytaneum or any other tribute that you use to honor benefactors?²⁹⁸ I do not believe so. Why is that? It is certainly not because you are ungrateful or unfair or

---

²⁹⁵ Drymus and Panactum were on the frontier of Attica and Boeotia. On Oropus, see 19.22.

²⁹⁶ On Aeschines' (supposed) plan to have the Thebans restore the Delphic property removed by the Phocians in 355, see 19.21. The "genuine Amphictyons" are the Phocians. Philip appropriated their seats on the Amphictyonic Council for himself.

²⁹⁷ Demosthenes is complaining that the monetary fines inflicted on the Phocians, which were supposed to go to the Delphic treasury, never found their destination. Hurling a criminal from the precipice known as Hyampeia was the traditional punishment for impiety in Delphi. Athens traditionally enjoyed the right to consult the oracle first, but it lost that right in Philip's settlement of the Third Sacred War (Dem. 9.32).

²⁹⁸ See 19.31n on dining in the Prytaneum.

mean, but because you would say that those envoys always acted to advance Philip's cause and never ours, which is a true and fair statement. [331] Now, do you think that this is your view of things but that Philip sees it differently, and that he gives so many generous gifts to these men because they carried out their missions by advancing your cause in noble and honest fashion?²⁹⁹ It's not possible. You see how Philip received Hegesippus and the envoys who went with him. I omit other matters but note that Philip officially banished the poet Xenoclides, who is here in court, just for entertaining the envoys, his fellow-citizens.³⁰⁰ Such is the treatment that he bestows on those who honestly speak their minds on your behalf, but those who have sold their services he treats like these men. Do these facts need still more witnesses or still greater proofs? Will anyone remove them from your mind?

[332] As I was coming into court earlier today, I was told one of the most extraordinary things: Aeschines plans to denounce Chares and expects to trick you with that ploy.³⁰¹ Whenever Chares has been tried on any charge, he has been found to be loyal and trustworthy in advancing your cause to the best of his ability, and his many failures were caused by those who undermine our affairs in pursuit of money. But I won't insist on that point; in fact, I will go even further: let's admit that everything this man will say about Chares is true. Even so, it is absolutely ridiculous that he should denounce Chares. [333] I do not blame Aeschines for anything that occurred in the war, the generals being accountable for those matters, or even for the city's agreement to make peace, but I put aside everything up to that point. What, then, do I mean, and from what point do I begin my accusations? From the point when in the midst of the deliberations on peace he supported

---

²⁹⁹ See 19.114, 145–146 for examples of Philip's largess to Aeschines and Philocrates.

³⁰⁰ Hegesippus, a strongly anti-Macedonian politician (see 19.72n), led an embassy to Philip in early 343 in an attempt to revise the terms of the Peace of Philocrates in Athens' favor. The attempt failed. Xenoclides, who had lost his rights in Athens (Dem. 59.26–27), had been living in Macedon.

³⁰¹ Aeschines, indeed, attacks Chares (2.70–73), Athens' most active general during the mid to late fourth century. Demosthenes' claim that he learned of Aeschines' tactic while on his way into court is rhetorical. The appearance of spontaneity and improvisation enhances the appearance of sincerity.

Philocrates and not the proponents of the best policy; when he took bribes; when, later on the Second Embassy, he wasted time and followed none of your instructions; when he tricked the city and destroyed everything by creating the expectation that Philip would do whatever you wanted; when, later, as others were advising you to beware of the author of so many crimes, he advocated Philip's cause.

[334] These are the accusations I make; these are the accusations you are to remember, since for a peace that was just and fair, for men who sold nothing and did not lie subsequently, I would express admiration and urge the bestowal of a crown. But if some general wronged you, it is no part of this present audit. What general lost Halus, who destroyed the Phocians? Who lost Doriscus? Who lost Cersebleptes? Who lost Hieron Oros? Who lost Thermopylae? Who opened for Philip a route through allies and friends right to Attica? Who put Coronea, Orchomenus, Euboea under foreign control? Who nearly put Megara under foreign control just the other day? Who strengthened Thebes? [335] These are diverse and important places, yet none of them was lost because of the generals, and none was conceded in the peace treaty and belongs to Philip because you consented to it. They were lost because of these men and their corruption. Now should Aeschines evade these charges, should he digress and try to speak of anything else, address him thus: "We do not sit in judgment of a general; you are not being tried for those matters. Do not tell us that someone else is to blame for the Phocian disaster, but show us that you are not to blame. If Demosthenes committed a crime, why do you tell us now rather than accusing him during his audit? For that reason alone you deserve to die. [336] Do not tell us what a wonderful and beneficial thing peace is. No one blames you for the city making peace. Rather, tell us that this peace is not a shameful and reprehensible one, that subsequently we were not deceived many times, that all was not lost. For in our eyes you have been shown to be responsible for all these acts. And why do you continue to heap praise today on the man [302] who has done such things?" If you citizens watch Aeschines in this way, he will have nothing to say. He will have lifted his voice and done his vocal exercises in vain.

---

[302] Philip.

[337] In fact, perhaps I need to add a word about his voice. I hear he takes considerable pride in it and expects to overwhelm you with his delivery. In my view, it would be the most peculiar behavior on your part if, when he portrayed the sufferings of Thyestes and the heroes of Troy, you stopped him by driving him noisily from the theater and practically stoning him to the point where he gave up his career playing bit parts,[303] yet when he has wreaked such disaster not on stage but upon the city's most important, communal interests, you pay him heed because of his beautiful voice. [338] Do not do it. Do not be so foolish. Rather, consider this: when you examine candidates for the office of herald,[304] you must look for someone with a good voice, but when you examine candidates to serve as envoy and to promote the city's interests, you must look for someone who is honest, who is really proud to represent your interests but is content to be your equal—as indeed I did not respect Philip, but I did respect the prisoners of war and saved them, sparing no effort. But this man groveled before Philip, sang paeans,[305] and scorns you.

[339] In addition, when you find cleverness or vocal brilliance or some similar distinction in an honest and magnanimous person, you should all share in the satisfaction and training, for it will be a common benefit to all the rest of you. But when you find this quality in a corrupt and wicked person, one who cannot resist any chance at gain, you should all shut him out and listen to him with rancor and animosity,[306] because wickedness that has acquired in your eyes the status of authority is destructive to the city. [340] See how much trouble plagues the city as a result of the attribute for which this man is renowned. Abilities of other kinds contain their effectiveness more or less in themselves, but the ability to speak well is foiled if you in the audience resist. So listen to him in that spirit, for he is wicked and corrupt and will never say anything true.

[341] Understand too that in addition to everything else, our rela-

---

[303] On Demosthenes' gibes at Aeschines' acting, see 18.129n, 262, 265.

[304] After candidates were chosen for office by lot or election, they submitted to an examination (*dokimasia*) to establish their eligibility. Only when they passed the examination did the candidates assume office.

[305] See 19.128 on paeans.

[306] Aeschines begins his response by rejecting this demand (2.1).

tions with Philip make it absolutely expedient to convict Aeschines. For if one day Philip finds it necessary to treat the city fairly, then he will change his ways. Now he has chosen to deceive the many and court the few, but if he hears that these men have been ruined, he will want to manage future affairs in a way that serves you, the many whose authority is supreme. [342] But if he does not abandon his present unconstrained insolence, then, if you convict these men, you will at least rid the city of men who would undertake anything on his behalf. For if they behaved in this way when they expected to be punished, what do you think they will do if your response to them is lax? Do you think there is a Euthycrates, a Lasthenes, any traitor whom they will not surpass?[307] [343] Is there any other citizen who will not become corrupt when he sees that those who sold everything gain money, status, resources, and Philip's friendship, but those who proved themselves honest and chose to spend their own money gain trouble, malice, and spite from some people? Do not let that happen. It will not bring you any advantage to acquit this man—not for your reputation or your piety or your security or anything else; so punish him and make him an example for all men, both in Athens and throughout Greece.

---

[307] On the Olynthian traitors Euthycrates and Lasthenes, see 19.265.

APPENDIX 1. THE SPURIOUS DOCUMENTS FROM DEMOSTHENES 18: ON THE CROWN

The medieval manuscripts and some ancient papyri of the speech *On the Crown* contain passages in several places that purport to be the documents that Demosthenes had the clerk read out to the court as evidence for his case. If any of the documentary passages were authentic or based on authentic documents, vital historical information would have been preserved. Yet after thorough scrutiny, it has been demonstrated beyond doubt that all the transmitted documents in the speech are utterly spurious and bear absolutely no relation to the documents that Demosthenes had the clerk read out to the court.

Ancient papyri have established that these passages were intruded into the text as early as the first century BCE. They are either outright forgeries or school exercises. The fabrications are often abysmal; in many cases, the context is blatantly misunderstood, names and dates are obviously wrong, or wording is lifted from surrounding passages or Aeschines' speech in prosecution (Aes. 3). The original documents were probably never preserved in the manuscript tradition, but if they were, they have vanished without a trace.[1]

[29] In the Archonship of Mnesiphilus, on the last day of Hecatombaion, during the presidency of the tribe Pandionis, Demosthenes, son of Demosthenes, of Paeania, proposed: whereas Philip sent envoys in regard to peace and has accepted the terms that were agreed to, it is decided by the Council and People of Athens, in order that the peace voted in the first Assembly be ratified, to choose at once five envoys

---

[1] The text used for the translations of the spurious documents is Dilts 2002. For more information on the spurious documents, see Yunis 2001: 29–31.

from all Athenians, and that upon election, they shall travel without delay to wherever they may discover Philip to be, and shall accept the oaths from him and give them to him as quickly as possible according to the terms agreed upon by him and the Athenian people, and they shall include the allies of both sides. The envoys chosen were Eubulus of Anaphlystus, Aeschines of Cothocidae, Cephisophon of Rhamnus, Democrates of Phlya, Cleon of Cothocidae.

[37] In the Archonship of Mnesiphilus, an extraordinary assembly called by the generals and Presiding Officers, a resolution of the Council, on the twenty-first day of Maimacterion, Callisthenes, son of Eteonicus, of Phaleron, proposed: no Athenian shall spend the night in the countryside for any reason, but only in the city or Piraeus, except those assigned to the garrisons, and all of these shall stay at their assigned post and not leave it during the day or night. [38] Whoever disobeys this decree shall be subject to the penalties for treason unless he shows that compliance was impossible for him; whether it was impossible shall be decided by the general of the infantry, the general of the budget, and the secretary of the Council. All property shall be conveyed from the countryside as quickly as possible: that lying within 120 stades, to the city or Piraeus; that lying beyond 120 stades, to Eleusis, Phyle, Aphidna, Rhamnus, or Sunium.

[39] Philip, king of the Macedonians, sends greetings to the Council and People of Athens. Know that we have passed inside Thermopylae and have the territory around Phocis under our control, that we have established garrisons in all the towns that surrendered voluntarily, but those that disobeyed we have taken by force and destroyed, and we have enslaved the inhabitants. Hearing that you are preparing to aid them, I have written you to save you any further trouble on their behalf. Your policy as a whole seems unreasonable to me, inasmuch as you agreed to peace and at the same time would take the field against us, especially since the Phocians are not even included in our common agreement. So unless you abide by the agreements, you will gain no advantage apart from hastening to do wrong.

[54] In the Archonship of Charondas, on the sixth day of Elaphebolion, Aeschines, son of Atrometus, of Cothocidae, indicted Ctesiphon, son of Leosthenes, of Anaphlystus, before the Archon for an illegal

proposal, on the grounds that he proposed an illegal decree, namely, that Demosthenes, son of Demosthenes, of Paeania, should receive a golden crown and proclamation should be made in the theater at the Great Dionysia at the performance of new tragedies, that the people should crown Demosthenes, son of Demosthenes, of Paeania, with a golden crown for his merit, for the loyalty he always displays towards all Greeks and the people of Athens, and for his bravery, and because he always acts and speaks in the best interests of the people and readily does whatever good he can, [55] that all these things proposed by Ctesiphon are false and against the law, since the laws forbid, first, placing false proposals in the public records, second, crowning a citizen subject to audit (Demosthenes is commissioner of the walls and oversees the theoric fund), and further, proclaiming a crown in the theater during the Dionysia at the performance of new tragedies; rather, if the Council confers a crown, it is proclaimed in the Council-house, if the city does, in the Assembly on the Pnyx. The fine is fifty talents. Witnesses to the summons are Cephisophon, son of Cephisophon, of Rhamnus; Cleon, son of Cleon, of Cothocidae.

[73] In the Archonship of Neocles, in the month of Boedromion, an extraordinary assembly called by the generals, Eubulus, son of Mnesitheus, of Coprus, proposed: since the generals announced in the Assembly that the admiral Leodamas and the twenty ships dispatched with him to the Hellespont for the grain convoy have been diverted to Macedonia by Philip's general Amyntas and are being held under arrest, the Presiding Officers and the generals shall undertake to have the Council convened and envoys to Philip chosen [74] to meet with him and discuss the release of the admiral, the ships, and the soldiers; and if Amyntas took this action in ignorance, they shall say that the people make no complaint; if he did it because he caught the admiral in any way contravening his orders, they shall say that the Athenians will investigate and punish him in accord with the seriousness of his negligence; but if neither of these is the case, and the aggressive behavior was an intentional act of either the person in charge or the person charged with carrying it out, they shall say this too in order that the people may be made aware of it and deliberate about what to do.

[75] In the Archonship of Neocles, on the last day of Boedromion, by resolution of the Council, the Presiding Officers and generals took

up business with a report of the proceedings in the Assembly, that the people decided to choose envoys to Philip regarding the recovery of the ships and to give orders in accord with the decrees of the Assembly. They chose the following: Cephisophon, son of Cleon, of Anaphlystus; Democritus, son of Demophon, of Anagyrus; Polycritus, son of Apemantus, of Cothocidae. In the presidency of the tribe Hippothontis; proposed by Aristophon of Collytus, president.

[77] Philip, king of the Macedonians, sends greetings to the Council and People of Athens. Your envoys, Cephisophon, Democritus, and Polycritus, met with me and discussed the release of the ships commanded by Leodamas. In general you seem to me extremely naïve if you think that I was unaware that your ships were dispatched ostensibly to escort the grain from the Hellespont to Lemnos but in fact to help the Selymbrians, who were under siege by me and were not included in the terms of friendship mutually established by us. [78] The people were unaware that the admiral received these orders, which came from certain officials and other individuals now in a private capacity who wish in every way to have the people take up war in place of their current friendship with me and are more intent on seeing this accomplished than on helping the Selymbrians. They see in this policy a source of revenue for themselves, but I do not believe it is a good idea for you or for me. Therefore, I release to you the ships that were recently diverted to us, and as for the future, if instead of endorsing leaders who recommend this malicious policy, you choose to punish them, I will undertake for my part to keep the peace. Farewell.

[84] In the Archonship of Chaerondas, son of Hegemon, on the twenty-fifth day of Gamelion, during the presidency of the tribe Leontis, Aristonicus of Phrearrii proposed: whereas Demosthenes, son of Demosthenes, of Paeania, does the people of Athens many great services, has through his decrees aided many of the allies previously and on the present occasion, has liberated a number of Euboean cities, is ever loyal to the people of Athens, and through speech and action confers whatever good he can on the Athenians themselves and the rest of the Greeks, it is decided by the Council and the People of Athens to praise Demosthenes, son of Demosthenes, of Paeania, to crown him with a golden crown, to proclaim the crown in the theater at the per-

formance of new tragedies, and to entrust the proclamation of the crown to the presiding tribe and the official in charge of the festival. Proposed by Aristonicus of Phrearrii.

[90] In the priesthood of Bosporichus, Damagetus proposed in the Assembly with the permission of the Council: whereas on previous occasions the People of Athens were ever loyal to the Byzantians and their allies and to their kinsmen the Perinthians and did them many great services, and on the present occasion when Philip of Macedon invaded the land and the city to destroy the Byzantians and Perinthians, burning the countryside and laying waste to the trees, they came to our aid with one hundred and twenty ships, food, arms, and soldiers; saved us from great dangers; and reestablished our ancestral constitution, laws, and burial places, [91] it is decided by the People of Byzantium and Perinthus to confer on the Athenians the privileges of intermarriage, citizenship, ownership of land and houses, seats of honor at the festivals, first access to the Council and People after the sacrifices, and, for those wishing to inhabit our city, exemption from all civic obligations, to erect in the Bosporeion three statues sixteen cubits high, representing the People of Athens being crowned by the People of Byzantium and Perinthus, to send delegations to the panhellenic festivals, the Isthmean, the Nemean, the Olympian, and the Pythian, and to proclaim the crowns bestowed by us on the People of Athens, in order that the Greeks know the merit of the Athenians and the gratitude of the Byzantians and Perinthians.

[92] The Chersonesians who inhabit Sestus, Elaeus, Madytus, and Alopeconnesus crown the Council and People of Athens with a golden crown of sixty talents and dedicate an altar to Gratitude and the Athenian people, because they are responsible for all of the Chersonesians' greatest blessings, having saved them from Philip's forces and restored their countries, laws, freedom, temples. And in all time hereafter they will not fail to be grateful and do them every good they can. This decree was voted in the common Council.

[105] In the Archonship of Polycles, on the sixteenth day of Boedromion, during the presidency of the tribe Hippothontis, Demosthenes, son of Demosthenes, of Paeania, introduced a trierarchic law to re-

place the old one that established associations of trierarchs. It passed by a vote of the Council and the People. Patrocles of Phlya indicted Demosthenes for an illegal proposal; he did not get his share of the votes and paid five hundred drachmas.

[106] The trierarchs to be called, sixteen for each trireme from the associations by companies, from age twenty-five to forty, taking equal part in the public service.

The trierarchs to be chosen according to the assessment of their property at ten talents for each trireme. If the property is assessed at a higher amount, let the public obligation be proportionate up to three ships and a tender. Likewise the same proportion for those whose property is less than ten talents, forming an association for up to ten talents.

[115] The Archon Demonicus of Phlya, on the twenty-fifth day of Boedromion, a resolution of the Council and People, Callias of Phrearrii proposed: it is decided by the Council and People to crown Nausicles, general of the infantry, because when two thousand Athenian infantry were in Imbros defending the Athenian inhabitants of the island, and storms prevented Philo, elected general of the budget, from sailing and paying the troops, he paid out of his own funds and did not charge the people, and to proclaim the crown during the Dionysia at the performance of new tragedies.

[116] Callias of Phrearrii proposed on the advice of the Presiding Officers, a resolution of the Council: whereas Charidemus, general of the infantry and on duty in Salamis, and Diotimus, general of the cavalry, when some soldiers were disarmed by enemy forces in the battle by the river, at their own expense equipped the young men with eight hundred shields, it is decided by the Council and People to crown Charidemus and Diotimus with a golden crown; to proclaim it at the Great Panathenaea at the gymnastic competition and at the Dionysia at the performance of new tragedies; and to entrust the proclamation to the Thesmothetae, the Presiding Officers, and the officials in charge of the festival.

[118] In the Archonship of Euthycles, on the twenty-second day of Pyanepsion, during the presidency of the tribe Oineis, Ctesiphon, son of Leosthenes, of Anaphlystus, proposed: whereas Demosthenes, son of Demosthenes, of Paeania, as commissioner for the repair of the walls spent on the work three talents of his own funds and donated that amount to the people, and as commissioner of the Theoric Fund donated to the theoric officials of all the tribes 100 minas for sacrifices, it is decided by the Council and the People of Athens to praise Demosthenes, son of Demosthenes, of Paeania, because of his merit and the generosity that he always displays on every occasion to the Athenian people, to crown him with a golden crown, to proclaim the crown in the theater during the Dionysia at the performance of new tragedies, and to entrust the proclamation to the official in charge of the festival.

[120] For those receiving a crown from any of the demes, the proclamation of the crowns is to be made in each case in the particular deme, except when crowns are bestowed by the People of Athens or by the Council; in such cases it is possible in the theater during the Dionysia [2]

[135] The following bear witness for Demosthenes on behalf of all: Callias of Sunium, Zeno of Phlya, Cleon of Phaleron, Demonicus of Marathon, that when the people elected Aeschines to be their advocate before the Amphictyons regarding the temple on Delos, we in Council deemed Hyperides better suited to speak on behalf of the city, and Hyperides was sent.

[137] Teledemos, son of Cleon, Hyperides, son of Callaeschrus, Nicomachus, son of Diophantus, bear witness for Demosthenes and have taken oaths in the presence of the generals that they know that Aeschines, son of Atrometus, of Cothocidae, went at night to Thraso's house and consulted with Anaxinus, who was convicted of spying for Philip. This testimony was given before Nicias on the third day of Hecatombaion.

---

[2] The text breaks off abruptly.

[154] In the priesthood of Cleinagoras, at the spring meeting, it was decided by the Accompanying Delegates, the Councilors of the Amphictyons, and the General Assembly of the Amphictyons, that whereas the Amphissians tread, sow, and graze their flocks on sacred ground, the Accompanying Delegates and Councilors shall go out and mark the boundaries with stones and forbid the Amphissians from treading there in the future.

[155] In the priesthood of Cleinagoras, at the spring meeting, it was decided by the Accompanying Delegates, the Councilors of the Amphictyons, and the General Assembly of the Amphictyons, that whereas the men of Amphissa have divided up the sacred ground and farm and graze their flocks on it, and when they were prevented from doing this they appeared under arms, forcibly resisted the common Council of the Greeks, and even wounded some, Cottyphus of Arcadia, elected general of the Amphictyons, shall go as envoy to Philip of Macedon and ask him to help Apollo and the Amphictyons in order that he not allow the god to be wronged by the impious Amphissians. And [he shall announce] that he is chosen general with full powers by the Greeks attending the Amphictyonic Council.

[155] The Archonship of Mnesitheides, on the sixteenth day of the month Anthesterion.

[157] Philip, king of the Macedonians, sends greetings to the magistrates of the Peloponnesian allies, to the councilors, and to all the other allies. Whereas the Ozolian Locrians, who inhabit Amphissa, commit crimes against Apollo's temple in Delphi, tread the sacred ground under arms, and pillage, I wish to join you in helping the god and stopping those who transgress against any of the sacred customs of mankind. Therefore, assemble in Phocis under arms with food for forty days in the present month known as Loios in our calendar, Boedromion in the Athenian, Panemus in the Corinthian. For those who do not assemble in full force we shall make use of the sanctions established in our treaty. Farewell.

[164] In the Archonship of Heropythus, on the twenty-fifth day of the month Elaphebolion, during the presidency of the tribe Erechtheis,

a resolution of the Council and generals: whereas Philip has seized some neighboring cities and destroyed others and in sum is preparing to come to Attica, utterly disregarding our pacts, and undertakes to break the oaths and the peace, contravening the common agreements, it is decided by the Council and People to send envoys to him to talk with him and urge him above all to preserve the friendship and agreements with us, but if not, to give the city time for deliberation and to arrange a truce until the month of Thargelion. Simus of Anagyrus, Euthydemus of Phylae, Boulagoras of Alopece were chosen from the Council.

[165] In the Archonship of Heropythus, on the last day of the month Munychion, a resolution of the Polemarch: whereas Philip attempts to alienate the Thebans from us and has made preparations to occupy positions near Attica with his entire army, violating his existing agreements with us, it is decided by the Council and People to send to him a herald and envoys to ask and exhort him to conclude a truce so that the people may deliberate to the extent possible; for as yet they have decided not to mount an expedition in the event of a fair response. Nearchus, son of Sosinomus, Polycrates, son of Epiphron, were chosen from the Council, and Eunomus of Anaphlystus was chosen from the people as herald.

[166] Philip, king of the Macedonians, sends greetings to the Council and People of Athens. I am not unaware of your original policy towards me or of your zeal in seeking to win over the Thessalians and Thebans and also Boeotians. Since they are more prudent and are unwilling to put their policy in your hands but take a stand on their own interests, you now turn around, send envoys and a herald to me, remind me of the agreements, and ask for a truce, though we have not harmed you at all. However, after listening to the envoys, I accept their offers and am ready to conclude a truce so long as you reject those who advise you wrongly and punish them with the appropriate dishonor. Farewell.

[167] Philip, king of the Macedonians, sends greetings to the Council and People of Thebes. I received your letter in which you renew friendship and peace with me. However, I have learned that the Athe-

nians are using every effort to induce you to accept their proposals. Previously I condemned you for being ready to give in to their hopes and agree to their policy. But now that I have recognized that you would rather have peace with us than follow the advice of others, I am pleased and willingly commend you for many reasons, but most of all for your wise decision on these matters and for your loyalty to us. I expect, if you preserve this attitude, it will bring you no small return. Farewell.

[181] In the Archonship of Nausicles, during the presidency of the tribe Aiantis, on the sixteenth day of Scirophorion, Demosthenes, son of Demosthenes, of Paeania, proposed: whereas in the past Philip of Macedon openly violates his peace agreements with the people of Athens, disregards his oaths and the traditions of justice common to all Greeks, seizes cities that do not belong to him, enslaves some cities that belong to Athens without any provocation from the people of Athens, and now advances greatly in power and cruelty; [182] and whereas he puts garrisons in some Greek cities and abolishes their governments, razes other cities and enslaves the inhabitants, in yet other cities establishes barbarians in place of Greeks and installs them over temples and tombs, thereby doing nothing at odds with his country or character, arrogantly enjoying his current fortune, and forgetting that from a meager, ordinary background he has become [great] against expectation. [183] So long as the Athenian people saw him subdue barbarian cities and his own cities, they took little notice of the wrongs done to them, but now, since they see him assaulting some Greek cities and laying waste to others, they consider it terrible and unworthy of their ancestors' fame to ignore the enslavement of Greeks; [184] therefore, it is decided by the Council and People of Athens to offer prayers and sacrifices to the gods and heroes who watch over the city and territory of Athens, to bear in mind the courage of their ancestors who chose to protect the freedom of the Greeks ahead of their own country, to put two hundred ships to sea, that the naval commander shall sail to Thermopylae, that the general and the commander of the cavalry shall lead the infantry and cavalry to Eleusis, to send envoys to the rest of the Greeks, but first of all to the Thebans inasmuch as Philip is nearest their territory, [185] to encourage them to have no fear and to resist Philip for the sake of their own freedom

and that of the other Greeks, because the people of Athens, holding no grudge for any previous dispute between the cities, will send aid in forces, money, weapons, and arms, for they know that it is honorable for Greeks to contend with each other for supremacy, but to be ruled by a foreigner and deprived by him of supremacy is unworthy of the Greeks' reputation and their ancestors' courage. [186] Further, the people of Athens do not view the people of Thebes as alien to them in blood or kinship, but they recall the services that their own ancestors rendered to the Thebans' ancestors; for they restored the children of Heracles to their paternal domain when the Peloponnesians tried to take it, defeating in battle those who sought to oppose the descendants of Heracles, they received Oedipus and his family when they were exiled, and we did many other notable acts of kindness for the Thebans. [187] Therefore, the people of Athens will not spurn the interests of the Thebans and the rest of the Greeks. An alliance with them is concluded, the right of intermarriage established, and oaths given and received. The envoys: Demosthenes, son of Demosthenes, of Paeania; Hyperides, son of Cleander, of Sphettus; Mnesitheides, son of Antiphanes, of Phrearrii; Democrates, son of Sophilus, of Phlya; Callaeschrus, son of Diotimus, of Cothocidae.

APPENDIX 2. TIMELINE

404   End of the Peloponnesian War, regime of the Thirty Tyrants
in Athens

403   Democracy restored in Athens

384   Birth of Demosthenes

371   Thebans defeat Spartans at Leuctra

362   Battle of Mantinea, end of Theban hegemony

359   Philip's accession to the Macedonian throne

357   Social War (between Athens and its allies, until 355)
Philip takes Amphipolis and Pydna, outbreak of war between Athens and Macedon

356   Birth of Alexander the Great
Phocians occupy Delphi, outbreak of Third Sacred War

352   Philip elected Archon of Thessalian League

351   Dem. 4: *First Philippic*

349   Philip invades Chalcidice, threatens Olynthus
Dem. 1–3: *Olynthiacs*

348   Philip takes Olynthus

347/6   Demosthenes member of Council of 500 in Athens

346   Spring: First Embassy to Philip in Pella
Peace of Philocrates adopted and ratified by
Athens and its allies
Second Embassy to Philip, waits in Pella

        Summer: Philip meets Athenian envoys, ratifies Peace of
Philocrates
Demosthenes indicts Aeschines for misconduct
on Second Embassy
Philip occupies Thermopylae, Athenians prepare
to defend Attica

Fall: Amphictyonic Council under Philip's control
ends Third Sacred War, punishes Phocians

Dem. 5: *On the Peace*

346/5 Aeschines prosecutes Timarchus (Aes. wins case, Demosthenes' speech for Timarchus not preserved)

344 Dem. 6: *Second Philippic*

343 Philip sends Pytho of Byzantium on diplomatic mission to Athens

Philocrates accused of treason, flees Athens

Demosthenes prosecutes Aeschines for misconduct on Second Embassy (Dem. 19, Aes. 2), Aeschines narrowly acquitted

342 Philip supports tyrannies in Euboean cities

341 Diopeithes (Athenian general) makes gains in Chersonese at Philip's expense

341/0 Athens gains control over Euboea, alliances with Euboean cities

Demosthenes' diplomatic mission to Peloponnese, alliances with Peloponnesian cities

Dem. 8: *On the Chersonese,* Dem. 9: *Third Philippic*

340 Philip attacks Perinthus and Byzantium, seizes Athenian grain fleet

Athens declares war against Macedon on Demosthenes' motion

Demosthenes' reform of trierarchic law

Athenian expedition to Byzantium

339 Spring: Philip retires from Byzantium, campaigns in Scythia

Amphictyonic war against Amphissa

Summer: Thebans take Nicaea, near Thermopylae

Fall: Philip takes Elatea

Alliance of Athens and Thebes, organized by Demosthenes

338 Summer: Battle of Chaeronea, Athens and allies defeated

Winter: Demosthenes delivers funeral oration

338/7 Common Peace, formation of League of Corinth

337/6 Demosthenes commissioner of Theoric Fund, commissioner of city walls

336   Ctesiphon proposes a crown for Demosthenes, indicted by
        Aeschines

        Philip assassinated, Alexander accedes to the Macedonian
        throne

335   Thebes revolts, destroyed by Alexander

334   Alexander's Persian campaign begins

331   Fall: Alexander defeats Persian army at Gaugamela

330   Spring: Revolt of Agis III of Sparta fails

        Summer: Aeschines prosecutes Ctesiphon for proposing
                 crown for Demosthenes (Aes. 3, Dem. 18),
                 Ctesiphon acquitted by huge margin

324   Demosthenes goes into exile as a result of charges arising
        from the handling of public funds (Harpalus affair)

323   Death of Alexander, Greek rebellion led by Athens, Demos-
        thenes recalled

322   Greek rebellion crushed, death of Demosthenes

BIBLIOGRAPHY FOR THIS VOLUME

Adams, C. D., 1927: *Demosthenes and His Influence.* New York.

Badian, E., 1995: "The Ghost of Empire: Reflections on Athenian Foreign Policy in the Fourth Century BC," in *Die athenische Demokratie im 4. Jahrhundert v. Chr.,* ed. W. Eder. Stuttgart: 79–106.

————, 2000: "The Road to Prominence," in *Demosthenes: Statesman and Orator,* ed. I. Worthington. London: 9–44.

Blass, F., and K. Fuhr, eds., 1910: *Demosthenes. Ausgewählte Reden für den Schulgebrauch erklärt,* part II: *Die Rede vom Kranz.* 2nd ed. Leipzig.

Burkert, W., 1987: *Ancient Mystery Cults.* Cambridge, MA.

Carlier, P., 1990: *Démosthène.* Paris.

Classen, C. J., 1991: "The Speeches in the Courts of Law: A Three-Cornered Dialogue," *Rhetorica* 9: 195–207.

Dilts, M. R., ed., 2002: *Demosthenis Orationes,* vol. 1. Oxford.

Fornara, C. W., 1977: *Translated Documents of Greece and Rome,* vol. 1: *Archaic Times to the End of the Peloponnesian War.* Cambridge.

Fox, W., 1880: *Die Kranzrede des Demosthenes.* Leipzig.

Fuhr, K., ed., 1914: *Demosthenis Orationes,* vol. 1, part 3. Leipzig.

Gabrielsen, V., 1994: *Financing the Athenian Fleet: Public Taxation and Social Relations.* Baltimore.

Goodwin, W. W., ed., 1901: *Demosthenes: On the Crown.* Cambridge.

Griffith, G. W., 1979: "The Reign of Philip the Second," in *A History of Macedonia,* vol. II: *550–336 B.C.,* ed. N. G. L. Hammond and G. W. Griffith. Oxford: 203–646, 675–726.

Hansen, M. H., 1991: *The Athenian Democracy in the Age of Demosthenes: Structure, Principles and Ideology.* Oxford.

Harding, P., 1985: *Translated Documents of Greece and Rome*, vol. 2: *From the End of the Peloponnesian War to the Battle of Ipsus.* Cambridge.

————, 2000: "Demosthenes in the Underworld: A Chapter in the *Nachleben* of a *Rhetor*," in *Demosthenes: Statesman and Orator*, ed. I. Worthington. London: 246–271.

Harris, E. M., 1986: "The Names of Aeschines' Brothers-in-Law," *American Journal of Philology* 107: 99–102.

————, 1994: "Law and Oratory," in *Persuasion: Greek Rhetoric in Action*, ed. I. Worthington. London: 130–150.

————, 1995: *Aeschines and Athenian Politics.* New York.

Kennedy, G. A., 1994: *A New History of Classical Rhetoric.* Princeton.

MacDowell, D. M., ed., 2000: *Demosthenes: On the False Embassy (Oration 19).* Oxford.

Mirhady, D. C., 2000: "Demosthenes as Advocate: The Private Speeches," in *Demosthenes: Statesman and Orator*, ed. I. Worthington. London: 181–204.

Ober, J., 1989: *Mass and Elite in Democratic Athens: Rhetoric, Ideology and the Power of the People.* Princeton.

Parker, R., 1996: *Athenian Religion: A History.* Oxford.

Paulsen, T., 1999: *Die Parapresbeia-Reden des Demosthenes und des Aischines. Kommentar und Interpretation zu Demosthenes, or. XIX, und Aischines, or. II.* Trier.

Pearson, L., 1976: *The Art of Demosthenes.* Meisenheim am Glan.

Pickard-Cambridge, A. W., 1914: *Demosthenes and the Last Days of Greek Freedom, 384–322 BC.* New York.

Rhodes, P. J., 1972: *The Athenian Boule.* Oxford.

Roberts, J. T., 1982: *Accountability in Athenian Government.* Madison, WI.

Rowe, G. O., 1967: "Demosthenes' Use of Language," in *Demosthenes' On the Crown: A Critical Study of a Masterpiece of Ancient Oratory*, ed. J. J. Murphy. New York: 175–199.

Rubinstein, L., 2000: *Litigation and Cooperation: Supporting Speakers in the Courts of Classical Athens.* Historia Einzelschriften 147. Stuttgart.

Rutherford, I., 1998: *Canons of Style in the Antonine Age: Idea-Theory in Its Literary Context.* Oxford.

Ryder, T. T. B., 2000: "Demosthenes and Philip II," in *Demosthenes: Statesman and Orator*, ed. I. Worthington. London: 45–89.

Sealey, R., 1993: *Demosthenes and His Time: A Study in Defeat.* New York.

Shilleto, R., ed., 1874: *Demosthenis De Falsa Legatione.* 4th ed. Cambridge.

Todd, S. C., 1993: *The Shape of Athenian Law.* Oxford.

Usher, S., ed., 1993: *Demosthenes: On the Crown.* Warminster.

Vickers, B., 1988: *In Defence of Rhetoric.* Oxford.

Wankel, H., 1976: *Demosthenes. Rede für Ktesiphon über den Kranz.* Heidelberg.

Weil, H., ed., 1883: *Les plaidoyers politiques de Démosthène.* Première série. 2nd ed. Paris.

Wooten, C. W., trans., 1987: *Hermogenes' On Types of Style.* Chapel Hill, NC.

Worthington, I., 2000: "Demosthenes' (In)activity during the Reign of Alexander the Great," in *Demosthenes: Statesman and Orator,* ed. I. Worthington. London: 90–113.

Yunis, H., 1996: *Taming Democracy: Models of Political Rhetoric in Classical Athens.* Ithaca, NY.

———, 2000: "Politics as Literature: Demosthenes and the Burden of the Athenian Past," *Arion* 8: 97–118.

———, ed., 2001: *Demosthenes: On the Crown.* Cambridge.

INDEX

236   INDEX

apotympanismos (execution),
157n.128
Arcadia/Arcadians, 47, 106, 108, 123,
174, 192, 200, 204, 205, 206
Archons, xx, xxii, 59, 59n.98
Areopagus Council, xxii, 65, 66,
66n.125, 176n.190
Arestidas, 205, 206
Argos, Argives, 47, 106, 193
Aristaechmus, 106
Aristodemus, 37, 124, 124n.20, 126,
147, 186, 187, 187n.220, 208
Aristogeiton, 198n.246
Aristoleus, 79, 79n.159
Aristomachus, 188n.222
Aristonicus, 51, 86, 87n.175, 110,
110n.238, 220, 221
Aristophon, 48, 49, 72, 72n.142, 85,
201, 203, 220
Aristotle, xxiii
Aristratus, 44, 79, 79n.159, 106
Artemis, 57n.93
Artemisium, 82
Arthmius, 195, 195n.239
Assembly, xix, xx, xxiii; speeches in,
xiii
Athena, statue of, 195, 195n.241
Athens, grain supply, 52nn.77–78,
91, 142n.80; legal system, xix,
xxi, xxv; political system, xix, xxv,
9, 12
Atrometus (father of Aeschines), 64,
64n.120, 198
aulos (wind instrument), 64n.118

Basileus (king archon), xx, xxi n.23,
59n.98
Battalus, 76
Black Sea, 108n.233, 142n.80,
169n.167
Boeotia/Boeotians, 4, 54, 76n.149,

84, 88, 107, 118, 126, 126n.33, 140,
148n.131, 154, 197n.245, 225
Bosporeion, 221
Bosporichus, 221
Bosporus, 49, 52n.77
Boulagoras, 225
bribery, 11n.5, 51n.71
Byzantium/Byzantians, 24, 49,
49n.66, 50, 52, 53, 53n.80, 88, 90,
91, 221

Callaeschrus, 223, 227
Callias, 191n.242, 195, 222, 223
Callisthenes, 41, 143, 144n.88, 218
Callistratus, 85, 85n.172, 203
Cardia/Cardians, 167, 167n.161
Cecrops, 204n.268
Ceos, 54
Cephalus, 85, 85n.172, 93, 93n.192,
94
Cephisodotus, 169, 169n.169
Cephisophon, 37, 201, 218, 219, 220
Cercidas, 106
Cersebleptes, 16n.152, 164, 170, 213
Chabrias, 200, 200n.255
Chaerondas, 220
Chaeronea, 88n.178, 90; battle of, 4,
5, 15, 24, 26, 28, 29, 30, 48n.52,
52n.77, 54n.83, 68n.133, 74n.147,
80n.161, 82nn.163–164, 84n.170,
92n.188, 97n.203, 102nn.217,222,
110n.238, 118, 118n.11
Chalcidice, 10, 114, 193, 194
Chalcis, 137, 153
Chares, 212, 212n.301
Charidemus, 59, 222
Charondas, 218
Chelidonian islands, 195, 196n.353
Chersonese, 50, 53, 67, 107, 115, 142,
142n.80, 167n.161, 221
Chios, 89